Foreword to the CL Press republication and acknowledgments

By Daniel B. Klein

CL Press colleagues and I are grateful for permissions from the editor Björn Hasselgren, the Introduction-author Lars Magnusson, and the publisher and copyright holder Timbro Förlag (which gives permission not only to reproduce softback copies bearing a CL Press imprint but also to post the contents at CLPress.net).

Thank you for your cooperation in the effort to bring your marvelous English-language sample of Erik Gustaf Geijer to a wider range or readers.

Here I offer a few words of guidance to those readers. First, Geijer is pronounced "Yay-yer."

Geijer (1783–1847) wrote in Swedish and for Swedes. He wrote as an esteemed professor and cultural luminary.

He shared with David Hume, Adam Smith, Edmund Burke, and Alexis de Tocqueville a spiritual approach to human existence. He was still of an age that understood that many great truths are saga. Compared to Hume, Smith, Burke, and Tocqueville, however, Geijer's intended reader was more localized. Geijer thought big, but first and foremost he was concerned to make Sweden hardy and wholesome. Tocqueville's implied reader might live in France, in America, or practically anywhere; Geijer's implied reader, for much of his writings, was a Scandinavian of one sort or another. But Geijer well understood the wider conversation.

I encourage the reader of this volume to start with the shortest chapter, which is the final one, "An Economic Dream," which appeared shortly before Geijer's death, and then consider the next shortest, "On Slavery." I advise that you turn last to the longest chapter, "Feudalism and Republicanism", which was Geijer's effort to integrate across times and themes, written in 1818 shortly after he was appointed to the highly regarded professorship at Uppsala University.

Into the 1830s, Geijer, in his fifties, had long been regarded as a nationalist influenced by German idealism and romanticism, and with good reason. G. W. F. Hegel, F. W. J. Schelling, and others from the German idealistic tradition were among his influences. After age 50, Geijer's liberalism became more pronounced. In 1838 Geijer announced to his public that he had revised his thinking and worldview and had gone over to liberalism. Swedish society took note and many were shaken. Several of his colleagues and friends erupted publicly with dissatisfaction. Geijer's new liberal stance has, ever since, generally been regarded as a substantive change of mind. I am not convinced, however. It was perhaps as much a coming out of the closet as a change of political persuasion. I do not see conflict between the early writings focused on nationalist themes and the later, more openly classical liberal writings. I think that Geijer agreed with David Hume, who wrote, "liberty is the perfection of civil society; but still authority must be acknowledged essential to its very existence." There needs to be a nation before there is a liberal nation.

FREEDOM IN SWEDEN

ERIK GUSTAF GEIJER

FREEDOM
IN SWEDEN

Selected works of Erik Gustaf Geijer
Edited by Björn Hasselgren
Translated by Peter C. Hogg

CL Reprints
CL Press
Fraser Institute

CL Press

Published by CL PRESS
A Project of the Fraser Institute
1770 Burrard Street, 4th Floor
Vancouver, BC V6J 3G7 Canada
www.clpress.net

Freedom in Sweden: Selected Works of Erik Gusfaf Geijer

Edited by **Björn Hasselgren**

Translated by Peter C. Hogg

New CL Press Foreword by Daniel Klein

First printed: April 2025

CL Press cover design: John Stephens

Cover image: Cover illustration titled "Gutenberg's Press" by Dave Grey, licensed under a Creative Commons Attribution-NoDerivs 2.0 Generic license.

Typeset (original to 2017): Tina Selander

ISBN: 978-1-957698-16-8

Contents

Editor's preface

ERIK GUSTAF GEIJER (1783-1847) was an internationally renowned scholar in numerous fields, most prominently a history professor at Uppsala University for nearly thirty years. He held a variety of significant positions, such as Member of Parliament, member of several prestigious academies, and Chancellor of Uppsala University. In addition, he was also a celebrated poet, musician and composer.

He was well versed in the academic and popular debate and published a vast number of articles, essays and books, though only few have been translated into English. Hence, this book will offer to many a first, primary introduction to Geijer's work.

My own curiosity towards Erik Gustaf Geijer stems from a fascination of Sweden in the latter part of the 18th century and its development into the first decades of the 19th century. This was an era of upheaval, during which the country went through a number of revolutionary phases. Beginning in the mid-1700's Sweden experienced pre-democratic parliamentarism, royal despotism, the murder of King Gustavus III, the dethronement of King Gustavus IV, with coup d'états-like events in 1772, 1789, 1792 and 1809.

In resonance with a wider, international vogue, Sweden saw raging debates on constitutional issues and in 1809 a hasty implementation of a novel constitution with several innovations. Simultaneously, its borders were reduced geographically with the loss of Finland in 1809 as the country faced a very real threat of a Russian invasion in the War of 1808-1809.

On top of this political turmoil, Sweden entered into the industrial revolution with all its well-known, radical social changes: The development of a middle class of industrialists, a swift reorganisation and rationalisation of agriculture, the emergence of a working class, and a growing number of people entirely without means.

Through all of these wide-ranging events Geijer is an excellent guide. He possessed the experience of a man who already during his childhood in his own words "sensed, like a distant roll of thunder, the outbreak of the French revolution", and devoted his professional life to continuous analysis of the long-term development and future challenges of Sweden.

Geijer contributed to the public debate in journals where lingering Royal regulations at times had to be dodged despite the new constitution's liberal Freedom of Speech Act. His elegant and novel literary style — both in poetry and creative prose — has had a lasting influence on the Swedish language.

The sample of texts included here and the introduction offers a broader framework of Erik Gustaf Geijer's work than is usually provided in the literary canon. Especially, it argues that while Geijer was inspired by the tradition of German idealists and romanticists, it is an understated fact that he also very much interacted with the Anglo-Saxon and British scholarly debate, and the unique Scottish Enlightenment. Freedom in Sweden and the freedom of the Swedish people were among the core themes in Geijer's work from the early 1800's. 'Freedom in Sweden' as a title of this volume is justified in both ways.

This volume, covering almost half a century, contains a number of pivotal texts from Geijer's extensive production, ranging from the Sten Sture-essay (1803) reflecting on the Swedish late 15th century regent, and Geijers first major published and price winning text, to his last published text, *An Economic Dream* (1847). Notably, *The Poor Laws*, one of few texts translated into English during Geijer's own lifetime, gives a perspective on his work in the late 1830's. In a chapter originally prepared as an academic article, I reflect on *the Poor Laws*.

The translation is primarily based on the 1873-75 edition of Erik Gustaf Geijer's collected works (Stockholm, P. A. Norstedt), and follows the original texts closely. Hence, special efforts have been made to convey Geijer's original use of Swedish terms and expressions.

Professor Lars Magnusson of Uppsala University provides the introductory chapter. Dr. Magnusson is an expert on economic history and the history of economic theory in Erik Gustaf Geijer's time, and author of several books on Sweden's economic history.

Peter C. Hogg has a wide experience from Scandinavian historic literature and has translated works by Carl Linnaeus and Anders Chydenius. His experience from working with the British Library has been most helpful, and it has been a pleasure to include him in this project.

This project has received financial support from Reinhold Geijer, The Royal Swedish Academy of Letters, History and Antiquities (Kungliga Vitterhetsakademien),

Jernkontoret (The Organisation of Swedish Steel Producers), and the Royal Patriotic Society (Kungliga Patriotiska
Sällskapet).

Professor Daniel B. Klein has kindly supported the
translation project with his profound knowledge in many
of the themes in Geijer's writings and with numerous
valuable comments. I would also like to thank Martina
Stenström, Timbro förlag, for guiding the project with insight and proficiency.

Björn Hasselgren, Stockholm, July 2017

INTRODUCTION

Erik Gustaf Geijer
– An Introduction

by Lars Magnusson, Uppsala University

During the last two hundred years Erik Gustaf Geijer (1783-1847) has reached an almost iconic status as *the* national poet in Sweden of the so-called Romantic era, as well as the founder of history as a modern academic discipline in Sweden at the University of Uppsala. Generally being regarded as a firm conservative and primarily as a follower of German idealism, he is said to have shocked his contemporaries in 1838 by proclaiming his defection from conservatism in order to join the liberal political camp. He has sometimes also been regarded as a Hegelian and even as a utopian socialist. It is also a matter of fact that Karl Marx read Geijer's work on Swedish history in the early 1840's (in German translation) and perhaps also took some influence from it. Lastly, Geijer read the works of left-Hegelians such as Ludwig Feuerbach and Bruno Bauer where he picked up the notion of "religion as the opium of the people". Still, all through his life he was a warm disciple of the Protestant state church in Sweden and Christian faith was always close to his heart.

Then what shall we make of this Erik Gustaf Geijer with so many bewildering faces, a man who seems to slip through one's fingers as soon as you think that you have him in your grip? After two hundred years, how can we characterize Geijer as a man and writer?

It is perhaps easier to explain the purpose of this book, which is to introduce Geijer to a wider non-Swedish reading public. Geijer was indeed a great European thinker and writer involved in the contemporary debates and discussions on moral philosophy, politics, political economy and how to write history. By introducing him – or rather re-introducing him, as he was not a totally unknown figure in the early 19th century outside his native country, some of his works having been translated into both German and English – we seek to bring him back to the context of all-European intellectual developments and transitions roughly from the Scottish Enlightenment up to the 1840's.

During most of his life he struggled with issues concerning the nature of Man, Society and History which were hotly debated during this period. Publishing the bulk of his works in Swedish, he has largely been forgotten outside Sweden, though sometimes appearing as a footnote in general intellectual history textbooks. Also as we have seen he is not easy to pin down as a specific representative of a certain school of thought – idealism, conservatism, liberalism, etc. – still stylised in most textbooks on intellectual or political history. Geijer was certainly a thinker with a mind of his own and interpreted the great contemporary debates in his own manner. By bringing his voice back we can learn much about the general (not only Swedish) possibilities and perspectives that were opened up during his period, but also about the closures concerning what never came to be. We can also hint at combinations of discourses and ideas that could have formed the basis for other solutions and possible futures.

With Geijer as the starting point we can acknowledge to what extent history is an open process, but also how it serves as a place for lost opportunities. Moreover we can learn that "schools" of thought which for us seem disparate for someone like Geijer were much more close and tangled.

THE MUSICAL PROCESS – GEIJER'S EARLY YEARS IN UPPSALA

When Geijer arrived in Uppsala in 1799 as a young student the radical political club called the Junta that had held its meetings in the big stone house at Sankt Johannesgatan number nine for a number of years was at its height. Its shining star, the philosopher Benjamin Höijer (1767–1812), had the same year been put up as first candidate for the chair in Theoretical Philosophy. However he was rejected by the university perhaps because of the involvement of its chancellor, king Gustavus IV himself – no doubt because of Höijer's alleged republican views. During the 1790's the Junta had been a club for radical Uppsala professors and students hotly discussing the latest events in France, the need for more political freedom and not least the new philosophies arriving from Königsberg, Berlin and Paris.

The prudent burghers of Uppsala as well as the more conservative professors of the university wondered what was going on at Sankt Johannesgatan. Höijer and the inner circle of the club were often depicted as dangerous Jacobins. Being rejected for the chair, Höijer went on a long journey that took him to Paris, Switzerland and Berlin. Kant had already been introduced in Uppsala and the earlier dominance of Wolffian theology and moral philosophy was slowly melting away. In Berlin Höijer socialised with Fichte, the brothers August Wilhelm and Friedrich Schlegel and others. Returning to Uppsala he was allowed to teach at the university but was several times rejected when seeking a position as lecturer or professor. Ultimately he did get his chair in theoretical philosophy in 1809 – but that was after king Gustavus IV had been removed from his throne as a consequence of the so-called revolution of 1809 (or rather a coup d'état by liberal-minded noblemen, who detested his absolutist rule and blamed him for Sweden's loss of Finland to the Russians in the 1808-09 war).[1]

What really had sent Höijer out in the cold with several other leading members of the Junta was an incident that occurred in 1800. Geijer was too much a newcomer to have been directly involved, but it is reasonable to imagine that he was a supportive bystander.

On the third of April 1800 Gustavus IV was crowned in Norrköping, where the Diet was summoned, in a storm so blistering that more or less no one was able to go outside to watch the parades. It had been decided by the academic authorities that Uppsala University should host a ceremony to celebrate the coronation. But everything went wrong in Uppsala. In its main building, the *Gustavianum*, oratorical speeches were delivered and the university's own academic orchestra was supposed to play. One of the musicians in the orchestra was one of the leading Junta members, Gustav Abraham Silfverstolpe. He had been able to trick the old *director musices* Lars-Fredrik Leyel into opening the musical performance with some passages of the Marseillaise hidden in a piece called *Bataille de Fleurus*. But the *rector magnificus* of Uppsala university, J A Tingstadius, was informed and stopped the performance.

So when arriving at the *Gustavianum* the musicians found the music sheets had been replaced by one of Haydn's symphonies. This resulted in Silfverstolpe and most of the other members of the orchestra storming out from the *Gustavianum*. Left were four musicians who (rather unsuccessfully as it seems) had to struggle with Haydn's composition, which required at least a couple of horns. Heading for a nearby tavern (Östmarks källare), the oppositional musicians toasted the republic and political freedom. Farcical as it might seem, the episode turned out to be anything but amusing for some of the rebellious musicians. Silfverstolpe was banned from the University for life, and lost his title of *docent*, while six others were punished with banishments for a longer or shorter period as well as having to face some days of incarceration in the University prison.[2] This was one of the most renowned political protests against the king at the time, and obviously something that coloured Geijer's perceptions of the political system and lack of intellectual freedom at the time.

Although later taking up history as his academic field, Geijer's roots were in philosophy. When Geijer arrived in Uppsala in 1799 professor Erik Michael Fant (1754–1817), the holder of the chair in History, lectured mainly on antiquarian topics and was occupied with historical artefacts and collections. Instead Geijer attended the lectures of

Jacob Fredrik Neikter (1744–1803), professor of rhetoric and government. Neikter was a follower of Montesquieu and during the first year Geijer was in Uppsala he lectured on "the history of Mankind".[3]

Besides this early experience of the European intellectual discourse Geijer emphasised, especially in his *Autobiography* ("Minnen"), the important role that Benjamin Höijer played for his intellectual development.[4] According to himself he attended every single lecture that Höijer held after returning to Uppsala in 1802[5]. For many Höijer was still looked upon as a suspect radical – perhaps even still with republican inclinations – and his pupils were rather few. Through him Geijer was introduced to the new idealist philosophies coming out of Germany: Herder, Fichte but also Schelling and Hegel. But Höijer was not the only influence on Geijer. The professor of Practical Philosophy Daniel Boethius (1751-1810) – the introducer of Kant in Uppsala – was regarded as a man of the 1790's still favourable to at least some aspects of the French revolution. It is clear that Boethius, even after Geijer had arrived, had some influence within the circle of young students to which Geijer belonged.

Over the coming years Geijer – following in the footstep of Höijer – would become increasingly more critical of the French revolution and certain strands of French enlightenment philosophy (Voltaire, Helvetius, *les encyclopédistes*, Condorcet). The revolution had been manipulated by demagogues leading to terror and dictatorship (Robespierre and Napoleon), he argued. At the bottom such an unfavourable development had been made possible because of a, according to Geijer, "sterile" or "mechanical" enlightenment discourse which made men into easy victims of outside forces. But even some years after Geijer's arrival in Uppsala the radicalism of the 1790's appealed to him. He was also looked upon by his superiors as somewhat of an extremist. For financial reasons he applied for a job as a personal tutor to a noblemen's son after three years in Uppsala. But the university did not recommend him to the post; he was said to be "a young man without steadiness".[6]

LIFE AND CAREER

Erik Gustaf Geijer was born in 1783 in the parish of Ransäter in the county of Värmland in the west of Sweden. His father Bengt Gustaf Geijer was the owner of an iron works (*järnbruk*), Ransäter bruk, and his mother Ulrica Magdalena came from a family of iron miners from Falun in Dalecarlia. At the time of Erik Gustaf's birth Värmland hosted a great number of small iron works, but most of them ran into serious economic difficulties, especially as a consequence of the Napoleonic wars and the establishment of the Continental blockade. This was also the case with the ironmill at Ransäter and no doubt the reason why it seemed difficult for Bengt Gustaf to finance more than three years of studies for his son at Uppsala.[7]

However, Erik Gustaf seems to have had a happy childhood at Ransäter in a mansion house with a great number of relatives and guests coming and going. The ironworks and the adjacent mansions in Värmland served as beacons of culture and enlightenment. Their owners formed a kind of gentry in an otherwise sparsely populated countryside. News from the outer world continuously arrived as well as books and journals containing new ideas and learned discourse. Hence at an early age Erik Gustaf was well informed about the French revolution and its twists and turns. No doubt he grew up in a *milieu* that was favourable to the new liberal ideas concerning both politics and economics, in particular as regards the value of free trade and commerce.

Returning home to Ransäter in 1802 without a finished exam or a job he felt miserable and worried about his future. Continuing his studies at home he more or less by chance applied to a prize essay competition put up by the learned Swedish Academy in Stockholm. He sent in the *Panegyric on the Regent Sten Sture the Elder* ("Äreminne över riksföreståndaren Sten Sture den äldre") which is included in this volume. Perhaps to his own surprise he won the first prize and a gold medal. It was a patriotic piece that fit with the anti-Napoleonic feelings at the time (with Denmark as the foe in this case). The text hails political freedom as an ideal and includes passages that bear witness to his readings in the contemporary literature on moral philosophy.

After almost two years Geijer was able to return to Uppsala in 1804 and commence his studies. It is possible that already at the start of this second round of studies at Uppsala University he formulated a strategy that he should concentrate on history and later on take over the chair held by Fant. While waiting for positions that could become available in that field – no doubt once again because of financial difficulties, as the problems for the Värmland iron establishments had become desperate, even if the Ransäter ironmill might not have been among the worst affected – he took on the job as a tutor for the son of a commercial councillor (*Kommersråd*) at the College of

Commerce in Stockholm, named Schinkel. Together with the son Erik Gustaf went off on a year-long study visit to England 1809-10.

Sailing from Gothenburg to Yarmouth the pair arrived in London on August 19 1809. Geijer was greatly impressed by London, its size and multitude of people, the City with the Royal Exchange and all the coffee-houses; a veritable "Babylon of bricks".[8] He enjoyed concerts and visited the opera house at Covent garden; Händel's Messiah was "without any comparison the most heavenly piece of music I have listened to so far ".[9] Beside some journeys to Bath and southwest Devonshire he also spent some time in Bristol where Geijer could watch the effects of the industrial revolution on the spot. "The English proletarian makes indeed a miserable character", he wrote in a letter back home.[10] Here began an interest in the situation of the workers and the less well off in society was initiated, an interest that would never leave him and that resonated with the sentiments in the traditional ironmill culture, with its patriarchal-style leadership.

Otherwise Erik Gustaf and his pupil spent most of the time in London. Geijer could combine his teaching duty with studies of his own, digging deep into the writings of the Scottish moral philosophers as well as contemporary political economy. Journals like the *Edinburgh Review* became his regular reading which he subscribed to when back in Uppsala in order to keep him updated on recent events and debates in Britain up to the 1840's.

Back in Uppsala Geijer began to teach history and became a senior lecturer in the subject. In the end his long-term strategy for a permanent position in the academy worked and he replaced Fant in the chair of History in

1817. During his long waiting time – apparently the old professor did not want to retire and died just half a year after he finally left the chair – Geijer was soon to join the Gothic Society (*Götiska förbundet*).

The Society had been established in Stockholm in 1811 and consisted at its height (in the 1820's) of around 100 members of the cultural and academic elite and some influential politicians. Its aim was patriotic and to emphasize the uniqueness of Swedish culture and history. It nostalgically looked back to a Swedish past of free allodial peasants and its idealised kings elected by a free people. Geijer was keen to contribute to such a patriotic task and wrote a large number of poems and other pieces on this theme during 1811 and the following years for the journal of the Gothic Society named *Iduna*. It was now that some of Geijer's most famous patriotic poems were published: *Manhem*, *Vikingen* (The viking) and *Odalbonden* (the Yeoman farmer). Up to the middle of the 20th century young pupils and students in Sweden were supposed to recite at least some of the verses from these poems by heart. Geijer himself, though, did not hold his poems in any particularly high esteem and did not see himself as a poet. In the first place came music, secondly philosophy and in the third place poetry and history.[11]

To be a patriot in the 1810's was not to be a conservative and still less a reactionary. The Swedish *Göticism* was rather a liberal ideology – similar to German patriotic discourse in Germany – emphasising the role of the *Volk* and its inherited liberties. To be a real conservative at the time was to be in favour of the restoration of the Bourbon monarchy in France and against every aspect of 1789. As we saw Geijer was certainly antipathetic to the anarchy

and bloodshed that the revolution had let loose, especially
in its Jacobin phase, which he disfavoured as much as the
dictatorship of Napoleon. On the other hand he returned
throughout his life to the revolution as something perhaps
inevitable in France, given its past history of absolutism
and feudalism. Revolution therefore was not necessary in
a more liberal country such as Britain and certainly not in
Sweden, which had never introduced feudalism proper or
serfdom. When France restored the Bourbon monarchy
with Louis XVII in 1814 Geijer was a stern opponent.[12]
He feared that this would also lead to *emigrés* returning
and the restoration of feudalism. In the same manner as
the Catholic Church, feudalism had perhaps been a necessity in the old time. But its role as a system of protecting
the people and keeping up order had vanished especially
with the emancipation of the cities and the rise of a middle class. The rule of the feudal nobles could no longer be
regarded as legitimate. Such developments were a theme
that he returned to in several of his texts in the 1810's,
perhaps most pertinently in the long essay *Feudalism and
Republicanism* included in this volume.

The critique of feudalism and serfdom he certainly
shared with most of the Scots as well as the German idealist philosophers that he adhered to at the time. Moreover he was critical of the so-called Holy Alliance after
1815, the main architect of which was the Austrian minister Metternicht. Geijer regarded it as a backward-looking
alliance of great powers and not very holy at all. Rather it
used the church as an instrument for reaction, he stated.[13]

We will return later to Geijer's no doubt close relationship to German philosophy. But what suffices to say here
is that his "romantic" turn in the 1810's did not necessari-

ly occur because he became more conservative in his political views. As a professor in Uppsala, serving as the *rector magnificus* or head of the University of Uppsala for several periods as well as being a delegate for the university in Swedish diets from the late 1820's and onwards, Geijer was of course supposed to stand up for law and order and to support the establishment.

Without doubt he was also a warm follower of the king, Carl XIV Johan, the French general who had been placed on the Swedish throne in 1818. But at the same time – especially during his first decade of ruling – Carl Johan was regarded as a liberal king in a European context. He undoubtedly had great personal power but still formally ruled according to the constitution of 1809, which was characterized by a balance of power between the king, the government and the Diet. The Diet consisted of the four estates of Noblemen, Clergy (in which Geijer sat as university professor), Burghers and Peasants.

The system worked in such a way that the king's appointed ministers (the government) put forward proposed legislation to the four estates separately. If any of the estates refused to vote in favour of the proposal it was turned down. But if there was agreement between all of the the estates and the king the proposal would become law. Suggestions for the replacement of the old estate system with something resembling the French constitutional assembly of 1789 were made from the 1790's onwards. However, it was not until the end of the 1830's that something of a real opposition to the system of four estates was formed, culminating at the Diet of 1840, which, although there were high hopes for reform, did not lead to many concrete results. The main argument for "reform of the representation", as it was called, was that the four estates did not represent the whole Swedish population; there was also a fifth estate in the form of a property-less proletariat of peasants and workers and servants that had no say in the Diet. Some in the middle classes also had little or no representation as the estate of the Burghers mainly voiced the interest of the merchants and craftsmen of the major towns.

Geijer was for a time a defender of the four estates system but gradually changed his mind. In the discussion concerning what was called the representation issue he first suggested reform within the old system. At the Diet of 1828 to which Geijer was a delegate he held a long speech outlining the view that reforms of any kind should not endanger the role of the free peasants. At the same time he worried about the estate system as a whole. It did not represent the great mass of people, he thought. In the burgher and peasant estates high income qualifications had become a way to prevent servants and workers from having any influence in political life.

Geijer warned of an upcoming conflict between the poor and the and the rich, a theme that he would develop even more in the 1840's. He gradually also came closer to giving support to a reform of the representation that would establish something like the House of Commons in Britain along the lines of the electoral reform of 1832 – but with significantly lower income requirements. Still, it would not be a house that represented everybody: women should be excluded because of their unique position as mothers and teachers of children (for a while Geijer played with the idea that other teachers of the youth such as priests and university professors should also be sheltered from the degenerating effects of political life, but he changed his mind).

Parliamentarism was most certainly not on his agenda: that a government should be formed according to a majority of voters. Instead he continued to emphasise the role of the king as the head of government with a right to appoint his ministers. In fact until 1840 very few in Sweden would have held any other view and certainly not Geijer. Until his death (1847) he was a firm believer in constitutional monarchy with a strong personal influence of a potent king – emphasizing the unique bond between the monarch and *his* people that Geijer regarded as an historical fact in Sweden.

As noted, the historiography of Geijer has put much emphasis on his alleged defection from conservatism in 1838. There is without doubt a grain of truth in this, but we should not exaggerate that shift to what has been called liberalism. Geijer was never a conservative of the kind that we might think of today. Nor was he a liberal in the way we use the term today. We must instead place him more firmly in his own historical context. Categories like "conservatism" and "liberalism" fit badly with the contemporary debates and discourses in Sweden during the first half of the 19th century.

It is still true that Geijer at the end of the 1830's shocked many of his friends and colleagues by talking much more in the affirmative about the so-called classical school of political economy and its discourse on freer trade and the positive aspects of the industrial revolution. As we saw when he was a young man visiting Britain, his first reaction to that revolution and the ongoing process of proletarianisation was a mixture of apprehension and remorse. The rise of widespread factory industry would break apart the social fabric and create a war between the rich and the poor, he thought. That was still his view at the end of the 1820's. But as he delved into the debates presented in *Edinburgh Review* and other British journals, such as the *Quarterly Journal*, he began to think otherwise. Yes, the political economy of the industrial revolution did create great upheavals. However, through a continuous process of division of labour productivity would rise and create more wealth. Such an increase of wealth would also create increasing incomes, which benefitted poor workers. This positive view of the benefits of industrial development he would retain during the rest of his life. However, as we will see, he would return to the plight of the proletariat during the 1840's with greater force than ever.

Hence his so-called defection reflected a certain shift in, or return to, a more clearly liberal stance in Geijer's overall economic views. On the other hand there was – as already noted – much continuity and a transgression in his thinking between positions which are hard to pin down and hard to label. Moreover, he would once again become more critical of classical political economy.

Still, one cannot help feeling that Geijer was very active personally in portraying himself as something of a radical maverick in 1838. He expressed the situation dramatically in a poem at the time: "Alone in a fragile vessel" ("Ensam i bräcklig farkost"). However, by this time Geijer was an established professor and a leading historian, with influential friends close to the Bernadotte monarch in Stockholm, and did not risk very much by his apparent defection to more liberal political standpoints. Geijer continued to teach history in Uppsala until the early 1840's, his final series of lectures being a long one on the *History of Mankind* ("Människans historia") in 1842 and 1843, in which he tried to combine a general history of philosophy since the end of the 18th century with an outline of his own intellectual development – and then resigned his chair in 1846. By that time he had moved to Stockholm, where he died the following year.

SCOTTISH FUNDAMENTALS

Geijer has often been misunderstood as a firebrand critic of everything that the Enlightenment stood for – at least after his Young Turk days in the 1790's. Moreover, his turn to German idealism in the early 1800's is often said to have made him a conservative. Along the lines of this stylised portrayal he remained so until his defection in 1838. After that he first became a doctrinal economic liberal and in the years before his death perhaps something of a proto-socialist. However, such a narrative is misleading in a number of ways. Firstly, it reflects a dated and to a large extent a distorted view, emphasising a great divide between "enlightenment" and "romanticism" (or "German idealism"). Secondly, it builds on a misinterpretation of Geijer's critique of enlightenment discourse. Thirdly, it takes a much too mechanical view of the relationship and conflicts between different versions of (moral) philosophy and politics. As has already been suggested, labels such as "conservative", "liberal" etc. are difficult to apply in Geijer's case. He easily crossed such borders – made manifest only much later – in his thinking and writing. Hence, by

28

forcing him into such anachronistic categories it becomes more or less impossible to understand what he was trying to say in his own time.

A starkly drawn line of demarcation between "enlightenment" and "romanticism" has a long pedigree in Swedish intellectual historiography.[14] After a period characterised as "the age of utility," in which especially French enlightenment discourse, including Voltaire and *les encyclopédistes* dominated the intellectual scene during the 1750's and 60's, something of a break occurred during the reign of Gustavus III (1771–1792). According to that version the Age of Utility was characterised by a cult of reason but especially of economic improvement, in which the state should play a fundamental role. A central figure here was of course the botanist Carl Linnaeus (von Linné), who was said to have paved the way for such "utilitarianism" (not to be confused with Benthamite moral philosophy). A version of political economy that emphasised the role of manufactures and a regulated economy often went hand in hand with views of that kind.[15]

During the Swedish so-called Age of Freedom (1721–1771) such a discourse was especially spurned by the 'Party of the Hats', an elite group of Stockholm export merchants and nobles. Moreover, a Swedish version of French Physiocracy was also regarded as part and parcel of this spirited utilitarian enlightenment. Hence agricultural reforms and regulations were regarded as pivotal for the rise of a new era of Swedish glory after the pitiful loss of the Baltic provinces in the peace of Nystad 1721.

A first fatal blow against this kind of enlightenment came as early as the mid-1760's, when the Hat Party (or rather proto-party) was replaced by that of the so-called

'Caps' as a dominating force in Swedish politics. A next step was taken by the *coup d'état* of Gustavus III in 1772, when he replaced the rule of the estates with his own in the form of enlightened monarchism (in fact closing down the Age of Freedom). Although Gustavus III was a friend of French enlightenment, a change of sentiments occurred during his reign opening the way for what in Swedish intellectual historiography has been named "early romanticism". This supposed stream of *belles lettres* in Sweden has been said to have been based on a diverse group of writers, poets, freemasons, members of learned societies and politicians.[16] What kept them together was an increasing distrust of the old "utilitarianism" and the kind of enlightenment views that went with it. Romanticism, in particular, was said to have had its breakthrough in Swedish discourse during the 1790's, after the French revolution and the introduction of *German idealism* (Herder, Fichte etc.). However, the romanticists held diverse opinions concerning the French revolution. Some were ready to listen to the kind of critique delivered by Edmund Burke, while others were keen supporters of the revolution. Some were radicals, like the famous Swedish author Tomas Thorild (1759–1808) – expelled from Sweden proper, he found a retreat in Swedish Greifswald – while others were outright reactionaries and followers of enlightened despotism, like Carl Gustaf af Leopold (1756–1829). The establishment of the Gothic Society, to which, as we saw, Geijer belonged, is traditionally seen as being part of this rather incoherent "stream" of new romanticism.

There are two problems with such an historical narrative, problems that also affect how we are to understand Geijer's intellectual development. First, it gravely underestimates the role of influence from countries outside France, particularly from Germany. The second is that it promotes a too monolithic view of what was in fact a variety of enlightenments. Hence the kind of enlightenment behind Swedish utilitarianism was much less of French origin than stemming from Prussian moral philosophy, especially as formulated by the great systematiser Christian Wolff in Halle. Consequently, the emphasis on a regulated society and economy rested on a view of a natural order created by God, "A Divine Economy" (*Oeconomia divina*), as defined by the intellectual historian Tore Frängsmyr.[17] Already in the 1730's several leading scientists from Sweden, such as Anders Celsius and Anders Benzelstierna, had visited Halle and brought the new philosophy back home with them. Together with Linnaeus and others they became very much the founders of Swedish "utilitarianism". The mainstream of political economy during the Age of Liberty in Sweden was highly influenced from the 1750's onwards by Wolffianism.[18]

To a large degree such enlightened "utilitarianism" was based on a specific interpretation of a moral jurisprudence put forward in the debate on natural law that had been going on in Europe since the 17th century. One main point of difference within that discussion concerned the relationship between Society and Man and the origins of the social contract. While those taking their departure from Thomas Hobbes emphasised original Man as one who had to be tamed by a Leviathan (or at least a patriarchal and highly regulated) state in order not to end up in a war of all against all. Grotius and subsequent natural natural law philosophers such as Samuel Pufendorf, underscored the social character of Man even before the

31

creation of omnipotent rulers.[19] This might seem to be a minor verbal quibble but the political consequences were great. Those who underscored the importance of regulation and a strong state took their point of departure from the first of those two positions while those who were critical of such measures took the second. Modern scholarship emphasises that especially the Scottish version of enlightenment to a large extent built upon the notion of man as a social creature already in the state of nature. It was on this foundation that Scots like Frances Hutcheson, David Hume, Adam Smith, Adam Ferguson and the historian William Robertson – of particular importance for Geijer – built their vision of the sociability of men and their moral instincts (or sympathies, which was the most commonly used term at the time).

From what Geijer states himself we know that he gained a deep inspiration from the Scots. He refers to Adam Ferguson's *Essay on the history of civil society* as his "first most cherished book of study".[20] William Robertson was somebody he already read in his youth and found great pleasure in. Robertson had as early as 1754 become a member of the Select Society in Edinburgh, which included David Hume, Adam Smith and Lord Kames.[21] Some of Robertson's historical works reached almost popular status and were widely read: *A History of Scotland* (1759), *A History of the reign of Emperor Charles V* (1769) and *A History of America* (1777).

The influence of what was typical of Scottish moral philosophy is very evident in Robertson's works. It is especially in his American history that he develops an anthropology of man which emphasises the natural habit of people to form associations (family and upwards).

He stresses that "the dispositions and manners of men are formed by their situation, and arise from the state of society in which they live".[22] He is clearly influenced by Montesquieu in claiming the importance of climate and geography, but more than anything else he underscores the importance of human labour in order to increase production, "the improvement and embellishment of the earth".[23] Especially in Geijer's *Feudalism and Republicanism* there is a strong echo of Robertson, Montesquieu, Hume, Smith and Scottish moral philosophy in general. Here we also find a critique of Hobbes along the lines of the Scots. He cites Hume at length – though not always in a positive manner. He disliked Hume's sarcastic treatment of religion, but so did William Robertson when he spoke about Hume he said "...with whom, notwithstanding the contraries of our sentiments both in religion and politics I live in great friendship".[24]

However, all through his life Geijer would return to the Scots. In one of his only two works translated into English (the second was an abridged version of his *Svenska folkets historia* translated as *A History of the Swedes*, where the author's name was said to be Eric Gustave Geijer[25]), namely *The Poor Laws and their bearing on society* (1840), he wrote that the "natural and the voluntary associations – on one side the family and on the other the corporation – are the two elements of society".[26] When Geijer states that "... the state existed at first solely as the loose connection between the families or tribes," that certainly is an echo from the great debates on natural law which also inspired the Scots moral philosophers. Moreover, in stressing productive labour as a driving force of civilisation we find traces of Adam Ferguson's *Essay on Civilization* as well as of the so-called Stages Theory developed by the Scots as well as by the famous economist and finance minister under Louis XVI, Anne-Robert-Jacques Turgot in France during the decades before 1789.[27] Some central aspects of The Poor Laws essays are reflected on in an article printed in this volume.

Finally, it is perhaps in his *Om det mänskliga naturtillståndet* ("Concerning man in the state of nature") (1818) that he is most explicit concerning his reliance on the Scots. He there refers to the tradition going back to Pufendorf on the social character of men, cites Ferguson with approval and makes a critique of social contract theories that is highly Scottish in kind. He states outright that "already in the state of nature there is society"[28]. In *Feudalism and Republicanism* too, he criticises social contract theory – this time along the lines of Edmund Burke. The contract is not simply a piece of paper by which people hand over their natural freedoms mechanically for the purpose of protection, he says. To the extent that it is a contract at all it must include the already dead and the ones that have not yet arrived, the inborn rights of men and their social and moral aptitudes.

In several texts over the years – certainly both before and after his apparent defection – Geijer talks about a "false enlightenment," acknowledging that there is also another enlightenment that is sound and worth preserving. The "false" version he also often calls "mechanical" enlightenment. After taking notice of his Scottish roots we can better understand what he was actually aiming at. According to Geijer any version of Hobbes' social contract – people having to hand over their natural freedoms in order to gain security – was false and mechanical. Such views, neglecting the social nature of men, were at the same time the reason why the French revolution, which had promised so much, turned into bloody terror and political dictatorship.

Any view that treated man as a blank page ready to be manipulated Geijer regarded as false enlightenment. It is true that he wavered on his opinion of Rousseau but in the end he also found him to belong to the "false" school.[29] We must acknowledge that he found the critical view of religion of Voltaire, the *encyclopédistes* and Helvetius disturbing (but perhaps understandable because of a corrupt Catholic Church). But that was not at the core of his critique of false enlightenment. It was the view which left men without moral propensities, feelings of compassion, without a history and the possibility of a better future built on reason. And, perhaps even more importantly, without liberty. Some of this he thought could be cured by a dose of German idealism.

GERMAN IDEALISM

When Geijer arrived in Uppsala in 1799 the leader of the discussion club the *Junta*, the philosopher Benjamin Höijer, was acknowledged to be a radical Kantian. Even in his old age Geijer rated him as his foremost teacher in philosophy and someone greatly underrated in his thinking. Höijer also seems to have been Geijer's guide to German philosophy at large, introducing him to Herder, Fichte, Schelling and perhaps also Hegel. But Höijer was not the one who introduced Kant in Uppsala. In 1799 the "battle" still raged between the so-called Lockeans and a Kantian party, the first led by the philosophy professor Per Nichlas Christiernin and the other by his colleague Daniel Boethius.

From the beginning Boethius had also been a follower of Locke's empiricism and its implied calculus of pleasure and pain, later identified with Jeremy Bentham. But Boethius swung over to Kant's position that moral categories could not be verified by sense-data. This undoubtedly pleased many of the radical young students and teachers, including Höijer. However he was already at this time attempting to take a next step: to transcend the dualism that he saw both in Kant and Fichte, between object and subject, spirit and nature, liberty and necessity. In a number of treatises, particularly in *Om den philosophiska constructionen* (1799), Höijer developed ideas along those lines, which have been said to have anticipated Schelling's attempt in the same direction.[30]

The degree to which Geijer followed in Höijer's footsteps has been discussed over a long time. John Landquist, who published Geijer's collected works in the 1920's and also wrote an influential biography of him, has perhaps gone furthest in the direction of emphasising the influence from German philosophy.[31] He mentions in particular the influence of Schelling's transcendentalism. He also insists that Geijer over time developed into a Hegelian.[32] By and large C.A. Hessler also follows the same path in his two books on Geijer's development as a politician. Hessler – as we have discussed – takes the position that it was German idealism that can explain Geijer's turn to conservatism after 1810. However, that was perhaps an appropriate strategy for a socialist-leaning doctor in political science in Gothenburg, such as Hessler, writing his books on Geijer before and at the end of the Second World War, for whom German idealism was something suspect.[33] On the other hand, he was rather hesitant in regarding Geijer as a full fledged Hegelian.

Others also have mixed feelings about the relation between Geijer and the Germans. The historian of religion (among other things), Per Meurling, emphasises that Geijer's fondness of Schelling essentially has to do with the fact that he regarded his thinking as an attempt to bring religion back into philosophy. At the same time he stated that Geijer was no doctrinaire Schellingian.[34]

Undoubtedly, however, Geijer, in his critique of false and mechanical enlightenment, the unfettering of man from being a victim of external forces and his search for an identity with spirit and matter, found the Germans very useful. Like Höijer, he believed that "reason does not take its laws from nature but it is reason that defines the laws of nature[35]."We have already mentioned the possibility of including God in, for example, Schelling's schemes.

Perhaps the most important thing that can be said of Geijer's involvement with German idealist philosophy is that he never adhered to any fixed position that enables us to pin him down as a true follower of any rigid "system". In this case and in general he was a sceptical soul, insisting upon the right to mix elements from different sources.

Perhaps the best guide to his own intellectual development is his previously discussed lectures from the early 1840's on the *History of Mankind* published in the form of lecture notes from a number of his students. Rather than as a series of lectures on historical narrative, Geijer here delivered his matured views on the history of (moral) philosophy from Plato onwards. From his earlier works we recognise the critique of "mechanical enlightenment" from Locke up to Voltaire and the French *encyclopédistes*. Given the emphasis that interpreters of Geijer have placed on his defection from conservatism in 1838, this might seem awkward, but Geijer's supposed turn to liberalism did not change his mind in the least in his critique of Lockeanism.[36] Furthermore, as we follow his lecturing, he talks in positive terms about Montesquieu, the Scottish moral philosophers and their emphasis on man being equipped with inherent social "sympathies".[37] Then he goes over to the Germans and "the new philosophy". He speaks in favour of Goethe and mentions Herder "as one of my first reading experiences". He calls Kant a "true humanist" and someone who placed Man in the centre of philosophy.[38] What he has to say about Rousseau is in the main sceptical ("he was in opposition to everything including himself").[39] After that he mentions his admiration for the Swedish philosopher Benjamin Höijer ("I did not miss a single one of his lectures"[40]). He regards Schelling's works as the best introduction to "pure idealism". Idealism ends at least for Geijer in religion: only God as creator can know what the essence or spirit of Man really is. He acknowledges that he himself has sometimes fallen victim to the cult of the genius to which the idealists were often prone. But he is now more sceptical and speaks of "pure idealism" as something of an epistemological cage from which there is no escape.[41]

It is also clear that in his lectures from 1840–41 Geijer was ambivalent about Hegel. On the one hand he describes his "system" as the fulfilment of the new idealist philosophy.[42] On the other he tells his students (in a deflecting sense) that to explain Hegel's system is perhaps "above his abilities". In his biography (*Minnen*) he had called Hegel's work "hard to penetrate".[43] The central message in his lectures 1840–41 seems to be that Schelling is still his favourite. This does not mean to say, of course, that Geijer was not influenced by Hegel. In 1825 – when he actually met Hegel in Berlin but was a bit disappointed by his petty insistence upon *formalia* in his philosophy – he said that he had not read Hegel until recently. He then most probably referred to *Grundlinien der Philosophie des Rechts* (1821) in which he certainly liked what Hegel had to say about the family and the different corporations as the basic institutions in society – but those were themes that he had explicated before he read Hegel's *Philosophie des Rechts* (for example in *Feudalism and Republicanism*).

Much of that Geijer could already have got from Schelling (or even Robertson!). Scholars who tend to call Geijer a fullblown Hegelian often refer to a piece, *Nytt ett och annat i fråga om den akademiska jurisdinktionen* ("New one or two things regarding the academic jurisdiction"), which was published in 1822 after he had read Hegel's book on *The Philosophy of Right*.[44] Geijer's aim here was to defend the academic freedom of his *Alma Mater* (including its corporate right to its own jurisdiction). There is no doubt that he here used Hegel to defend that right and went far in the direction of identifying the state as the result of human progress from the family to the corporations and to see both of these as natural institutions in a (future) ideal state.[45]

However, Geijer never before or later went beyond that but instead became more sceptical over time. Even in 1822 he emphasises that the family and different corporations would not be replaced or superseded by the state but would instead form an identity or even an organism. Regarding Hegel's view of the state as the fulfilment of the spirit, he might have felt that his perfect state was too similar to the (authoritarian) Prussian state for his liking. At the same time he was ready to accept Hegel's view of the state as something of a moral personality. But he never went as far as identifying the state as an "objective spirit" so that "it is only through being a member of the state that the individual himself has objectivity, truth, and ethical life."[46] Nor could he accept Hegel's high regard for Napoleon as an instrument of the development of the spirit or understand his discussion on the identity of civil society with the (Prussian) state. In the early 1840's he leaned over towards the left Hegelians as we will see in his critique of the contemporary state. Moreover his notion that civil society was something different than the state was reinforced when he read Tocqueville.

The distinction between Geijer and what is commonly known as the "romanticist turn" in Germany is perhaps most pertinent in the case of Adam Müller, the most important of the so-called "romantic economists" anticipating Friedrich List and the later historical school of economics in Germany. Much effort has been spent by Swedish scholars to establish a link between Müller and Geijer.[47] But it is difficult to pin down what "romantic economics" was, as it is evidently constructed as a "school" later during the 19th century in order to emphasize German exceptionalism.[48] The dichotomy between "Smithian economics" and "Romantic economics" emphasised in older scholarship hinges to a large degree on our understanding of what has been called 'Das Adam Smith Problem', more precisely the existence of what from a simplified analysis appears to be two different Adam Smiths; one concerned predominantly with commerce and trade, as in the *Wealth of Nations,* the other with moral philosophy, as in *The Theory of Moral Sentiments.* Few scholars today would admit that such a *problem* exists at all and argue instead that Smith must be placed in the Scottish tradition of moral philosophy. As a consequence, as noted by Richard Bronk, Adam Smith could very well be seen as "a precursor to the Romantic Economics"[49]. We should not for example be surprised over that someone like Adam Müller regarded himself as a person who followed in Smith's footsteps.[50]

This is not the place to explain the economic theories of Adam Müller's (1779–1829) or his famous book on money.[51] Geijer could to a large extent follow Müller's critique of early classical political economy and especially of Bentham. Geijer could also agree with Müller when he had defended Smith in vitriolic prose against Fichte following the latter's plea for economic isolation in *Der geschlossene Handelsstaat* (1800) – especially in *Elemente der Staatskunst* (1810) or in *Versuch einer neuen Theorie des Geldes* (1816). At the same time Geijer felt Smith to be much too focused on self-interest and the individual.

However, it is unlikely that Geijer ever approved of Müller's *state dirigisme* on economic and monetary matters or his idealisation of the middle ages. Müller was surely too entangled in the German cameralist tradition for someone like Geijer, who had been brought up in Värmland, among independent iron-masters who cherished less regulation and instead had the tradition of a Swedish version of mercantilism or cameralism which was much more open to free enterprise and to some extent freedom of trade.[52]

41

GEIJER AS AN HISTORIAN

When Geijer made the choice to become a professor of history in the 1810's the subject was being transformed. At the new university in Berlin named after the great Wilhelm von Humboldt and with Johann Gottlieb Fichte as its first *rector* the aim was to establish a more scientifically based discipline of history. Even though Leopold von Ranke did not become history professor in the Prussian capital until 1825, his definition of these new efforts, which had started earlier, has become seminal: to deal with history "wie es eigentlich gewesen". However, when Geijer was inaugurated in the chair in Uppsala in 1817 "critical history" had not yet arrived there. As we saw, Geijers' predecessor in the chair, old Fant, was mainly interested in antiquarian issues. During the 18th century at least two general histories on Sweden were published by native authors, the first by Olof von Dalin, a man of letters, and the second by Sven Lagerbring, professor of history at the University of Lund. Both were patriotic in tone and mainly centred on the period up to the 17th century, particularly on the development of Sweden as a great power. Especially Dalin spent many pages on the chronology of pre-medieval mythical kings who probably never existed. His history was to a large extent story-telling, while Lagerbring on the other hand was more critical towards his sources.

With Geijer, however, there was a break. In the 1820's Geijer set out to introduce Berlin-style history in Uppsala, establishing it on a more factual basis. Moreover, his interest lay less in details or the collection of artefacts than in something which at the time was named "philosophical history". Taking his departure from the broader sweeps of history provided by 18th century writers such as Montesquieu up to the Scottish tradition with Hume and Robertson he was aiming to write synthetic histories of civilisation in a broad sense, not only dealing with political history but also with social issues, economy and culture.[53] Geijer held the chair in Uppsala from 1817 to 1846. Besides his academic duties, including lecturing to students, other writings and duties in state commissions and the Diet in Stockholm, he also composed two major works on Swedish history, *Svea rikes hävder* (1825) and *Svenska folkets historia* in three parts (1832-1836). A planned fourth volume dealing with "modern times after 1654", where the third volume ended, was never published. However, in 1836 Geijer published a separate treatise on the Swedish Age of Liberty (1721-1771), *Teckning af Frihetstiden*, in which he painted a rather dark picture of that period. This has puzzled many readers, as Geijer was at that time moving towards his famous defection and into more liberal politics.[54]

However, he did not regard the rule of the Diet before Gustavus III's *coup d'état* as particularly liberal. Where others saw the introduction of freedom of the press in 1766 and the lively debates at the different Diets in the middle of the 18th century as signs of progress in political freedom, Geijer instead saw party fractions and corruption.

The rule of the Diet was in fact a façade for a rule of the elites, leaving the majority of the people without a voice. In his critique of the Age of Liberty he could rely on his negative view on "mechanical" enlightenment and the kind of "utilitarianism" which dominated Swedish polity and economy at the time. It is also to a large extent coloured by his belief in a strong monarch serving as the father of his people. The king should hold a mediating position between different social strata and carry out rule by law.

Especially in his *A History of the Swedes* Geijer has a tendency to emphasise the historically progressive role of kings – writing about Charles IX at the end of the 16th century, he even said something like "Swedish history is that of its kings". He did not really mean that literally, of course, but definitively preferred a strong monarch before the rule of selfish elites.

GEIJER AND CLASSICAL
POLITICAL ECONOMY

Towards Adam Smith Geijer was no doubt in sympathy in his earlier days, given his interest in the Scots. But like so many others he was influenced by the general reinterpretation of Smith which took place already from the 1790's by Edmund Burke and others, from someone who emphasised the social sentiments of Man to someone who spoke in favour of the naked economic "laws" in the manner of Malthus and later on Ricardo.[55] Geijer never explicitly says that Smith belongs to the "mechanical enlightenment" but instead, perhaps like Müller, sees him as something different from the followers of Smith and the Classical political economists.

As noted above, Geijer was a keen reader of the English political economists – in the *Edinburgh Review* in particular – ever since his visit to England in 1809-10. He was undoubtedly disturbed by the plight of the proletariat as a consequence of the industrial revolution, the fifth (propertyless) estate as he called it from a Swedish perspective. No doubt he blamed its hardship on the selfishness of the "dismal science" put forward by the Malthus-Ricardian school and by Benthamite moral philosophy.

Being occupied by other matters, teaching and writing history as well as performing his duties as professor in Uppsala, he only returned to such issues in the 1830's. During that decade the so-called social question was on everybody's lips. There was talk of the *classes dangereuses* and their challenge to law and social stability.[56] Examples could be taken from the factory towns in Lancashire in England, where machine wreckers put their clogs in the spinning machines, or in the countryside, where threshing machines were destroyed in the name of a mysterious Captain Ludd.[57] Also in Silesia in the east there was talk of social unrest and from Paris rumours spread of secret societies of proletarian anarchists, which were supposed to take to arms. Without doubt Geijer was following such discussions closely.

Up until the middle of the 1830's he was sceptical about the British industrial revolution, for two reasons: first, as mentioned, because it created a multitude of propertyless and poor workers, but secondly also because it destroyed the basis for handicrafts, which he saw not only as beneficial from an employment point of view but also as a stabilising force in society. But gradually Geijer changed his mind. In his *Blå boken* ("The Blue book"), where he made personal comments, he noted in 1835 some articles from the *Edinburgh Review* that he had found particularly interesting. In two books concerning the history of the cotton industry he had found evidence of the tremendous growth of output and income which had been the consequence of the introduction of industrial methods in that industry. This must mean that, although many complaints could be levelled against abuse of child labour etc., the introduction of machinery and the factory had been on the whole beneficial also for the poor workers.[58]

Equipped with such the Smithian rising-tide-raises-all-boats theory, Geijer also published articles in which he showed himself to be positive to a greater liberty of trade. He also placed himself as a liberal in an article concerning Poland in which he protested against the great powers in Europe dividing up of the country. Moreover Geijer was also seen among liberal circles in Stockholm, where friends of free trade gathered; he seems to have become especially close to the iron industrialist Jonas Waern.[59] Those who had regarded Geijer as a stern follower of the establishment began to wonder. Had he become a follower of liberalism and given up his old values? We must then ask if there is any sense to talk about a defection?

Without doubt Geijer had become more liberal concerning the old *dirigisme* after reading the discussion in the *Edinburgh Review* in the middle of the 1830's. But it is to go too far to say that he had changed his deeper values regarding society and religion. As we already stated, it is difficult to pin him down as either conservative or liberal in any modern sense of such labels. He had become more positive towards contemporary economics concerning the beneficial effects of the industrial revolution but was still critical towards the Benthamite calculus of pleasure and pain and to the individualistic approach of classical political economy. And he changed his mind again – at least partly – when we arrive in the early 1840's.

Moreover, Geijer's liberalism at the time was to a great extent coloured by his reading of the French writer Alexis de Tocqueville. He had come across Tocqueville's *De la démocratie en Amérique* in an English translation during the winter of 1835–36.[60] Geijer commented that it was one of the best books he had ever read.[61] To the extent that Tocqueville can be seen as a liberal at all, Geijer's liberalism at the end of the 1830's was close to what he could distil from the great Frenchman's interpretation of American society. America was something new and fresh, with institutions still to be formed. It had a democratic and republican spirit. It definitely had room for a civil society besides a state, giving a fresh input to, for example Hegel's dialectics. It put freedom and ideas of equality at the forefront. All of this inspired Geijer greatly. About his supposed defection, he himself noted in 1838: "My defection from the historical school – because I have become evermore convinced that past history can not do more than modify human action which is rather the outcome of the work of each generation".[62] This was very much a *Lesefrucht* from Tocqueville.

GEIJER AS A UTOPIAN SOCIALIST

From the end of the 1830's Geijer involved himself in two different political issues. The first concerned the poor laws and the second the so-called representation reform and subsequently a reform of the old Diet and the four estates system. In 1839, in a series of articles in his own journal *Litteratur-Bladet*, Geijer presented his view on the necessity of reforming the Swedish poor law system. The articles were translated into English and, as mentioned above, published as a booklet in 1840, entitled: *The Poor Laws and their bearing on society*.[63] He took the issue very seriously indeed, writing nine articles running over more than two hundred pages. He goes far back in history to explicate how the poor have been treated in Sweden. To a large extent he presents a historical sketch which closely follows the one he presented in *Feudalism and Republicanism*.

Geijer goes on to emphasise that two methods have previously prevailed to treat the poor: either charity or penal correction. A third alternative he also rejects, especially because modern industrial societies have trade crises and thus create involuntary unemployment: to leave the poor to take care of themselves. Instead he prefers the kind of method that we would today call a system of workfare – anticipating a later Swedish model for the labour market – in which society takes a certain responsibility. However the main road here is something that Geijer calls "the liberation of labour". This is not only a Swedish matter, in fact the liberation of labour which has endured long birth pains "is the work of civilisation."[64]

In defining such a liberation he made use of the Classical political economists, especially J R McCulloch and Ricardo. A free labourer will work more diligently than a worker fettered by the old regulations. Better labour in turn will "increase both production and the number of producers". More productive labour will cause prices to fall, which at the same time "is fully compatible with a rise in the value of labour".[65] Interestingly enough he thus rejects what has been regarded as a central ingredient in the Classical political economy: the so-called iron-law of wages. He might have got this from the American economist Carey's *Principles of Political Economy* published in 1837, but such a critique of the Ricardo-Malthus model was commonplace both in America and Sweden at the time, emphasising the possibility of increased productivity and the great supply of land and other resources in industrialising countries.[66]

However, Geijer undoubtedly takes a further step in his discussion of the liberation of labour. He talks of the "collectivisation of labour" as the consequence of industrialism, on which nations will in the future have to rely or their livelihood. In this context he speaks much more about reciprocity and the rights of labour than do the classical political economists. Something that he calls "labour for labour" is "the divine ordinance which through the law of reciprocal right comes more and more into realization".[67] Moreover he talks of the "emancipation of labour" and asks whether this emancipation does not also have its dangers. Most certainly it has, he says, but these are "the dangers of liberty". Moreover, he speaks about "the luxurious repose of the Capitalist" as not after all "the purpose of humanity" and talks of the capitalists as "an aristocracy of drones and sluggards".[68] Was Geijer in fact already treading the path of a social utopian in 1839?

The second concern of Geijer around 1840 was the representation reform and the future of the four estates system. As we have seen he was even much earlier in favour of reform according to the British model of 1832. But when he returns to the issue some years later he takes a more radical stance. He now speaks in favour of a totally new institution to replace the Diet of estates. The Diets have played out their historical role, he says. The main reason is the rise of a fifth estate of workers who are pivotal for the future wealth of the nation and will thus have to take their place in the political system in the future. As we saw, women and perhaps others would still not be represented but income should not on principle be an excluding factor. At the beginning of the 1840's this was undoubtedly to take a quite radical position on a debate that would continue until 1865, when a parliament with two chambers was established in Sweden – but with higher income qualifications than Geijer would have preferred.

Geijer's reputation as an utopian socialist stems largely from his longish essay based on lectures partly included in this volume, *On the internal social conditions of our time* ("Om vår tids inre samhällsförhållanden") (1844). Here he put forward a critique of industrial capitalism, once again emphasising that "the fulfilment of the capitalist's wellbeing...is not the goal of mankind". Further, he speaks of the third estate (the burghers) as trying to block the "rights" of the working people. They sing the song of freedom of trade while at the same time striving for a class monopoly.[69] Yes, Geijer here uses the word "class" in several places as opposite social strata with different interests to defend. Further he talks about the capitalist class increasing its hegemony over the working-class.

Talking now about the hardships of the proletariat and the establishment of "the power of the strongest," he now again turns more critical towards the classical economists. The industrial revolution had undoubtedly increased production and income, but the question was if the price was worth paying. He now insisted that the liberalisation of work – that he had talked about in the 1830's – did not merely imply an unfettered labour market. It was something deeper than that. Now in 1844 his text is filled with references to his reading of "left" Hegelians such as Ludwig Feuerbach and Bruno Bauer. When he talks of the issue of justice as being "the first in society" and the "fulfilment of the complete man," that echoes the recent debates originating from Germany.

However, it is not only the "young" or "left" Hegelians who appear in this remarkable piece. He also refers to what he has picked up from the British debates on the social issue. C. A. Hessler has has noted Geijer's interest in the Chartist movement. No doubt when he refers to the importance of the "association principle," especially for working men, he refers to the young labour movement in Britain.[70] He regards its effort to put forward a representation reform according to the principle of one man one vote. Hence a "forward moving social principle" could only be achieved by the association of workers, "a more comprehensive social formation". Still, Geijer was not uncritical of the Chartists, even at times calling them "demagogues". As usual he could not make up his mind totally. He perhaps feared a return of something like the French revolution fifty years earlier. But for Geijer there was no way back: labour must be liberated even if certain risks lay ahead. This is also the picture Geijer gives in his last published essay *An economic dream* ("En ekonomisk dröm") from 1847, included here, originally published only two months before he died in 1847.

WRAPPING UP

Closing as we began, we put the question: what can we make of Erik Gustaf Geijer's life and letters? Undoubtedly, he lived in a time which saw the emergence of a new civilisation built on industry and capital – but also the beginning of a process of emancipation of labouring men and women. This new civilisation's contradictions were also his. Geijer, like many others, observed the mighty forces unleashed by machinery and the power of capital. The old world of chivalry and feudalism was on its way out. The great issues of the day were how to solve the social question. Could this be done without too much bloodshed? Could increased democracy and representation be introduced without the loss of societal stability? Lastly, could industrial capitalism be made to become more inclusive?

It was on such questions that Geijer reflected during most of his life. In fact we are still doing so. In order to find good answers he made use of many different sources. All through life he was a receptive and reflective reader. When we take part in his intellectual journey from the 1790's up until the middle of the 1840's we acknowledge both change and continuity. But we also get a hint that intellectual developments over this long period have to some extent been misunderstood. Where intellectual historians see cemented "schools" in opposition to each other Geijer saw possibilities and openings. When we feel that he crosses demarcation lines between different traditions or schools he would not himself have acknowledged that in many cases. As pointed out in contemporary intellectual history, the divide between the enlightenment – especially in its Scottish form – and the German romanticists was never as wide as it has often been depicted. When reading the essays of Erik Gustaf Geijer in this volume we find ourselves in a great laboratory of ideas where issues were discussed almost two hundred years ago which to a great extent are still with us today: to create decent and inclusive societies which combine the creation of wealth with a sense of equality.

Notes

1 Birger Liljekrantz, *Benjamin Höijer: En studie över hans utveckling*. Lund: H Ohlssons boktryckeri 1912.

2 Göran B Nilsson. *Musikprocessen och andra historiska processer*. Stockholm: P A Norstedts & söner 1984, p. 9f.

3 Henrik Schuck and Karl Warburg, *Illustrerad Svensk Litteraturhistoria*, del V. Stockholm: Hugo Geebers förlag 1897, p. 422f.

4 Geijer, *Minnen*.

5 A statement that perhaps not is totally true as Geijer was away from Uppsala for some time after Höijer had returned. But perhaps Höijer did not give any lectures during those years.

6 Cited after Schuck and Warburg, p. 429.

7 For this and the following biographical overview, see Svenskt Biografiskt Lexikon, "Geijer"; Schuck and Warburg; and John Landquist, *Erik Gustaf Geijer. Hans levnad och verk*. Stockholm: P A Norstedt & Söner 1924.

8 Erik Gustaf Geijer, *Minnen*. Stockholm: Minerva (no year), p. 49.

9 Ibid, p. 79.

10 Ibid, p.72.

11 Schuck and Warburg, p. 452.

12 See for example C. A. Hessler, vol. I, p. 259.

13 Ibid, p. 195f; Geijer, *Samlade skrifter,* II, p. 384f

14 Especially Sten Lindroth, *Svensk lärdomshistoria*, del II. *Stockholm: Norstedts 1997.*

15 See for example Lars Magnusson, "Comparing Cameralisms: The case of Sweden and Prussia". In Marten Seppel and Keith Tribe (eds), *Cameralisms in Practice.* London: Boyden Press 2017.

16 See especially Martin Lamm, *Upplysningens romantik, I-II.* Stockholm: Hugo Geebers förlag, 1918-20.

17 Tore Frängsmyr, "Den gudomliga ekonomin. Religion och hushållning i 1700-talets Sverige". *Lychnos 1971-72*; and Tore Frängsmyr, *Wolffianismens genombrott i Sverige.* Acta Universitatis Upsaliensis. Uppsala 1971.

18 Lars Magnusson, "Corruption and Civic Order – Natural Law and Economic Discourse in Sweden during the Age of Freedom".. *Scandinavian Economic History Review*, vol XXXVII:2, 1989; and Tore Frängsmyr, *Wolffianismens genombrott.*

19 Istvan Hont. " The Language of Sociability and Commerce: Samuel Pufendorf and the Theoretical Foundations of the Four Stage Theory". In Anthony Pagden, (ed), *The Languages of Political Theory in Early Modern Europe.* Cambridge: Cambridge University Press 1987.

20 Geijer, *Samlade skrifter*, part IO, *Människans historia*, p. 41.

21 Dugald Stewart, "An Account of his life and Writings"(1801). *The Works of William Robertson.* London: Longman & Co, 1882.

22 Robertson, *The works*, p. 785.

23 Robertson, *The works*, p. 783.

24 Cited from Dugald Stewart, p. 12. On Hume and
   Robertson, see J. G. A. Pocock, *Barbarism and Religion,
   II.* Cambridge: Cambridge University Press, p. 200f.

25 Eric Gustave Geijer, *A History of the Swedes.* London:
   Whittaker & Co (no year).

26 Geijer, *The Poor Laws*, p. 29.

27 Ronald Meek, *Social Science and the Ignoble Savage.* New
   York and London: Cambridge University Press, 1976.

28 Cited Hessler, I, p. 252 Cf, Geijer, *Samlade skrifter*, part
   II, p. 403f.

29 Geijer, *Samlade skrifter,* vol. 10, p. 49, 115f.

30 On Höijer, see "Benjamin Höijer" Svenskt Biografiskt
   Lexikon.

31 John Landquist, *Erik Gustaf Geijer. Hans levnad och verk.*
   Stockholm: PA Norstedt & Söner, 1924.

32 Landquist, p. 443f. Also Sven Ingemar Olofsson *Geijer
   som samhällsekonom.* Stockholm: Rabén och Sjögren
   1959, p. 153f, 188.

33 C. A. Hessler, *Geijer som politiker.*

34 Per Meurling, *Geijer & Marx*, p.119.

35 Citation from Meurling, p. 111.

36 Especially evident in his lectures on *The history of
   Man* in the beginning of the 1840's when he said
   that Locke's conceptualised Man as a "calculating
   machine". Cf Geijer, *Samlade skrifter*, vol. 10, p. 29.

37 Geijer, *Samlade skrifter*, vol. 10, p. 42.

38 Ibid, p. 44f.

39 Ibid, p. 35, 49, 115f.

40 Ibid, p. 82.

41 Ibid, p, 135.

42 Ibid, p. 135f.

43 *Minnen*, p. 216.

44 For example Hessler, I, p. 264f and Olofsson.

45 Geijer, *Samlade skrifter*, vol. III, p. 276f.

46 Hegel, Philosophie des Rechts, *Grundlinien
    der Philosophie des Rechts*. Georg Wilhelm
    Friedrich Hegel: Werke. Band 7, Frankfurt a. M. 1979,
    section 258.

47 Olofsson, p. 114f and Landquist, p. 417f.

48 Richard Bronk, *The Romantic Economists*. Cambridge:
    Cambridge University Press, 2009.

49 Richard Bronk, p. 62 Cf, also Keith Tribe, *The Economy
    of the Word*, Oxford University Press, 2015.

50 On the relation between the Germans and Smith, see
    Knud Haakonsen, *Natural Law and Moral Philosophy.
    From Grotius to the Scottish Enlightenment*. Cambridge:
    Cambridge University Press 1996. Here of course Kant
    was a bridge, p. 148f, 166f.

51 Bronk, p. 154f.

52 Magnusson, "Comparing Cameralisms".

53 On this and the following, see Bengt Henningsson,
    Geijer som historiker. Stockholm: Scandinavian
    University Books, 1961.

54 In 1844 the popular historian Anders Fryxell wrote
    a treatise in a critique of Geijer's critical attitude
    towards the historical role of Swedish aristocracy, "Om
    aristokratifördömandet i svenska historien", which was
    much discussed at the time. See Henningsson, p. 105f.

55 Emma Rothschild *Economic Sentiments: Adam Smith,
    Concordet and the Enlightenment*. Harvard University
    Press: Cambridge, 2001, Lars Magnusson, *The
    Tradition of Free Trade*. London: Routledge, 2004.

56 On this theme see the seminal Louis Chevalier,
    Laboring Classes and Dangerous Classes. Princeton:
    Princeton University Press, 1973.
57 See for example Eric Hobsbawm and George Rudé,
    Captain Swing, Harmondsworth: Penguin University
    Books, 1973.
58 We can follow this in detail in Hessler, II p. 104f.
59 Hessler, II, p. 69.
60 Hessler, II, p. 131.
61 Geijer, *Samlade skrifter*, vol. VIII, p. 227.
62 Cited from Hessler II, p. 159. In Geijer, *Samlade skrifter*,
    vol. XIII, p. 553.
63 Erik Gustaf Geijer, *The Poor Laws and their bearing
    on Society. A series of Political and Historical Essays.*
    Stockholm: L J Hjerta 1840. In 1842 a second printing
    occurred now by a British publisher: Hatchard & Son
    in London.
64 Ibid, p. 134.
65 Ibid, p. 163.
66 Lars Magnusson.
67 Geijer, Hjerta's ed, p. 157. See also p. 137.
68 Ibid, p. 63f.
69 Geijer, see this volume.
70 C. A. Hessler, II, p. 219, 283f.

Literature

Bronk, R., *The Romantic Economist*, Cambridge: Cambridge
   University Press, 2009

Chevalier, L., *Laboring Classes and Dangerous Classes in Paris
   During the First Half of the Nineteenth Century*, Princeton:
   Princeton University Press, 1973

Frängsmyr, T., "Den gudomliga ekonomin. Religion och
   hushållning i 1700-talets Sverige", *Lychnos*, Uppsala:
   Acta Universitatis Upsaliensis, 1971

Frängsmyr, T., *Wolffianismens genombrott i Sverige*, Uppsala:
   Acta Universitatis Upsaliensis, 1971

Geijer, E. G., *A History of the Swedes*, London: Whittaker &
   Co, 1832–36

Geijer, E. G., *The Poor Laws and their bearing on Society. A
   series of Political and Historical Essays*, Stockholm: L. J.
   Hjerta, 1840

Geijer, E. G., *Minnen*, Stockholm: Minerva, 1834

Geijer, E. G., *Samlade skrifter II*, Stockholm: Norstedts,
   1849–1855

Geijer, E. G., *Samlade skrifter III*, Stockholm: Norstedts,
   1849–1855

Geijer, E. G., *Samlade skrifter VIII*, Stockholm: Norstedts,
   1849–1855

Geijer, E. G., *Samlade skrifter XIII*, Stockholm: Norstedts,
   1849–1855

Geijer, E. G., *Samlade skrifter 10*, Stockholm: Norstedts,
   1849–1855

Geijer, E. G., *Människans historia,* Samlade skrifter 10,
   Stockholm: Norstedts 1923-31

Hegel, G. W. F., *Grundlinien der Philosophie des Rechts,*
   Frankfurt: Felix Meiner Verlag, 1820

Haakonsen, K., *Natural Law and Moral Philosophy. From Grotius to the Scottish Enlightenment*, Cambridge: Cambridge University Press, 1966

Henningsson, B., *Geijer som historiker,* Stockholm: Scandinavian University Books, 1961

Hessler, C. A., *Geijer som politiker, Hans utveckling fram till 1830*, Stockholm: Almqvist & Wiksell förlag, 1937

Hobsbawm, E., and Rudé, G., *Captain Swing*, Harmondsworth: Penguin University Books 1973

Hont, I., "The Language of Sociability and Commerce: Samuel Pufendorf and the Theoretical Foundations of the Four Stage Theory". In Anthony Pagden (ed) *The Languages of Political Theory in Early Modern Europe*, Cambridge: Cambridge University Press, 1987

Lamm, M., *Upplysningens romantik I-II*, Stockholm: Hugo Geebers förlag, 1918–20

Landquist, J., *Erik Gustaf Geijer. Hans levnad och verk*, Stockholm: Norstedts, 1924

Lindroth, S., *Svensk lärdomshistoria II*, Stockholm: Norstedts, 1997

Liljekrantz, B., *Benjamin Höijer: En studie över hans utveckling*, Lund: H Ohlssons boktryckeri. 1912

Magnusson, L., "Comparing Cameralisms: The case of Sweden and Prussia". In Seppel, M. and Tribe, K. (eds), *Cameralisms in Practice*, London: Boyden Press, 2017

Magnusson, L., *The Tradition of Free Trade*, London: Routledge, 2004

Magnusson, L., "Corruption and Civic Order – Natural Law and Economic Discourse in Sweden during the Age of Freedom", *Scandinavian Economic History Review*, vol. XXXVII:2, 1989

Meek, R., *Social Science and the Ignoble Savage,* New York and London: Cambridge University Press, 1976

Meurling, P., *Geijer & Marx,* Stockholm: Bokförlaget Tiden, 1983

Nilsson, G. B., *Musikprocessen och andra historiska processer,* Stockholm: Norstedts förlag, 1984

Olofsson, S. I., *Geijer som samhällsekonom,* Stockholm: Rabén & Sjögren, 1959

Pocock, J. G. A., *Barbarism and Religion II,* Cambridge: Cambridge University Press, 2001

Robertson, W. and Stewart, D., *The works of William Robertson,* Palala Press, 2016

Rothschild, E., *Economic Sentiments: Adam Smith, Condorcet and the Enlightenment,* Harvard University Press: Cambridge, 2001

Schuck, H. and Warburg, K., *Illustrerad Svensk Litteraturhistoria V,* Stockholm: Hugo Geebers förlag, 1897

Stewart, D., "An Account of his life and Writings" (1801), *The works of William Robertson,* London: Longman & Co, 1882

Seppel, M. and Tribe, K. (eds), *Cameralisms in Practice,* London: Boyden Press, 2017

Reflections on Erik Gustaf Geijer's Poor Laws Essays

by Björn Hasselgren

Introduction

DURING THE EARLY 19th century, Sweden was going through a fast transition from a relatively stable and closed society organised in traditional estates (nobles, priests, burghers and peasants) to a more modern industrialised and urban structure. Population growth and reform of the agricultural sector, with enclosures of land, was leading to a situation where more and more citizens were left outside both the traditional estates and the means of living, other than from day-to-day work.

This situation threatened to drive a situation where drastic changes both to the economy and individual rights could no longer be postponed. People increasingly sought to organise, both in economic activities and to express political views. But economic and political development was still hampered by economic regulations and political privileges.

One effect of the general developments was an increase in the number of poor and unemployed. At the same time the traditional way of organising support for the poor was unreformed; in principle local parishes were expected to finance poor-houses etc. The situation clearly demonstrated a need for reforms.

In this context, Erik Gustaf Geijer (1783-1847), a professor of History at Uppsala University, and the chancellor of the university, who was also a member of a number of Royal Academies, a Member of Parliament, and something like a national icon, as well as a poet, a composer and a historian with an interest in political economy, was in the midst of a reorientation. In a number of essays and books Geijer had illustrated and laid out the economic, political and historical development of Sweden, based on an unusually broad outlook, intense scholarly studies, extensive travel in Europe and deep insights into German idealism, the Scottish Enlightenment and developments in America and other continents.

Following a period inspired by the sentiments of the late 1790's up to the early 1810's, characterised by Enlightenment-inspired liberalism, Geijer turned to analysing the situation from a nationalistic and conservative stance. Sweden and its history had to be restored following the loss of Finland and other overseas territories in the 1809 wars, all according to the young men forming the Gothic Society (*Götiska förbundet*), in order to work with and foster knowledge of Sweden's ancient history.

The Gothic Society, including some of the most emblematic young Swedish intellectuals of the time, took a conservative outlook on society. Stability and conservative historicism were among the landmarks of the research, novels, poetry and music that flowed from them. Geijer established himself as one of the leading conservative intellectuals and politicians in Sweden at the time (Hessler 1937-47, Hallberg 2010).

From the mid-1830's, and most evidently from 1838, however Geijer started a drastic political and scientific reorientation. Geijer himself, and subsequent Geijer studies, called the reorientation a defection (*Affallet*). The old way of describing society, the driving forces of history and the economy no longer satisfied Geijer. There was an obvious need for new concepts and a new agenda. Erik Gustaf Geijer published a large number of articles and essays in his own intellectual journal (*Litteratur-Bladet*) that he established and edited from 1838, with the first issue published on February 5, 1838, and published for some years to come.

In *Litteratur-Bladet*, Geijer gave public access to his changed analysis of the challenges of Swedish society and of many other questions in domestic and foreign policy and research. Among these was the political representation in the Swedish diet (the Riksdag), the growing middle class and the proletariat, liberalism and economic development, and the situation of the poor in society. In these essays, Geijer is a precursor of economic and social analyses as presented by many scholars in the years to come. Based on previous literature and current discussions, he points to a future which, according to his view, has to deal with the inequalities and liberalisation of society.

The Poor Law essays

The nine essays originally published by the late 1830's, were translated and published together as *The Poor Laws* (Geijer, 1842). The essays deal with the following themes (as translated):

- The ancient slave state
- The Roman empire, poverty and wealth
- Christianity and its attitude to the poor
- Worldly and religious communities in medieval Europe
- On the increase of population and its bearing on welfare in society, Malthus etc.
- Applications to Sweden (two essays)
- On corrective punishments
- On negative means to reduce pauperism
- On positive means to reduce pauperism

Here the focus is on essays 4 and 7-9, which most obviously deal with the specific challenges at the time of Geijer's analysis and the question of the growing inequalities in society and the situation of the poor.

ESSAY 4 – ON THE INCREASE OF POPULATION AND ITS BEARING ON WELFARE

Geijer begins to discuss the origins and effects of a growing population in Europe. Here Geijer, as is often the case in his historically inspired texts, takes on a long-term perspective. He tries to deduce the origins of population growth through the different periods in the development of mankind from nomads/hunters to farmers, and the

64

advents of civilisation and industrialisation. Innovation and private ownership/property holdings have, according to Geijer, been a prerequisite for growth and welfare gains, and thus for population growth. The industrialisation-process in England since the 18th century, and more specifically since the 1760's, a period that Geijer identifies as a time of relative peace, has drastically changed the situation for the less well off in England.

Though industrialisation had brought on the improvement of living conditions for many, it also led to a greater number of poor people in the cities, and a need for new forms of poor relief. Geijer here mentions the English Poor Law of 1795, which had increased the scope for parish support to the poor. But it had also shown for Geijer one of the difficulties with these systems; they become difficult to alter once introduced, and their effects (discussed in the following essays) are in many ways detrimental to society by introducing negative incentives, reducing the willingness to take ordinary work.

Geijer goes on to discuss Malthus's famous work, *An Essay on the Principle of Population* (1798), with its largely negative outlook on the future of mankind, as a result of the inevitability of over-population. It is interesting to read Geijer's remark (p. 53) that Malthus's "geometrical and arithmetical series" contain mere "sophisms" and is unconvincing, which Geijer though is prepared to overlook, since the work is still of value as such. Geijer did not have an interest in mathematical expressions or analysis. Geijer elaborated further on the causes of overpopulation and different development or growth paths for the economy and the population. Growing populations can, in those cases characterised by "improvement", be consistent with increasing wealth and limited poverty. He takes a more positive view than Malthus.

These cases are, according to Geijer, exemplified by industrialisation in England and the introduction of "machines" which amplify the rates of production. Industrialisation has "opened the possibility of greater welfare for more individuals than formerly". Geijer points to the fact that mortality has been reduced owing to the general increase in welfare. And, once again, welfare depends on innovation, trade, private property and liberty.

Geijer sees a series of "orders" according to which society and the economy is organised, that over time has led to increasing wealth and reduced poverty. These have been "conductors" for better growth and welfare. Among these are increased trade following the break-down of feudal systems in Europe, the establishment of the colonial system and the introduction of industrialisation. Geijer, well-known for his many language-forming expressions in Swedish, summarises this development with a splendid sentence referring to the economic trends he is analysing (p. 62):

> "The conductor for our age is manifested in the experience which we have placed foremost in the profit and loss account of the present period, namely the means of employment now far more extensively varied than formerly, owing to the development of industry."

Social change and shifts from one "order" to another is generally combined with social unrest and disputes. This is true also for the ongoing industrialisation process, according to Geijer. The age is one of "transition" which is characterised by "a stream of destruction". It is important that the new class of industrialists be aware of their duty and the necessity to act as a kind of a contemporary "nobility", where a certain degree of ethical conduct and sense of citizenship is at the core. Those capitalists who only live as "drones and sluggards" will see its "very origin ruined", and probably be met by revolutionary tendencies from the workers. Geijer here exposes a vision, expressed as the "third order", where a widespread citizenship is a goal and where ethics (and religious belief) are part of this new citizenship and order of society.

ESSAY 7 – ON CORRECTIVE PUNISHMENTS

While an industrialised society and economy represent the best way to alleviate poverty in the modern world, poor people will always exist, according to Geijer's view. In essay 7, Geijer discusses different ways of counteracting poverty and the effects of poverty.

To begin with, Geijer notices that the responsibility to take care of the poor and to introduce corrective measures to hinder poverty and its effects gradually has been transferred from the church and the local public sector level, the municipalities, to the state. This responsibility, according to Geijer, involves different activities such as the police, poor law administration, and education. These different activities form a system of instruments that the state has to work with in order to hinder poverty in society. But we shall also see (Essay 9) that Geijer considers "positive" means as equally important in the state's arsenal of measures. These are measures implemented in order to avoid or reduce poverty and its origins through economic policy and other measures.

An introductory remark from Geijer is that, even though he believes that the state is the proper provider of the different activities mentioned above, the state has "far too much on its hands" to carry out these activities in a successful manner. And even though Geijer believes that it is in general a positive development that the state has taken over the duties from corporations like the church and professional guilds, when it comes to corrective punishments, the state has also to seek the support of civil associations in the future. The idea that voluntary associations will play an important role in the future development of citizenship-based societies was at the center of Geijer's philosophical program, a theme Geijer often returned to, with inspiration from Tocqueville and others.

The rest of Essay 7 is devoted to discussing, in great detail, one of the big issues in 19th century social debate: the proper organisation of prisons and other correctional facilities. One example is the (modern) invention of classification of prisoners into different groups in order to reduce the risk of strengthening detrimental tendencies from older to younger criminals.

Another classification or measure is to have separate cells for prisoners and to organise meaningful work for the prisoners, though it is remarked that, if too successful, such operations could run the risk of introducing an unfairly strong public sector competitor in the market, something that Geijer exemplifies with American experiences. If Geijer, in the former essay discussed above, gave many references to the English society and based his views on journals such as the *Quarterly Journal* and the *Edinburgh Journal*, in this essay he is drawing to a large extent on records from the USA as well as on European sources such as Beaumont and Tocqueville's *Système pénitentiaire des Etats Unis* (1834). Geijer shows good knowledge of the contemporary organisation of correctional facilities and social discourse. He seems to view prisons and criminal policies, if organised in a modern way, as a natural part of a system of incentives that will hinder poverty. This is obviously part of his view of the new "order" of industrialised society, even if that is not stated explicitly.

ESSAY 8 – ON NEGATIVE MEANS AGAINST PAUPERISM

In Essay 8 of the Poor Laws, Geijer makes a considerable effort to formulate and classify into a coherent structure many of the basic aspects of poverty, its causes and remedies. Geijer here also deals with the balance between voluntary measures and compulsory measures, and between measures taken by the state as compared to measures taken by local authorities, like municipalities.

Geijer states initially that there is in principle three different approaches or classes of activities towards poverty:

- Negative – including punishment (discussed in Essay 7)
- Palliative – only short term relief – and often "feeding the disease" at the same time as it gives support
- Positive – active measures of the state in order to remove "the evil of poverty"

69

He discusses under what circumstances the palliative and positive measures might be effective. A great part of the discussion has to do with the division between approaches for voluntary measures like communal workhouses which, according to Geijer, in the longer run almost always give way to compulsory forms of work institutions. This is because they introduce detrimental incentives for the poor. Only those who are in need of support should be attracted by these voluntary support measures, but they have, says Geijer, a tendency to attract also such people who are able to work under normal conditions, but who do not care to seek ordinary work. This is the reason why voluntary work-houses cannot survive in that form. They have often turned from voluntary work-houses to correctional facilities, and after that into parts of the penal system of the state. Or, as Geijer puts it (p. 135):

> "The more extensive the scale and the more liberal the
> equipment, the more rapidly they have sunk under their
> own weight, leaving behind all the greater deficiency
> and want from the impossibility of maintaining
> permanently by extraordinary sacrifices such easy
> and abundant opportunities of employment as they
> opened."

Why then is it that Geijer still calls for state action in this field? It seems to be, based on the observations by a number of government investigations (in England and in Sweden), that communal poverty relief and workhouses have been found to be operating with the "greatest abuses". Geijer does not believe in a reformation of the communal level but calls for state action and more legally based poverty relief.

Geijer observes that it is important for the giver or supporter to be careful and design poverty relief in a way that does not undermine the moral and economic self-reliance of the receiver. The support-level should therefore not be too high and on the other hand not too low. The balance seems difficult to strike, but the principle is something we strive for also today. Geijer also calls for the cooperation between the public sector, the local authorities, and families. They have all important roles to play in poverty relief.

Geijer also discusses situations where people are interested in taking on ordinary work but where demand in the economy is too low to generate enough production, which leads to too few work opportunities. Today we would probably say that there is a recession in the economy with too low aggregate demand to make use of all available workers in the labor-market.

In such "emergency" cases, Geijer calls for the "society" to "come forward as an extraordinary labour-contractor". Such labor should be directed to "such undertakings that promote the future demand for labour". Geijer mentions, in reference to Sweden's geography "with a surface... [with] only too much room", that such public sector undertakings should preferably be directed to "increased facilities of communication", which will in the long run support the functioning of the economy and the labor market.

Education as part of the poverty relief measures is the theme that is least discussed in this essay. This was, at the same time, a theme into which Geijer put much effort in other texts. Perhaps Geijer considered those sufficient for the present purpose.

Geijer also has a final word to give when it comes to the occupation of beggar; this should definitively be punished and forbidden. People who beg as a livelihood should instead be given compulsory work by the state in "work houses". Geijer is not fully clear on the motivation for this definitive view as regards begging, but he inserted a reference to an 1839 English Parliamentary Committee's observations on some of the less positive aspects of begging. Geijer reads widely and is prepared to incorporate new findings into his analysis.

ESSAY 9 – ON POSITIVE MEANS AGAINST PAUPERISM

Having described and discussed the origins of poverty in modern society and how poverty might be mitigated, Geijer, in this last essay, turns to the broader question of "how may the welfare of society be promoted?" Geijer does not say explicitly that increased welfare will be the best way to reduce poverty, by positive means, but this is clearly the theme of the essay. Geijer answers his own question in many ways in this essay. On the one hand, he says that the question is too broad and cannot be answered definitely, since welfare is more or less never increased for all but instead leads to different effects for different people.

It is better then, on the other hand, to try to determine the necessary conditions for a positive development in society. Geijer specifies some of these conditions, which are laws, morals and piety. Here connections to both Scottish moral philosophers like Smith and Hume and to the German idealists like Schelling are obvious. What we need for a positive development of society and increased welfare is for these 'institutional frameworks' to hold a necessary "quality". Geijer does not explain exactly what kind of quality he is aiming for in this respect, but the concept of institutions is clearly important for Geijer.

Institutional development is, according to Geijer, something of a historical necessity. The conservative and traditional view that society is organised to the best of all knowledge and should be preserved as is, in order to achieve a good state of society, is rejected. Geijer sees an ever evolving state of human conditions, with the "wants" of members of society developing over time. The situation perceived as "the best" at one time cannot simply be expected to be seen like that when "wants" have developed. The conservative view is defined by Geijer as the "stationary" view.

Against this, Geijer describes opposite mistakes where the structures in society, or the institutional frames, are changed through "revolutionary" processes. These will end with "illegality, immorality and impiety". A good thing, according to Geijer, cannot be achieved by "evil", which here stands for revolutionary processes. Geijer was, as were many of his contemporaries, appalled by the French Revolution and the following Napoleonic wars. Revolution had to be avoided.

But then: how to solve the necessary progress of society in order to pave the way for growth and wealth generation? Here Geijer has a solution. It is only through the continuous "movement" of society that "juster laws, more humane customs, more genuine piety" can be developed in order to reach "more secure prosperity", which is the only "true maintenance" of society. This is the only way that "liberty" develops and "confirms itself". In this way,

73

Geijer means that a truly liberal view of society is at the same time the truly conservative view. It is only through continuous change that stability can be preserved. Here we can see that Geijer is trying to mold change and stability as two different aspects of a good society open to the increase of welfare.

To further understand evolutionary paths in the development of society Geijer adds that laws can be seen as the work of "justice" in society while morals are developed as an effect of "reason" and religion is a work of "love". Conservatives have focused (too much) on the value of religion and morals, which has according to Geijer been described as an "opiate which may produce slumber". Revolutionaries at the same time have focused (too much) on justice, which often leads to reactions that forgets the values of love and moral.

Geijer takes a clear stand in this contradiction; society can only be changed in accordance with the law, if anarchy is to be avoided. His proposal is therefore the "obedience to existing law, but free right to demand a better, and free discussion of the means towards its accomplishment."

There is only one way forward for Geijer. That is the introduction of reforms in the field of "economical legislation". This is in fact the core of Geijer's positive means to reduce poverty by increasing growth and welfare in society.

Such reforms have to be based on the principle that the reform extends to the "rights of all", which is more or less parallel to the "third estate" (all the citizens in the "third order" see above) in society, which was Geijer's focus in societal discourse from the mid-1830's.

Those economic reforms should liberate "labour" which, according to Geijer, is the basic productive force in society. The right to supply one's labor in the market is on the one hand something that will be a consequence of the long-term historical developments and something of a natural right to Geijer. He sees it as an inevitable process: "The liberation of labour – a long birth pain – is the work of civilization" (p. 154). Further liberalisation is what will improve the functioning of the economy at large. The improvement of technology and skills among the workforce will be the basis for the success of economic development. One of the effects of the economic development is the further growth of "collective labour" organised in industries and corporations, which through specialisation will increase the output of the economy.

Quality of the workforce can be measured by the content of "intelligence" in the labor-force. Intelligence and intellectual occupations will increase, as economic liberty, manifested in increased trade and industrialisation, grows. Geijer foresees that intellectual and "material" work will soon become intertwined and equal, which as such is a sign of the "emancipation of labour". This growing intellectual nature of production will, as an important side effect, lead to more stability both in the economy and for the individual workers. Consumption will grow and so will production, giving way to more and better workplaces.

The abolishment of restrictions on the domestic economy should according to Geijer also be combined with the abolishment of restrictions on domestic and foreign trade and commerce (p. 173):

> "As freedom of labour thus more and more prevails, it already involves in itself the application of its principles in the exchange also of productions; that is, to internal and external commerce and traffic."

Geijer was, for example, a supporter of free trade of agricultural products, also through his conservative years. Free trade would support a growth of supply of agricultural products and thus enable lower prices on food, a development that would counter the fears of overpopulation.

Monetary questions are also part of the positive economic legislation that Geijer considered. Money is primarily seen as a value transfer tool, based on the value of labor performed. He discusses whether monetary systems should be based on a basic metallic reserve or if they could also operate primarily based on trust that the market actors perceive in the system. Geijer gives no clear-cut answer but is cautious to point out that monetary policy plays an important role among the positive means and that it has to be considered in relation to the economy.

Another important area for Geijer is questions related to price formation. The primary interest in this essay is to point to the fact that falling prices is generally the sign of an efficient production system, well-functioning competition and trade. Falling prices are thus not a sign of people in general becoming poorer, an idea that Geijer tried to counter.

Geijer also discusses some of the possible conflicts that might arise from the foreseen liberalisation of economic life. One of them is a tension between fixed capital and "moveable" capital where moveable capital, both industries and labor, will become more important over time.

This might lead to conflicts with the fixed capital such as land that constituted wealth in the old economy. Conflicts between old and new structures in society can and will probably, according to Geijer, stem from the development of industrialisation and liberalisation.

Geijer believes that such conflicts will be resolved. The markets will evolve and the tensions between different types of capital will be ironed out over time. Capital inherited is not a fixed value but often deteriorates over time (in parallel e.g. to Schumpeter's arguments) and therefore is not a major obstacle. The further development of society will depend on the associations, one of Geijer's core social concepts, where free citizens unite in order to arrange collective action in different fields, in a society without old corporations, guilds and privileged social groups like the nobility, priests and burghers.

The essay ends with a detailed description and analysis of liberal market reforms in Prussia and other German regions. Here Geijer observes many of the positive signs in the development that he has described earlier. This is exemplified by a number of references to official reports and statistics.

Discussion and conclusions

Erik Gustaf Geijer was an insightful analyst and researcher of history and long-term development, with a solid basis in Swedish history and culture, but also with a broad knowledge of European and American social life, politics and economics. He took part in and deeply influenced

77

many of the major social discourses in Sweden during nearly 50 years, and also was a participant in similar discourse in Germany, France and England.

Through his academic life, Geijer was analysing and considering how Swedish society, and European societies generally, were changing, evolving from one historical situation and to a new situation. He used different methods and scientific explanations and held different views over time on the driving forces behind its development, as well as on what constitutes the good society.

Starting as an Enlightenment libertarian, he became a romantic nationalist and conservative. From a leading conservative role in the 1810's to the mid-1830's, when he championed the preservation of the present political and economic system, he changed his views and directed his research interest in history towards the present time and the future development of society. The social unrest that seemed to be an effect of the industrialisation was a specific concern for Geijer. And he was worried that industrialisation could lead to a situation with large swaths of poor people without any possible means of support. There was indeed a question of growing inequality in many Western societies.

In the *Poor Law Essays*, Geijer took a long-term perspective on the development, starting with the medieval or even Ancient Roman societies as a reference, and discussing feudalism and hierarchical structures before moving on to the present situation. By the end of the 1830's, Geijer had clearly taken a liberal stance on these questions. The situation of the poor had to be dealt with, both with criminal justice policies, mitigating measures, and most importantly with liberal reforms, under the name of "positive measures" to be taken by the state in the economic field. Geijer provides both a theoretical framework to increase the wealth of society and reducing poverty, and a more practical discussion of how these goals can be achieved in reality.

Only by the liberalisation of markets and labor can society be prepared for the new era that is coming, an era of more egalitarian organisation of economic and political life. Through cooperation between the state, municipalities, individuals and associations, a new stable development of society can be secured.

Analysing poverty as a social dilemma, Geijer introduces a number of themes that have been widely used and discussed thereafter. One of them is the importance of institutional frameworks and how they evolve over time. Another one is the importance of incentive structures, when the government acts in economic life. A third is the need for the government to be able to act as a (short-term) supporter of demand in times of crisis in order to avoid poverty. Here Geijer is clearly pointing to the future, with something like a pre-Keynesian attitude. A fourth is his focus on entrepreneurial discovery and creative destruction connected to industrial and commercial activity, which resembles themes from Schumpeter.

Geijer presents a framework for the better understanding of the roots of poverty as well as a social and political program for the alleviation of poverty and for the further development of society, where increased growth and welfare is at the centerpiece of the arguments. Geijer in many ways is a precursor of later analysts of social developments and challenges in the mid-19th century. Some scholars have pointed to the similarities between his analysis and the works of Karl Marx. It seems reasonable to believe that there are indeed connections, but Geijer is a liberal and a firm believer in market economics and religion, things that Marx also discusses but whose positive value he rejects. Geijer's analysis and program add to the general picture of the 19th policy and economic discourse. Not only in Sweden, but also overseas, Geijer played a significant role in the scientific and scholarly debate at the time.

ACKNOWLEDGEMENTS

Revised following valuable comments from Daniel B Klein and Annie Cot.

Literature

Hallberg, P. (2010) Mirrors of the Nation: The Construction of National Character and Difference in the Historical Writings of E.G. Geijer, *Scandinavian Journal of History*, 6:1, pp. 25-52.

Hessler, C. A. (1937/47) *Geijer som politiker, del 1-2*, Hugo Geebers Förlag, Stockholm.

Geijer, E.G. (1842) *The Poor Laws and Their Bearing on Society, A series of Political and Historical Essays*, Hatchard and Son, London.

ESSAYS

1. Panegyric on the Regent Sten Sture the Elder
1803

Non civium ardor prava jubentium
Non vultus instantis Tyranni
Mente quatit solida.
HORACE

THERE IS AN important juncture in the progress of human civilisation, which is the one when mankind from its cradle, surrounded by hostile forces, had struggled to the stage at which its survival was secured, enabling it to engage in steady and free activity to improve itself. The stooping son of toil, who wrests his most pressing needs from an ungenerous nature, who moistens his meagre harvest with his sweat and his tears and may perhaps save it from the rapacity of the tyrant or the attack of an enemy, is not free to engage in peaceful mental exercises, happy intellectual occupations and the nobler feelings of the heart. The powerful voice of necessity speaks to him, and under its ravaging impact the higher human abilities wither. It is only when a country has reached a general level of prosperity, when general industriousness among its citizens sustains that prosperity which it has provided, when an enlightened and just government protects it, when inner strength has produced external security, when the storm of raw passions has sub-

83

sided over the ages, when the state respects the citizen, because the citizen begins to be worthy of respect, when the wild wilfulness of nature has been tamed and it has been given a more pleasant appearance by human hands; it is only in such a land that the quiet flame of mankind, like the heavenly fire that gave life to Prometheus' perfect statue, will set the hearts of humanity alight, be nourished in them, warm them and develop in them a full and rich character.

I have sketched out this picture. What did I depict? The present time, perhaps? Perhaps a time that glimmers in the view of the friend of humanity from a distant future? I have no opinion on that. One thing I do dare to affirm. We have approached nearer to it. We have seen mankind extend its victories over nature by new ones; we have seen illusions flee from the light of our epoch and during the upheavals of parties and divided minds a mighty party also arise: that of the honest and wise; we have seen the level strength of humanity increase and peoples increase, without the ponderous mass being raised by the hand of a single great man and falling when that hand faltered.

It has not always been thus. I look through history and pause at a time from which ours reckons four centuries. What do I see? The rulers fight with growing power against defiant vassals and they in their turn oppress powerless slaves; the uncertain foundations of the states shaken, statecraft an abomination, the religion bloodthirsty, the ways of thinking crude, customs barbarous. I also see the light breaking through; but then the flame of burning towns glares through the dark night. Now a general danger appears. Who will be the saviour? Who dares to deal with those dreadful circumstances? Who will unite those conflicting forces? See mighty spirits awaken during the general destruction, in whose breasts Providence has gathered the strength that mankind lacked! See them rescuing the peoples with strong arms from their distress! Should not humanity, saved from shipwreck and enjoying happier days on the bank of the calm river erect an altar to them and gratefully preserve the memory of their rescuers? The fatherland has erected that altar. An unknown citizen ventures to emerge from the shadows and place there the wreath of gratitude. I dedicate it, citizens, to the benefactor of the fatherland during an ungrateful era, to the regent of Sweden for twenty-eight years: Sten Sture the elder.

First part

With a timid and still powerless hand Europe is seen in the first, barely perceptible dawn slowly shaking the fetters with which oligarchy and hierarchy had shackled it during the darkness of the night. To break its bonds it did not have sufficient power of its own. But disunity, crusades and the rise of the cities had undermined the former. The disorder of the succession in the church, the depravity within it, which culminated with a Borgia, and the doctrine of Huss, disseminated despite bonfires and excommunications, had weakened the latter. Mutual conflicts had increased the destruction. Among ruins the kings established their thrones, summoned the third estate to their aid and would soon be victorious over both their antagonists and their allies.

In the Nordic countries a spectacle appears which, though produced at an early date by incidental causes, prepared for in various ways and with various outcomes, nevertheless corresponds to the general conditions of the time and its silent inclination to promote autocracy. The three crowns of Scandinavia were placed on a single head, and the epoch that saw the plans for expansion of Louis XI, the desire for power of Ferdinand the Catholic and the almost unlimited power of Henry VII had seen a woman residing by the entrances to the Baltic and ruling over three powerful kingdoms. The Union of Kalmar is known as to its origin and its consequences. A hazardous and conflicted union between nations related by their location, origins, languages and customs but jealous of their independence and their honour; uncertain neighbours, who were to become embittered citizens. A dividing wall existed between them, consolidated for centuries and strong, as it had been the only one. The audacious nature of Margaretha dared to demolish it, and those mutually inhibiting forces, which had previously sustained each other in a friendly equilibrium, clashed together destructively. The spirit of freedom turned into rebellion, the distrust into hatred, the competition into envy. The royal power, which was to be strengthened, was shaken by constant internal storms and was divided between parties. The subjects, whose potential was to be enhanced by the access to their respective resources, were impoverished by their rulers and their rulers' slaves, who competed in rapacity. And that extensive kingdom, washed by the waves of the Baltic and the Arctic Ocean, was a power that raged against itself and was among the nations a name without honour. The desire for power, the pressing lack of it and irresponsibility had gambled with the triple crown, when Sweden, tired of its misfortunes and provoked by the violence, chooses as its king the noblest among its citizens, Karl Knutsson Bonde, the greatest man in his fatherland at that time, had Engelbrekt not existed. It had seen him, the king of two countries,[1] overthrown and exiled and through the endeavours of the great men and the spiritual leaders a foreign ruler invited. It had seen Kristian fall when he offended the individual who supported him.[2] It had seen Karl Knutsson recalled and again expelled. – I pause.

In those terrible times, when fate seems to have emptied its full measure of afflictions over a pitiful people, when the mind wanders anxiously among dreadful objects and the heart is oppressed by constantly new sorrows, the eye of the friend of humanity rests with sweet pleasure on a consoling sight. It is your bright image, Sten Sture, that emerges from the background of that dark picture; it is a noble youth, the hope of Sweden, soon its support and its honour, who goes into battle to free his native country from a foreign yoke. How striking is not his civic virtue in every situation! How much more striking in an era in which it was a rarity! That faithfulness to the fatherland, that bravery, those battles won, that resolute activity, which restored to an unhappy king his crown and to an oppressed people a longed-for ruler: all of that would have been enough for the honour of a citizen, and if you, Sten Sture, harvested, had fallen in your prime, snatched away too soon from the hope of Sweden, at your fall an unhappy people's tears would have flowed, and at your grave the youth of Sweden would have stood to absorb courage to fight for their freedom and for revenge against their tyrants. But now the observer does not dwell on the beauti-

ful dawn light of your life; he hurries towards that bounti-
ful day when you, in the strength of your manhood, stood
by the royal throne, guiding both it and the happiness of
Sweden, at once its avenger and benefactor.

That time has now arrived.

Karl Knutsson bent his grey head to again accept a
crown, twice removed, and returned – to sit down on the
ruins of his fatherland and die. Sten Sture stood by that
deathbed and received from the faltering hand of the king
responsibility for the people that he had wished to be able
to make happy, with these remarkable words: Do not seek
the crown, that ambition has ruined my happiness and
cost me my life. – What a scene! There he lies, that king
of powerful lands, on whose gaze a thousand eyes were
turned, on whose words the fate of thousands depended for better or worse; there he lies alone at his terrible
height and laments the lost happiness of his life, He grasps
his golden crown – the metal is cold – and that sceptre?
– it is heavy to the dying hand – and that lustre around
the throne? – in the dim regions of the grave it vanishes. – Honour, fame, far-reaching plans, the ambition that
embraced two kingdoms, flaming figures from his youthful years? – sinking phantoms. Everything that was vain
disappears before the stern gaze of death; the brilliant rai-
ment falls and the human being remains. – Fearfully, he
now looks back over the course of his life and, like a man
travelling to distant shores who with tenderness gathers
around him at the moment of departure what had been
dearest to him, he now tenderly and admonishingly recalls
memories: here a lightened burden, a tear wiped away;
there justice and steadfastness; here pure, unfeigned intention – a moment of calm – another gasp from the la-

bouring chest – the flickering flame of life is extinguished – he is no more. Sten Sture had observed that victory of transience; he had seen the throne transformed into a deathbed and the yawning grave, and the shining will-o'-the-wisps are extinguished, and virtue, irradiated by the rosy dawn of eternity, remain: from death he had learnt to value life.

He had gone, Karl Knutsson, and his departure was that of a scudding cloud that settles below the horizon in the dark blood-coloured light of evening, a portent of new storms. Sten Sture was to become the support of Sweden during them, appointed by the will of the deceased king to a position that brought with it regal power and the perils of regal power, almost everything except its title. He who bore that title was fallen, and with him an obstacle for Kristian. He flatters, he threatens. Parties arise. Dissension begins to flare up. The spiritual leaders greedily extend their hands. But the voice of the common people, the love for Sten Sture, the hatred for Denmark and the danger of delay overcome all doubts. He is confirmed by the estates in the role of regent.[3] From the grave of Karl Knutsson the hope of Kristian for the throne of Sweden was again revived, but that hope was premature. He had rejoiced in having lost one enemy, and he had oppressed the Swedish nation.

Denmark prepares itself to exact the vengeance of a king. With a calm and fearless mind the regent awaits the danger, observes those numerous sails, counts those menacing flags that flutter around the coasts of Sweden and approach Stockholm. That fleet carries an army, gathered from several nations, fired by its commander's courage and implacable towards the name of Sweden; it carries that king, so dangerous due to his power, his skill and his followers, before whom the freedom of Sweden had already tottered. It is Kristian, accompanied by force and treachery. To calculate his own resources, to assemble them, make use of all his assets, discover new ones where none had existed, and where they were absent, to find them within himself, to give movement and impulse to everything, instil his spirit into the minds of the people, meet the attack of the enemy in Götaland, defeat it while Kristian negotiates, capture its fortresses and, victorious, hurry to join Nils Sture in the environs of the capital: see there the labours of Sten Sture during a relatively short period!

I have come to a brilliant act in the life of the hero. My thoughts penetrate the intervening space of ages and hover around that town, around those places, where the most important battle is to be decided. I see that army of enemies pouring from the ships. Splendid in their march, their faces defiant, their hands appearing to extend fetters. In awesome groups they encamp around the capital of Sweden.[4] On the other side I see that troop of simple, brave soldiers, mostly inexperienced in the arts of war but inspired by one and the same burning spirit. They assemble in a terrible silence, raise their arms and shake their swords. Already they approach, already the decisive moment has arrived, marked by the seething passion in thousands of breasts. Already – but wait! Sten Sture still offers a settlement. Human hero! – It is rejected – and now the fearsome masses came to blows. It is not a drama of those highly organised armies, the pride and shame of later ages, where the soldier sacrifices his blood without any interest in the conflict for which it flows. It is a people, oppressed, that fights against a people of oppressors. The passion surges in every breast, the hatred burns in every eye and vengeance directs every arm against its victim. The Swedes have made four assaults against that terrible ridge, where the ground slips beneath their feet, where every step against a stubborn and valiant enemy must be purchased with blood, where death with all its terrors hovers – they fall back – oh, fate! – but now the ambush is sprung on the pursuing enemy. The army attacks it again. The garrison of Stockholm sets fire to its camp and cuts off its retreat. Its king is in danger. Its troops are scattered. Sweden breathes. It is free. And Sten Sture – he bends his knee on the free soil of Sweden and raises his burning eyes to heaven. I shall not describe his feelings, for I will not profane the sacred.

Hardly had the existence of the realm been assured by that victory when the regent applies all his powers during a lull that it so much needed to heal its wounds and improve its prosperity. He recaptures the fortresses that had not yet been taken, settles the internal discords that, like the waves of the sea after a storm, still disturb the country, becomes reconciled with enemies[5] and rewards friends.[6] Brilliant were the deeds of the hero; they are still remembered with admiration. His first act as regent is forgotten, but it is sacred, for it gave bread to the hungry and taught the unhappy ones to shed tears of gratitude. The people complained, for it was oppressed by want, and it was a hard time in the country. Sten Sture brought about an abundance, which our annals still record.[7] Thus the eternal one, when he has purified the air by thunder and storms, lets the earth be favoured with the blessing of summer rains.

The realm is peaceful – but the enemies of peace will find all the more opportunity in that peace to prepare new disorders. Only now does Sten Sture find time to properly assess the difficulties he faces in his regime. He has beaten off an attack by the enemy, but has he therefore ceased to be dangerous?

And does he not have others? And does he not see the most dangerous one lying concealed within the fatherland? We shall return from the more clamorous external dangers, which have held our attention, to that internal evil, poisonous by nestling within the very body of the state, which will sooner or later cause violent ructions, if not destruction.

There was a time when Sweden encompassed among its forests and rocks a free and large-minded race, the savage and powerful sons of nature. It was ruled by hereditary kings. Wars were their pastime, the sword their property and Odin their god. The savage, the foster-child of nature, often bears in his character that expression of simple greatness, but the first spark of civilisation lights in him a conflagration of conflicting forces. He tears himself free from the benign hand by which he was led, does not possess sufficient strength to place his reliance on the support offered to him by the new light and falls into the abyss.

Barbarism is the first step taken by humanity.

That epoch, the beginning of which one could justifiably set for the Swedish people when the Christian religion was introduced, was here accompanied by the most important changes: the transformation of the kingdom into an elective monarchy, the breeding ground of misfortunes and crimes; the sharper differentiation of the estates; the council as a mediator between king and people;

the exclusion of the peasants from legislation; the unlimited power of the nobility over its retainers; the height of minority rule and the reduction of royal power.

With the change in religion another change was directly associated. A seed is cast into the bosom of the darkness; grown under barbarism, fostered by superstition, it reveals to the dawning light an immense tree with monstrous fruits. The dominion of Rome, the cruellest of all as it extended its fetters to mankind from heaven, the most terrible of all as it ruled consciences, had grown into an amazing power in Sweden. We see its servants detached from those of the state and soon from all human connections; impoverished provinces sighing under the oppression of their wealth and oppression; spiritual occupations, held by members of the noblest families, associate the interests of the nobility with those of the priests, without associating those of the priest with those of the nobility; the bishops having a higher status in the council than the regent; their voice the most powerful during the parliaments; their power increased with the contest between Danish and Swedish factions; their audacity deposing and appointing kings.

Such is the dual evil that the fatherland nourishes in its own bosom. And that internally divided kingdom is surrounded on every side by uncertain or hostile neighbours. To the west Denmark with its alleged rights, its active intrigues and its never ceasing envy; to the east an enemy, the very name of which caused dread among people in an era that was in any case replete with crimes; again, on another side, the Hanseatic towns, which under the guise of pretended friendship sought to undermine the foundation of the state: its industriousness. If I add that the union with Denmark was welcomed by a part of the Swedish nobility and suited the interests of the Swedish clergy, that Russia was incited by Danish kings to its cruel ravages and that the Hanseatic towns merely waited for the attacks of those enemies to trade on Sweden's distress, then the dark picture of the interconnected troubles that threaten the fatherland from within and without is completed; one could then justifiably ask: who is the bold man who promises to ward them off, who is confident of his ability to provide peace, or even happiness, to a country so encircled by enemies and so productive in its own destruction? No, Sweden, you would have fallen in the midst of the rapid, independent development of your powers, loaded with foreign shackles; you would have fallen and with the demise of your freedom seen the sources of your virtues poisoned, had you not possessed within yourself a man who in troubled times dared to hope for the salvation of his fatherland – and that man is Sten Sture.

His victory had deterred the external enemies. He makes use of that precious calm to turn his efforts towards the internal ones. It was a difficult enterprise to bring together interests that, being naturally diverse, had been made incompatible by many years of disputes and growing bitterness, to unite minds that had been confused by the misery of the times and, as it were, to first create the state whose regent he had become. Sten Sture approaches that task, and we follow his progress with emotion, as we know that that internal discord was the enemy that he could never defeat, which deprived his days of happiness, his old age of tranquillity, and even long after he had been laid to rest in the earth would tear apart his unhappy fatherland. That evil cannot be broken by naked power.

It meets violence with violence, it has forced its way into the heart of the state. It cannot be diverted by mildness. Self-interest is so rarely deceived, and gratitude acts only in noble breasts. What means then remained? One did remain: to hold out against those powerful forces by mutual fear in mutual inactivity and in the meantime to arouse a third one and prepare it for the recovery of lost rights. That is Sten Sture's plan, a plan that his conduct will further explain.

Kristian, forced to refrain from violent enterprises by such bloody losses, wants to negotiate his way to a crown that he had been unable to seize. Meetings between Danish and Swedish delegates are arranged, broken off, resumed.[8] Negotiations follow negotiations. Kristian himself attends. There is no lack of great promises, nor of eloquence, nor of any of the arts of political shrewdness. One concedes, one appears to hesitate. The Danes do not lose hope but are no closer to their goal after trying for many years. Sten Sture, not always seen but always active, is the one who masterminds that display and produces the amazing effect. His sharp eye follows the thousand springs, moved by a thousand individual passions, here working around each other, keeps them apart in their contexts, calculates their movement, their power, and foresees their intended effect. Now it is due to appear overtly; a quick, imperceptible turn – and the plan is disrupted, and the course of the game is changed.

A secret discord rules within those terrible parties themselves. If they are effective, then it will be to their own destruction. If they combine, if they seek aid from Denmark, then the commoners of the realm will rise against them, powerful in their unity, powerful in the

95

spirit of Engelbrekt, which still hovers over the oppressed. Common indignation against Denmark, common feelings for the regent – hatred, love – those powerful motives of human nature, more powerful still for simple minds, have unified the rough mass, given power and unanimity to its movements. Such is the wider view. But if we were to look for the more detailed composition, the inner organisation of that world, how could we admire less the creative intelligence that operates with the same force in the detail as in the larger context that adapts the whole to the manifold parts and each part to the perpetuation of the whole. We would see Sten Sture disguising his authority among haughty peers and yet retaining it; putting it aside among lesser people and yet not losing it; arrogance believing itself to be pursuing its own path and yet following his wishes; ambition being harnessed, selfishness deceiving itself and working for his goals; we would see passion to him being merely weakness, cunning merely a fault of character; people of all ages and estates following his gently guiding hand; those who were not guided by his wisdom being captivated by his charm, and envy, the only one of all the passions over which the great man has no control, as it is not satisfied except by the humiliation of its victim – shamefacedly following the crowd; but to a deceived honest man we would see the honest man opening his heart. What – and is it a statesman I am describing? – Statecraft! – Curses are associated with that term, accusations, levelled by millions of victims. A hateful art, generated amidst the miseries of mankind, based on contempt for human beings and which alone has the effrontery to admit itself free of all human connections. And yet I arise and bless it in the great regent, as the mild protection for mankind until it comes of age; revere it in the noble man as the highest form of freedom and fullness of human character – a character that adapts itself with delightful ease to the most difficult circumstances, walks confidently along abysses into which others fall; that, never losing its composure and its beautiful harmony, displays to the enchanted observer the supreme spectacle: the serious mystery of life resolved into a sublime game.

Sten Sture justly reminds us of that ideal. The steady integrity of heart, combined with that flexible genius and that gift of mixing with people, that depth, that openness of character not only makes Sten Sture what he is, the honour of Swedish men, but into an arresting and delightful sight for people of all nations and ages, into an example of a more pleasing humanity in an era when integrity was mixed with brutality, genius marked by forcefulness, but by hardness, and statecraft the art of Louis XI.

But while my eyes rest on that bright apparition, they discover a new trait in it. I lower my sight to a blessed deed that spreads its warmth through the ages, on which the dearest hopes of the nation rest. I have wandered through these halls, sat at the feet of these teachers, nourished my soul from the treasures of this calm wisdom; among the praises of thousands my quiet gratitude has also arisen and embraced the memory of the great man; with a kind of pride I have said: Sten Sture, you are my benefactor, too. Centuries pass and oblivion wins out. But if there is a man who ought to be assured of his immortality, it is he whose name the growing citizen learns along with his first duties, which can be forgotten, though not before posterity has forgotten to care for its own culture, when barbarism has again made that land uncivilised which he wished to enlighten and when that which is greater than him is neglected. Who does not concur with that voice of my emotions that recognises in Sten Sture the founder of Upsala University, that contemplates him in the glory of all the great names in which that institution rejoices, that in thought encompasses the extensive and important benefit which that nursery for a youth eager for learning has presented to the fatherland, that finally, as in a sacred place, recalls memories of the most fortunate days of a happy age?

From the East there now arose, as its dominion fell, a feeble glimmer in Europe, less a dawning light than the last quivering flame visible on the horizon of a fire that subsides and dies. One has also exaggerated the importance of that enlightenment, which a few refugees from the tombs of antiquity brought with them to the lands where they found a refuge. The light could only be given to Europe by itself, and it was maturing towards that condition. A concealed restlessness of awakening forces began to be revealed. Great geniuses emerged, important inventions were made, although in a violent era, and among the most important was the art of printing. If Sten Sture founded Sweden's first seat of learning, he carried into effect what had already been contemplated earlier,[9] being encouraged in that by a constantly felt lack that forced Swedish youths to seek abroad what was not available at home, yet it is an honour that he shares with the spiritual leaders of that time, above all with the most outstanding one among them;[10] but when he gave the fatherland that art so precious for knowledge, at a time when, still young, it had not gained all the attention that it deserved, when he introduced the printing of books to Sweden, it is an honour that belongs to him alone; as a patriot, not to have neglected any means that he had in his power to promote the education of his fellow-citizens; as a great man, to have set an example to his era.[11] Who knows in what happy future his thoughts were moving, where the most abundant fruits flourished in his hopes from those seeds that he now hesitantly entrusted to an environment that displayed so little gratitude! His era was a hard one, when human beings with anxiety and sweat were barely able to establish feeble defences against harsh necessity – and the muses are divinities. They want to be worshipped in temples. Sten Sture knew that the physical needs of humanity demand to be met before the moral ones can become active. To give sciences and arts an abode in Sweden was more a wish than a hope of his. Creators of peace and light in human minds, they shun the days of violence and darkness. He assessed the demands of his time and used every free moment to promote the well-being of the country by a ubiquitous consideration and a diligence that was inexhaustible. A wise husbanding of the resources of the realm; the greatest possible alleviation of the distress of the commoners; defining the duties of farmers who cultivate someone else's land; the founding of towns; the abolition of abuses in those that existed; the opening up of new mines; increases in the productivity of the old ones; the improvement of the coinage; protection of the means of livelihood; security established for the person and property of the citizen against the customs of a barbarous age; peace and abundance extended around his dwelling, in so far as it was within his ability: how many new and extensive reasons for contemporary and future gratitude.[12]

Ten years had meanwhile passed since the time when he took over the government of the fatherland: ten years, marked by benefactions. We have seen him as hero, great ruler, outstanding statesman, a friend of scholarship and protector of industriousness. What could be lacking in his honour? Yes, the severe judges of posterity answer, something still remains before we can deem him worthy of our respect. Every human being has his own world, in which he is a creator, in which he lives, acts and enjoys his life. Let it fall; we judge the human being as he stands on the ruins of his hopes. We must admit the justice of that objection, and fate does indeed reserve for Sten Sture the test of misfortunes to its fullest extent. The calmer days that were gained through his victories and preserved by his solicitude, on which we have dwelt with such great pleasure, soon passed. Right up till then we see him, victorious over his opponents, successfully realising his intentions; like a god in his creation we see him standing in the undisturbed circle of his activity; but now great changes are at hand. The prospects cloud over, the misfortunes multiply, internal and external enemies equip themselves with greater power; but brighter and purer will his image emerge from those gathering shadows.

He will stand the test.

Second part

Kristian died,[13] missed in Denmark as a benign king and a prince with many excellent qualities. I do not defend him. But I praise him as a fortunate man whose life flows quietly like a river within the banks of simple duties, which provides blessings and fertility for the immediately adjoining fields. The world ought to pity the kings and pass a mild judgement on their remains. The governors of states, against the bonds of which unruly human power resentfully struggles, with an endless vista before them, a world for their capability, how often have they been accused of errors, where one ought to recognise human limitations and turn away – to go about one's business. Or cultivate one's land, or plant a tree from which the immediate posterity will gather the fruit! – Thus I judge more mildly, sons of Sweden, the ruler against whom your accusations are levelled, but for whom the nature of the era and the example of his predecessors made it necessary to entrench the union of Sweden with Denmark – when I see the efforts of a thirty-year regime devoted to that end, when I know how easily people mistake a great aim, long borne in their minds, for what is the highest purpose in life; how everything is seen in the light of it and how one finally, due to the bias in one's views, fails to notice the criminality of one's means. But Kristian paid dearly for having so eagerly pursued an aim that could not in reality be attained without destroying the character of a people: a hostile assault and one that only Kristian the Tyrant[14] possessed sufficient criminal strength to realise, using the appropriate means. The first Kristian paid for it dearly. Like an evil genius he stood for the larger part of his life between the two nations, himself a mighty obstacle to the union he wished to promote; around his deathbed he had gathered curses, and by avenging fate it was only over his grave that a glimmer of hope would arise for the possibility of success in the aim for which he had lived.

Johan inherited his father's throne, his principles and plans, which he sought to realise with all the impetuosity of youth. Sten Sture soon realised the renewed danger to Sweden. He sought to anticipate the wishes of the spiritual leaders by granting them fiefs;[15] emissaries were sent to Norway; an alliance was concluded between the two kingdoms to share the same fortunes and have the same king; Norway rose in arms to avenge its oppression; the chain of the union appeared to be bursting. Delusional prospects! Norway recognises a Danish king within a year; the spiritual leaders just as eagerly support a union that, while loosening the power of the state, increased that of the church,[16] and, even more importantly, Sten Sture sees his people – that people which he had for so many years sought to keep apart from Denmark – perhaps more inclined towards the union at that moment than when he was given the governance over it.

Kristian was no longer there. The menacing figure, who seemed ready from the shore of Zealand to summon destruction across the borders of Sweden, had disappeared from the scene and appeared to have taken with him to the grave the memory of his violent acts, along with the memory of the merit that protected Sweden against them. One ceased to value so highly a defence, of the indispensability of which one was no longer so vividly reminded, and with Kristian no longer alive, Sten Sture became for the nation less than he had been.

Count on gratitude, ye benefactors of the peoples! What does it amount to? A ghost-light over a tomb. – Another occupied the throne that the feared one had left. His claims were known, but he himself was not known. Hope still cast its aura around the young monarch. One had defended oneself against Kristian, for the hardships of war were preferred to the misery of oppression. If Johan was forced to establish his claims by arms, the misfortunes of war were certain. If one submitted to his rule, who knows whether it would be as harsh as his father's? Could one perhaps purchase his leniency by submissiveness? Had he perhaps learnt from his father's fate that power based on violence simultaneously approaches its apogee and its downfall? And was the expedient of war still an option? And would it be more difficult to topple from his throne a king who had made himself hated than to prevent him from ascending it?

Those were the thoughts of the great mass of the people who hasten to extract from the moment its apparent advantage; that is at least how those expressed themselves who, though more clear-sighted, were nonetheless predestined by passions to be promoters of the union, out of the self-interest that desired to see personal advantage in the general misery; out of the arrogance that desired to use the opportunity to overthrow a hated authority; out of the craving for power that wished to usurp it; out of the hatred and envy that needed to strike its victim even if the fatherland should bleed to death from that blow. There was no motive, in a word, no incentive that had ever acted in the interest of Denmark that did not on that occasion gain new force and recover its dangerous activeness. What should Sten Sture do? Give way to necessity? For that he respected himself too much. By openly combatting it, be crushed or conquer? For that the fatherland was too precious to him. Sten Sture followed neither of those lines of conduct; with a skill possessed only by fortunate souls, he combined the two: gave way to the necessity but precisely thereby prepared for himself the chance of another victory. And we recognise him in that regard as being true to his character.

What could no longer be preserved was conceded, though on conditions that deprived that compliance of the greater part of its significance. Johan was elected king of Sweden, but with provisos: to relinquish Denmark's claim to Gotland; to restrict his royal power by guaranteeing the properties and privileges of the spiritual leaders, by allowing the nobility to fortify its manors and exercise unlimited power over its tenants;[17] to impose no tax without the agreement of his subjects; to begin no war without the advice of the council and never to transfer the revenues of the crown abroad. How many stumbling-blocks for the ambitions of that king! And Sten Sture possessed sufficient power to keep a watch on his behaviour, to give added strength to every discontent. To bring it to terrible outbursts. He had on his side the commons of Sweden, who abhorred a treaty for which they had not been consulted; who worshipped in him a benefactor, hated in Johan the son of Kristian. He possessed more: trust in himself, his virtue and his God. Oh, let us with him still hope for the salvation of the fatherland!

What Sten Sture expected did happen. Johan wanted to avoid settling the dispute about Gotland before he ascended the throne. One knew what that meant and refused to recognise him as king. He would willingly have seized by force what was not already granted to him, but he remembered his father's misfortunes,[18] and what could he indeed achieve against a man whose vigilance was not dulled by any worries, who lived in his own court as in an armed camp, surrounded by young nobles, formed into heroes under his eyes, one who with constantly ready armed forces was prepared to meet an attack and for whom the Swedish peasantry would gladly sacrifice their property and their lives.[19]

At the core of the state he thus wished to light the flame of rebellion, provoke a cruel enemy into an attack from another direction and then impose himself on that people oppressed by internal and external misfortunes and conquer the defeated. He sought a commander for a rebellion and soon found a born Danish subject, so powerful that he had warred with kings,[20] by inheritance and enfeoffment the richest man of his time in Scandinavia, a relative of Sture, now in conflict with him and therefore an all the more implacable enemy. Ivar Axelsson Tott is his name and his memory too despicable to be preserved by history, had his power not given him the honour of being mentioned as the enemy of Sten Sture. Russia, sufficiently incited by rapacity and a desire for revenge, hardly needed any encouragement to let Finland bleed once more under the feet of its barbarians. Sten Sture saw the threatening moment approach. He, too, sought new support against those dangers and was obliged to receive it from the Hanseatic towns, which defended the Swedish subject while turning him into a beggar. He then boldly confronts the danger, convenes a parliament, where it is decided to go to war with Denmark and to summon Ivar to answer for long-known conspiracies. Ivar answers defiantly that the regent and his council can come to him, rejects all offers of conciliation, makes an attempt on Sten Sture's freedom when he tries to make that possible, is declared an enemy of the realm and declares war on the fatherland. Sten Sture now turned on him the force that Denmark should have feared, besieges Borkholm by means of Svante Sture and with the aid of brave commanders seizes his fortresses Raseborg, Nyköping, Stegeborg and Kalmar. Ivar escapes with difficulty to Gotland, vindictively handing over that island to the king of Denmark, who allowed him to die in his own lands, depressed by poverty and contempt. Are not at times of the most hopeful prospects hidden intimations often glimpsed in the mind, which are disturbing and portend misfortune? Did Sten Sture have a presentiment that he would experience a time when a powerful faction would take the place of the lone rebel to declare himself the enemy of the fatherland and seek to carry out on him the sentence by which he now punished Ivar?

King Johan had held a meeting with Sten Sture that merely let him experience the victory of prudence over treachery, when the storm from the Russian side broke out. With an immense force the barbarians overran the unfortunate province of Finland during that and the following years and distinguished their campaign by an unparalleled savagery. Knut Posse defended himself bravely against the enormous mass, but every new victory was a new loss. – The regent himself came over with troops.[21] Here, while his eyes sweep across those fields, now a dreadful wilderness, where, among the corpses of murdered people and smoking ruins of destroyed villages, bloodied human figures wander about without a roof, without bread, in a horrid season; here, while his tears fall on that unhappy soil, while his heart shuns all human consolation and, shuddering, demands it from heaven; here – the bans of the church of sole salvation descend on his head.

His country was ravaged at the hands of his opponents, torn apart by internal strife. He was surrounded by enemies, by friends who were more dangerous than enemies, and his name was cursed in Christendom. – Gentle guardian spirit of humanity, ah hope, come and pour your consolation into his heart, all too deeply wounded by such cruel trials! Preserve him for Sweden! Or why was he not formed into someone hard, cold, with feelings only for honour, who sees only himself and builds his stronghold on the ruins of a world? See the flower longingly opening itself towards the eternal sun and drinking in its light. A toxic gust of air blows across the neighbourhood, silently enters its veins, and its head droops, still unbroken by the storm. Thus fate occasionally has a toxin for a sensitive and lively mind that is more dangerous than its storms, as it arms the noblest powers of the soul against itself. – But what then? Is it weakness, hopelessness in Sten Sture, if we were to see him for a moment abandon the fatherland to its fate? Is it not rather the greatest proof of his wisdom and courage? Does not the body of the state, like that of the human being, have moments of sickness and conflict, when the care of the physician is useless, when he has to leave nature to its own strength? Sten Sture ventures on that dangerous attempt, for he knew the people for which he lived, and he knew it well enough not to despair of its salvation. There was no lack of strength here, but of unity, of composure. To teach the nation to realise the danger it faced was to save it. What was required for that was a decisive, heroic step, and Sten Sture proceeded to take it.

Before the estates of the realm gathered in Södertälje Sten Sture returned the dignified office with which their trust had honoured him and which he had honourably held for twenty years and requested to be released from a burden that he no longer believed himself capable of bearing.

But he would for once experience the pleasure of being rewarded by the fatherland and through the highest and most sacred pleasure – the awareness of a people's love and gratitude, which demanded its salvation from him – to be reconciled with himself, with mankind and with his fate. The entreaties of the estates were unanimous, that he should not tire of governing. They decided unanimously to show him full loyalty and obedience, to avert war and live in concord, as history records.[22] What a triumph over envy, one that justifies his action, even if it had merely been politically shrewd, illustrated his courage, cast down that of his enemies and allowed him with greater security to continue on his difficult path!

It is with satisfaction that I choose this point in the life of Sten Sture, one of the few, when gratitude in its gentle light recognises his merit, so often thankless and unappreciated; I choose it with satisfaction in order to re-call here one of the greatest benefactions that the noble man provided for his fatherland. Sten Sture betrayed and wretched and Sten Sture, the benefactor of his native land – my eyes cannot accustom themselves to the proximity of those two images.

There is one class of the people, almost everywhere disfavoured, that here share fully in the rights of citizen-ship, possess their own place in the constitution alongside the estates that in other countries oppress them and are the masters of the soil from which they were born – that is the free commonalty of Sweden, which has among the nations given the Swedish one the reputation of possessing an enlightened social order. Hardly any state in Europe has been exposed to more severe crises: enemies have pressed upon it on every side, storms have shaken its governmental structure, and yet, as one of its greatest kings once said,[23] it has in its times of need always found its aid in God and in itself, healed its small wounds itself and from the depth of decay rapidly risen to honour and prosperity. – What is the reason for that? – I dare to express it. There is no Swedish man who is a slave. It lies in general civic freedom and the civic spirit to which that gives rise; in that inner sacred life of the state, which no misfortunes can harm. If that is true; if it is also true that the state that is based on violated human rights imposes terrible vengeance on itself; that there is no easy transition from serfdom to freedom, as one appears to have believed; that the slave breaks his fetters when he acquires the strength to do so, and that sooner or later he does acquire it: how much gratitude does the man then not deserve who equalised the social rights of those who bore the brunt of society's hardships; who restored to the most numerous class of the nation the portion in the legislative system of the realm that it had possessed from ancient times;[24] who thereby destroyed the seed of inevitable ruin that began to grow inside the fatherland itself and safeguarded its existence and happiness for centuries to come! – Ask that commonalty whom it has to thank for its good fortune, It does not know him. And should the eulogist of Sten Sture complain about that? His benefaction still survives, and that shadow which surrounds its originator seems to remind us of the high virtue which, hidden and thankless, has a beneficent effect, and for which every thank-offering made by contented people to God is a benediction.

Let us return to the events. An initial glance reveals to us how Danish ways of thinking had begun to be expressed among the clergy and to gain more of a footing among the higher nobility, reveals every new merit of Sten Sture rewarded with a further lack of gratitude. Foreign princes apply for the throne of Sweden and secretly make great offers to Sten Sture.[25] He discloses them to the council, and the council – in his absence – recognises Johan as king, despite the loss of Gotland, and the regent is compelled to assent to that, in order to avoid dishonourable suspicions.[26] To the realm whose elected king he was Johan arrives with a fleet and a power that seem far from portending peace. Fire and storms destroy an armament that the regent's vigilance had in any case made useless. The king then offers a thirty-year truce if one were willing to abandon the union with the Hanseatic towns and they were left to his vengeance. Sten Sture sees the injustice, realises the trap, avoids it and is rewarded by – the reproaches of the credulous. The Russians ravage Finland. Knut Posse was sent to defend it and is immortalised by the manner in which he gained victory.[27] The regent, who had persuaded Lübeck to engage Denmark, proceeds there himself with an army, sees the enemy withdraw within its own borders, orders troops to remain there to protect the country, returns – and finds a council displeased by his homecoming and at the diet that was summoned the dissension and disorder so great that nothing could be decided.

In the dark the plan of those who wished to build their own prosperity on the fall of the fatherland was still being fostered. All that they lacked for it to be acted upon was a pretext and the ability to present some great and respected name themselves around which no low intentions would be suspected. They found both. And in whom? In the noble Svante Sture, Sweden's hope, its future support, the greatest rival to the honour of Sten Sture. Left behind with relatively few troops to defend Finland, he had invaded the enemy's own country, captured Ivangorod, destroyed it and returned with his small victorious band, when the regent, who had just arrived with a larger force, ordered him to accompany him in a new attack. Svante Sture's soldiers were exhausted and grumbled. He himself, resentful at having been left as prey for an innumerable enemy, thought he had achieved enough with his small force and refused to obey, was angrily charged by Sten Sture with rebellion, returned to Sweden with his soldiers as his declared enemy and thereby gave the signal for civil war.

Posterity accuses Svante Sture of abandoning his duty but also reproaches Sten Sture with acting overhastily. The river of time has long since carried off the generation on whose life and activities our mind now dwells; for centuries those two men have now rested in the earth whose dispute we ought to settle; but, if it were possible, I would not fear to leave the judgement on himself and his great rival to the justice of Svante Sture himself; I would not fear to let him judge whether he had grounds to complain of a real injustice; if that were the case, whether it was now time for the fatherland to forget injustices; and in what light, alongside that action of his, he wished to regard the effort by which he later assisted Sten Sture in reconstructing what he now tore down; from him I would accept the judgement on the behaviour of Sten Sture, should it be found to reveal a lack of his former accommodating wisdom. He would then remark on that impulsiveness of character without which no great man can exist: an impulsiveness that, although inactive in the face of the indifference of the ignorant, the ingratitude of self-interest and the attacks of envy, nevertheless occasionally overflows when an elevated soul sees itself abandoned by those by whom it is understood and valued; and which causes the noble man, who tolerates the unfairness of his nation, not to put up with seeing himself misunderstood by his friend – he would remark on that and thereby perhaps have completed the defence of both Sten Sture and himself.

The time has come when the flash of lightning broke through the clouds that had for so long been menacing, when we see Sten Sture alone against so many destructive forces with his courage and his faithful friends in the midst of the horrors of a civil war that spattered with blood the fields that he would so willingly have protected for the peaceful cultivator, abandoned by fortune – when did he ever enjoy it? – but not by his virtue, with his arm supporting the collapsing shrine of Swedish freedom. I hurriedly pass by the dark images that appear to my sight. The council charges Sten Sture with responsibility, reproaches him with having exceeded his authority, of having left Finland unprotected. He defends himself manfully. His troops arrive and lend weight to his defence. The council deprives him of the office of regent. He replies in an open letter that it had been entrusted to him by the estates; into their hands and no others' did he wish to relinquish it; for all his sacrifices, his endeavours and the danger to his life, he had been ill rewarded. Johan declares war on him and, as if such enmity were a new merit on that account, he is again recognised as the king of Sweden. A manifesto, the content of which, dictated by the lowest form of hatred will not pollute my pen, is issued against him,[28] and the spiritual excommunication, issued by Jakob Ulvsson, then follows. He had himself destroyed the archiepiscopal palace in Upsala, besieged Svante Sture in Örebro, incarcerated the unruly prelate of Linköping,[29] and Jakob Ulvsson, shut up in his castle, already feared his vengeance, when Johan came to the aid of his supporters.

He had equipped a large fleet, gathered an army from several countries and attacked Sweden from two sides. Älvsborg is besieged. Kalmar is taken and the Swedish council hurries to offer its good wishes to the new conqueror on Swedish soil and to hand over to him as many fortified places as were in its power. With his fleet he approaches Stockholm, to which he had previously sent a part of his army. The siege of Stäket had to be raised and, by a victory over the assembled enemies, the way be opened to Stockholm, where Sten Sture is now shut in. Here, defended by ten thousand men and expecting thirty thousand Dalecarlians before jointly attacking the Danes, he was still quite formidable; but even that hope was to be dashed. The plan was discovered from captured messengers, the Dalecarlians were defeated after the most valiant resistance, without Sten Sture knowing about it or being able to assist them. He himself, deceived by the false banners of the enemy into making a sortie, surrounded by a superior force, was obliged to retreat after bloody losses, with the poor satisfaction of gaining the enemy's admiration, and – what was far worse for Sweden – that precious life is in danger of being shortened by a dreadful event.[30]

Now Johan offered a settlement – and I leave the scene, where those unfortunate events have crowded each other out of my sight, in order to follow Sten Sture in thought during his lonely deliberations – here in the deep silence of the night, when sleep, which soothes enmities and assuages worries, rests over everyone and he alone watches over the well-being of Sweden. Those moments – how different they are from those when, twenty-six years earlier, proud and triumphant after a victory that saved a people, his joy had not allowed him to rest; when from that elevated soul the plans for a coming future evolve in splendour and it finally alighted with pleasure on a vision that slowly emerged from the dawn of the future: Sweden saved from every form of foreign yoke, and Sten Sture its liberator! Twenty-six years spent in tireless activity for such a goal, only to be able to say at this moment, standing in the midst of the conflagration of his creation, alone with his memories: it was a mirage, a trick played by an arrogant imagination! The light came; it is no longer there. And yet – he feels it deep in his heart – that goal was something more; within him it possesses an indestructible reality, his endeavours gather around it there in perfect harmony, and he would be able to say with confidence 'I have not lived in vain', even if it became his lot to be buried under the ruins of his fatherland. – And would that not be his lot? Should he accept a settlement, the conditions of which he understands; throw away the fruits of so many years' labours in a cowardly manner; by his acceptance of it, see the country degraded whose loftiness he feels deeply as the Swedish regent and a Swedish citizen, and not before then summon his final strength for resistance, so that history might say of him: he died with the freedom of Sweden? But is he then helplessly lost? Is that commonalty not prepared to dare everything for his sake? Does he not conduct war in his own but the enemy in a foreign land, where every man of the peasantry is bitterly opposed to him? If he should manage to emerge victorious, and he himself by the gratitude of the citizens .... oh, Karl Knutsson! But – he sees it too clearly – that enemy, under whose feet his country bleeds, who now menacingly besieges its very capital, is not the most dangerous one. At the very heart of the state there are others more terrible: the envy and discord of citizens. Let the former be expelled – and how audacious is that hope! – and, recalled by the latter, it will return still more dangerous. Is there then no other prospect than an assured destruction or a fruitless victory?

Yes, there is a third one: Johan on the throne of Sweden, and Sweden still saved and free. – He separates that divided people into three classes: one whose self-interest and envy have attached it to the Danish cause; another that vacillates between the possible advantages of Johan's regime and fear of the usual manner of governing by foreign kings; the third, whose hatred of foreign rule he knows and of whose devotion he is certain. – He either renounces that art – the result of the experience of a long time in government – of looking into the minds of men; he either renounces his knowledge of Denmark's kings and their interests, the demands of Sweden and the character of its citizens, or will Johan, once he is king, disappoint the expectations of those by whom he had reached that position, by interfering with their rights decide the

115

course of the vacillating ones, arouse their hatred, increase it in those who had never been his friends and depose himself from the throne that he had won with such great effort. Did not Kristian run onto those rocks, and was he not greater than his son? What harmed him more in the eyes of the Swedish people: his own regime or the actions of his opponents? Sten Sture has therefore made his decision. He accepts the offer of a settlement while that can still be viewed as a merit; he reserves to himself a power by which he can confront unforeseen events and is himself secure – Johan governs, he falls; and the future leader of the country has won over a numerous class of citizens, attached another more closely to himself and can with their help create a counterweight to the third, in case it should find an advantage in new disorders.

Thus thinks Sten Sture and goes to resign his office as regent and to recognise Johan as Sweden's king, in return for receiving fiefs that make him the most powerful man in the realm after the king.[31] Do I deceive myself? Or is that step a not unworthy end to a regime that was a perpetual and glorious struggle against an adverse fate? Sten Sture appears to submit to the misfortune but transforms that into his plan and has conquered at the moment of his downfall.[32]

We cease for a moment to observe Sten Sture at the level of rulers, and that only supplies us with a transition from the virtues of the regent to those of the citizen. But what then? Is it not still he who keeps watch over Sweden, on whom the eyes of every friend of the fatherland are turned? Does he not still live and act towards the great goal at which his entire regime had aimed? We see him in this delicate situation firmly maintaining at once his security and his dignity, too deep-minded to be taken in by the flattery of the king, too clear-sighted not to notice the hatred that it covers and its secret designs; and we expect that. But if we see him at the request of Johan giving up some of his fiefs, along with the estates of the realm recognising his son Kristian as successor to the throne and, far from inflaming the general dissatisfaction that soon afterwards arose, informing the absent king of the danger that it poses to him – who would expect that who does not find an audacious contradiction in such conduct? He does not know Sten Sture. He ought to have considered more carefully the wisdom in the deliberations of the great man and realised the bold nature of his character.[33]

I hurry over the four years that cover the time when Johan governed Sweden to the remarkable resolution of those events. But if there is anyone who desires a point of rest among all these scenes and away from the designs of statecraft, which engage our reason, for a view that avails and satisfies the heart, let him come with me to enjoy the most pleasing sight: of Gustaf Vasa as a child by the side of Sten Sture, growing up under his gaze and preserved by him for the fatherland.[34] Here, on that innocent and juvenile mind the great and experienced man rests his gaze with pleasure, sees the surrounding world mirrored in it, like an attractive and lively beach on a quiet river, is delighted by its formation, by the great powers that are already revealed while he plays, and there deposits his virtues, which the world has so often rejected. – What a charming image! The martyr of freedom (should one not describe as such him who devoted his entire life to Sweden's freedom?) together with its immortal avenger! And who, on seeing that, does not forget a period of another twenty years of hateful fortunes for Sweden and in joyful imagination associate his hope for the salvation of the fatherland with the happy fulfilment of that hope!

The time has come, foreseen by Sten Sture, that would see the end of king Johan's rule for ever. The revelation of autocratic intentions, a desire for money that spared neither churchmen nor the secular and enraged both, harsh foreign administrators put in charge of the provinces, the loss of Gotland, the ravages of the Russians not averted but encouraged, and in addition general want and high prices: how many reasons to make his regime odious to a people that had never been favourably disposed towards him! The estates of the realm gather in Stockholm, where Sten Sture in a dignified manner presents the complaints of his fellow-citizens to the throne. But the king shows himself to be openly hostile, and at Vadstena the friends of the fatherland[35] pledged themselves to defend it against his despotism. At the forefront among them we see Sten and Svante Sture and Hemming Gadd, worthy by his intelligence and valuable services to be counted as a close friend of Sten Sture.

Johan leaves his kingdom, which withdraws its allegiance from him. The Stures march towards Örebro, seize it, besiege Stockholm, which surrenders to them, and shut up in the castle the fugitive garrison of the town and the consort of Johan. – The shaken realm requires a governor. From what trunk do the lesser trees find support during the storm? From which one but the majestic oak that has for ages provided its surroundings with shade and calm. Sten Sture is again unanimously chosen as regent. What images of a happy future present themselves to my eyes! A great regent, grown grey amidst important endeavours, who again receives his sceptre from the gratitude of a liberated people, a people that has learnt from an unhappy experience to find unity and calm, still governed for a long, happy period by his wise solicitude; with peace within its borders, industry and well-being in its dwellings; the milder virtues of humanity moderating its power; and again that regent at last at the goal of his life, who, rich in virtues and felicity, greeted as the father of his people, accompanied by the blessings of millions, moves from the hardships on earth to the peace in another world. Such is the description that presents itself to my pen, with which I had wished to conclude the praise of Sten Sture. Away with that illusion of the imagination! Does not the terrible fate of those times hang over Sten Sture? There still remains a decade of Sweden's unhappy years, and Sten Sture soon finds his peace – in the grave.

War occupies the final days of the aged regent, who had yearned for peace. King Johan's queen had to surrender, the king himself is repelled in a new assault, the archbishop is forced to renounce his loyalty to Johan, the fortresses of the realm are recaptured and its Southern provinces defended against the cruelty of prince Kristian. Sten Sture escorts back to the border the captive queen of Denmark, whom he has treated with his customary nobility, and then intends to continue the war energetically, when death cuts short the actions and the life of the hero.[36]

Grim times appear before my eyes after the death of Sten Sture! Storms that follow storms, until that terrible moment when the clouds gather on the horizon of Sweden, the atmosphere seethes, the flashing thunderbolt cleaves the sky, and Sweden, struck, stands up bloodied, shakes its fetters – and breaks them. – During those days of horror I once see some of Sweden's nobles gather round Sten Sture's grave; I see them in mournful silence gaze upon the space that encloses his mortal remains. I see one of them slowly approach the tomb. His eyes shed no tears – the memory of Sten Sture requires no feeble offerings – but he extends his hand over those sacred remains, raises his eyes to heaven and swears love for freedom and his native land.

Notes

1   He was also elected king in Norway but soon lost it. His own delegates gave away his right to that kingdom at the meeting in Halmstad, without his knowledge or instructions.

2   Archbishop Jöns Bengtsson, whom Olaus Petri calls an infamous rogue and no bishop, had together with his relatives of the Vase and Oxenstierna families forced Karl to flee and called in Kristian; but when Kristian had conveyed the prelate under arrest to Denmark, bishop Kettil Vase rebelled and, thanks to Sten Sture, won a victory in the Hellsjö forest in Västmanland in 1464, the first time that history records Sten Sture. His date of birth is unknown, his father was the state councillor Gustaf Amundsson of Rydboholm, his mother from the Bjelke family, a half-sister of king Karl. Karl was recalled but was again expelled by Kettil and Jöns Bengtsson; that he recovered his crown once more, which he wore for three years until his death, was due above all to the victories of Nils and Sten Sture.

3 At Arboga in 1471.

4 Kristian divided his force, which consisted of Danes,
Norwegians, Germans and Scots, into three sections,
one to protect the fleet, one on Brunkeberg all along
the sandy ridge and one by the convent of St Clare.

5 With Erik Karlsson Vasa, who still bore arms for
Kristian.

6 The Axelssons, Erik and Ivar, were given fiefs. The last-
named later rebelled against Sten Sture.

7 Dalin, pt II, p. 780.

8 Five during the life-time of Kristian; during the whole
of Sten Sture's time no less than fourteen.

9 In 1418 king Erik had received the pope's permission
to found an academy. When the learned archbishop
Nils Ragvaldsson held a church synod at Söderköping
in 1441 it was enacted that thought should be given to
founding a Swedish academy.

10 Archbishop Jakob Ulvsson's energetic support is as
undeniable as it was indispensable. The academy was
founded in 1477.

11 The art of printing was exercised here from 1483, and
it was only twenty years earlier that it had begun to
spread. Around 1490 Upsala, Strängnäs, Vadstena and
Söderköping all possessed printing presses.

12 Not all the economic decrees that are referred to here
were enacted during the first ten years of Sten Sture's
government; but they have been dealt with here, as
war and upheavals will hereafter occupy our attention.

13 1 May 1481.

14 [The reference is to king Kristian II of Denmark and
Sweden (1513-1523).]

15 Archbishop Jakob received a quarter of a silver mine discovered in Uppland and not long after that the whole of Norrland as a fief.

16 The spiritual leaders were the main force behind the union being renewed at the meeting in Kalmar in 1483.

17 "Every good man, spiritual or secular, shall be king over his own peasant" were the words of the resolution at Kalmar in 1483.

18 Queen Dorothea, his mother, always reminded him of them and advised against war with Sweden.

19 Dalin, pt II, p. 806. To keep a standing army had seldom been customary before; the peasantry was mobilised whenever danger threatened.

20 He had once earlier declared war on Kristian, when he came into conflict with him over confiscated fiefs and had joined Karl's party. Sten Sture was married to his fraternal niece.

21 In the autumn of 1488.

22 Dalin, pt II, p. 814.

23 King Gustaf Adolf in his autograph memoirs.

24 The peasantry actually possessed the entire legislative power in earlier times, in so far as that belonged to the people. It now first emerged as an estate.

25 Duke Frederik, the brother of king Johan, and prince Ferdinand, the son of the emperor Maximilian, applied in secret to Sten Sture for the crown of Sweden.

26 Rumours were spread that he himself coveted the crown.

27 We remember the famous 'Viborg explosion'. Knut Posse was richly and nobly rewarded by Sten Sture.

28 Dalin, pt II, p. 830.

29 Bishop Henrik, an ardent supporter of the opposite party.

30 In the throng of his own people he fell off the northern bridge into the water during the hasty retreat and could only with difficulty be rescued.

31 Sten Sture had the greatest extent of fiefs that any Swedish man had held since Bo Jonsson, consisting of the whole of Finland, the castle of Nyköping with a large part of Södermanland etc. The Dalecarlians were not satisfied with the peace until he also received Västmanland and Dalarna. When he came out into the camp to meet the king after the settlement, the latter asked him jokingly if he was well provisioned in the castle. Sture pointed to the bishops and answered: "gracious lord, these men who stand here by you are in the best position to know that, for they have themselves both brewed and baked."

32 History provides no evidence for such a plan, but no event contradicts it, and it thus possesses an entirely credible basis in the character of Sten Sture.

33 That conduct of Sten Sture towards Johan has been much praised as that which best evinced his noble disposition. I have not been able to regard it as commendable in that sense. Fidelity towards Johan is a virtue that could not be practised by Sten Sture. To dethrone him is more likely to have been his intention; but he would not do so until the people itself was convinced and called for a liberator with a common voice. Are his warnings to Johan not rather to be regarded as the pride of a genius, but one that well befits a great soul?

34 King Johan was so impressed by the qualities of the young Gustaf when he once saw him, still only in his ninth year, playing with his age mates, that he invited him to his court; but Sten Sture declined that perilous privilege for his relative.

35 In January 1501.

36 On 13 December 1503, during the return journey from the border, near Jönköping.

2. Feudalism and Republicanism

A contribution to the history of the social constitution, 1818

I T IS REFLECTING on the *dissimilarity* of various epochs that makes the engagement with history agree-
able for both the intellectual and the merely curious,
and we wish in no way to diminish the pleasure that may
be derived from it. Yet whoever looks for something more
in history than the charm of novelty must necessarily associate with that reflection on the dissimilarity of epochs
another, namely the reflection on the *similarity* between
different epochs. In reality, one cannot exist without the
other. For all observation of dissimilarity presupposes to
begin with that the objects should be similar in some respect, or else they could not even be compared with one
another. If one were to ask where that similarity, that
uniform and unchanging aspect by which all dissimilarity
and change is first perceived and gauged, is to be found
in history, it can be nowhere else than in the eternal notions regarding all forms of human society, which every
single epoch expresses, though in its own way. To explore
and consider those notions everywhere – and they can be
discerned, more or less clearly, everywhere; even from the
most corrupted epochs one can recover ex absurdo the
most compelling evidence concerning the social order, as
the bad is generally only the opposite or inverted version

125

of the good – to seek out and observe those notions, I say, is to reflect on the eternal in the midst of the transitory, which is undoubtedly the most worthy occupation of the human mind. There should be no need, therefore, to recommend it especially to our time. There is one reason, however, that makes such reflection particularly important for the present generation. Due to the exceptional nature of the experiences undergone by this generation, it is far too inclined to regard itself as placed beyond comparison with the preceding ones. And it is also true that so many of the long-existing social institutions have been destroyed by the upheavals of our time that little else is left upon which to build than the eternal foundations of all human society. But precisely they are all the more important, and that their importance is acknowledged is also shown by the active engagement with which constitutional questions are now embraced by almost all European peoples. As that interest, now more than in the past, is based on a real need to provide oneself with a constitution or at least to fundamentally consolidate and improve the existing one, so it has also more than in the past taken a practical direction. It seems that people have tired of building castles in the air, ceased to seek in paper constitutions the wonderful talisman that was to guarantee general welfare. Their intention is to base that welfare on the nature of human affairs and the foundation provided by experience. All of this will of necessity not only give greater significance generally to history, which contains that experience of the nations, but especially to what we have called the eternal and unchanging in history. For the latter is what remains applicable in every epoch, however divergent from the general rule it may appear to itself or actually be.

We have set our mind to investigate whether even in the social constitution of the middle ages some of those eternal social notions may not be found, for our instruction, and we have deliberately chosen that era, as there is hardly any other in relation to which the more recent and the present age has regarded itself as standing in such sharp contrast. Nor do we therefore intend to let ourselves be deterred by the apprehension of which the expression has for some time now become the battle-cry of many, namely that all the barbarity of the middle ages is imminent and will be introduced at the earliest opportunity by a certain other party, which eulogises that barbarity. We intend neither to eulogise nor calumniate. But one conviction we can at once declare: that the Middle Ages are a most instructive era and well worth knowing more about than that just beyond Luther and the discovery of America lies the great barbarism, rather as one says that just beyond Europe lies Siberia.

It has been disputed whether civil society is *artificial* or *natural* in origin. – The fact that both opinions have found numerous and skilful defenders, without either party having been able to refute the other, would seem to show the validity here of what conciliatory men in all kinds of disputes so readily propose, namely that both parties are right. Nothing much is gained by that, however, as such a concession by the conciliators, provided that there has been no subsequent reconciliation, can with reason be turned by the more zealous into the assertion that both parties are wrong: and by those two contradictory verdicts the issue itself is merely thrown into even greater confusion. In order to seek to contribute, according to our ability, to the investigation, we first wish to establish what is meant on either side. We thus say that those who assert that society is artificial in origin are the same as those who base society on a *compact* (the social contract, *contrat social*), whereas those others, who hold it to be of natural origin thereby assert not only that it has never actually come into being by a compact but also, theoretically, that it cannot be explained in terms of any compact. For the former, society is the product of *freedom*, by means of an agreement; for the latter, society is something originally created by *necessity*, and itself, far from it being possible to base it on a compact, on the contrary provides the basis for every compact and constitutes its first condition. Everyone can see that the difference between these two opinions is fundamental, even that they contradict each other. – But is the entire matter not after all merely an academic dispute, the subtleties of which have probably never had or been able to have any influence on life in general? – as more than one reader is likely to remark. – As if the academic disputes both in the past and increasingly so in more recent times, namely in so far as they have concerned the most important questions of humanity, have not also been of the greatest importance! The academy (I mean education through science and art in general) has always been the school of humanity, the training ground where all those questions that, having subsequently moved out into the wider, practical world, have most often had far too great consequences, were first raised, considered and recognised in all their significance. The history of philosophy is especially in this regard a prophetic history. Whatever happens later in the world has always happened there before. No change in the latter has been without the most remarkable influence on the former. One could say that the greatest revolutions have first occurred inside a single head. Not as if that head were itself the effective cause – that always lies beyond all individual ability and merit in such cases – but because it is precisely in it that the spirit of the time or of the future acts most powerfully and first reveal its specific character. Such a head gives birth to an idea – or rather: it simply expresses in a *word* what many have already in a vague presentiment thought and by means of which they at once think of it more clearly – and the thought becomes a general way of thinking and immediately puts not only thousands of heads but also thousands of arms and legs in motion; the former (or the heads) in the flow of events often not knowing any more than the latter (or arms and legs) from where the thought has come that activates them. For usually the epoch itself, with regard to the origins of its outlook – although the prophetic history of the sciences or the academy establishes those origins clearly enough – remains in a state of innocent ignorance. It believes that one cannot think in any other way with normal senses and faculties. Its *acquired* way of thinking appears to it as *natural*, or even as the only natural one, for which reason one also hears such a general outlook, a system of opinions that has emerged from everyday life, in a thousand voices describe itself especially as *common sense* (sens commun). Although the 18th century really brought that expression, with all its pretensions, into wide circulation, one nevertheless deceives oneself if one does not believe that each epoch has had its own. Those familiar with history know that it is well furnished with forms

2. FEUDALISM AND REPUBLICANISM

of common sense or various kinds of *sens commun*, all of which have, more or less, made essentially the same claims and also always asserted their soundness and infallibility most strongly when they have been about to give way to a new one.

Now with regard to our question, or the question of the basis and nature of our civil society, it is, although emanating from the academy, so little now confined to it that, on the contrary, no question occupies all minds more at this moment and even he who refuses to recognise it in our account and declares it to be a senseless quarrel may more than once have vehemently argued about it, at least in one of the various forms in which it may appear. – What most divides opinions at this time? Is it not everywhere the question of the old and the new? Of the right of the past, which attempts to assert itself, and the claims of the present, which will not allow themselves to be dismissed? – And who has not taken sides on these issues? Who, in cultivated Europe, is the fortunate one on whom our era has not imposed the answering of such questions?

I maintain that the debate1about all this, that is if one wishes to understand the subject itself, is in essence the same as the one we have just described and touches on the ultimate origin of society. – We have indeed come so far that the profoundest questions have become the questions of the day.

The debate, we said, is essentially the same. For what is this call for a *constitution* so often heard in the name of the nations other than an expression of the view that society itself is a compact and that consequently a new or improved social order can only and ought to be founded on another such explicit compact? If again, on the other hand, there are many and powerful individuals who deny or avoid such a demand and exclusively defend the old social institutions, does that not reveal the conviction that the social order ought to be placed above the arbitrary will not only of each individual person but also of every individual generation.

It is remarkable, and gives one reason to infer a special relationship between them, that each of these antithetical opinions, taken by itself and separately, in practice merges into the other or ends by leading to its own opposite. Thus the defenders of the social compact have, though erroneously, regarded themselves exclusively as the apostles of freedom and – in the belief that they alone sit at the source of all *liberal* ideas – branded their opponents as *servile* supporters of every kind of despotism. That the theory of the so-called liberals, taken one-sidedly and most liberally in the minds of blind supporters, leads straight to despotism, whereas that of the so-called servile ones, likewise in its one-sided form, may in practice lead to the most self-indulgent form of freedom is, on the contrary, a thesis that can reasonably be defended and which experience has confirmed. The names of both parties are therefore as meaningless as party names generally are and he who wishes to judge the matter merely by those designations would certainly be in rather deep error. For the liberals do indeed include *freedom* in the principle itself but here already so closely related to arbitrariness and chance that they must consequently summon *necessity* in its crudest form of violence and physical superiority and to their own surprise cannot, despite all the propositions regarding freedom, bring their society into being without the right to exercise force. The servile ones, on the other hand, begin with necessity as something once and for all given, but precisely that rigidity or even harshness of principle causes them, in its practical application, to always proceed in a *mitigating* manner. In order to be able to apply it at all they have to constantly make concessions in its application. But the more rigid the basic principle itself is, the more are all concessions associated with the danger of self-indulgence.

The history of Europe has already had time to provide examples of both of those outcomes.

We saw in our own day an entire nation rise up in protest against the existing social order and thereby cause a revolution, the repercussions of which, as the more clear-sighted at once predicted, soon spread around Europe. If one looks at the nature of that protest it is striking that the individual abuses complained of, which were its immediate causes, were by no means its real reason. How inconsiderable do the financial embarrassments that threw France into the turmoil of revolution not seem to a later generation, experienced in misfortune by enormous sacrifices! – What history had long before then instructed us about, namely that one should carefully distinguish between the *reasons* and the *causes* of revolutions – what the old proverbs meant, that a drop of water causes an overspill when the measure is full, that a spark causes a great fire where a large quantity of combustible materials is assembled, those everyday truths no epoch has had to learn again so thoroughly as our own. As the revolution gradually becomes conscious of itself (for none at first knows its exact intention, it *learns* it) it became clearer that it was not a question of individual changes but of one so surpassingly great and significant that it touched the innermost nature of society. For if I say that people in reality protested against the past and wished to sever every connection with it, that statement must be taken simultaneously in its most general and its strictest sense. It was not only the most recent past that the protest concerned; it was the influence of earlier times on the present in general, the right of the ancestors in some respect to decide and act on behalf of their descendants that one attacked and denied. Changes to the old had often been seen before. – What history does not provide examples of that? and how would it itself be conceivable without them? – However, the destruction that is more or less inseparable from changes had generally been regarded as a necessary evil rather than in itself desirable; and, by recognising something unchangeable and sanctified when entering into a new state, one had at least, preserved for oneself the living connection with the past that preserves that continuity in the life and consciousness of society. Here on the contrary, destruction became a purpose; for what mattered was to establish in principle the complete independence of the present from all previous time: an arrogance that was nourished by the conviction of that period itself of its incomparable perfection. The character of the revolution and what distinguishes it from all others of that name lies in the fact that it wanted to explain society in the strictest sense as merely a compact between the contemporaries and tried to give the world an example of the making of such a compact. If every generation now necessarily represents not only itself but also the preceding ones and demands to be represented by posterity; if society embraces not only those who live *with* but also those who live *after* each other; if there is, so to speak, also a society with a longitudinal and not only a latitudinal dimension; then the attempt,

133

to continue the simile, to abolish one of society's natural dimensions would, by the nature of the matter, necessarily fail. That universal upheaval did also have the outcome that Burke's prophetic vision already at the outset (alone) foresaw, namely as a military despotism that threatened all of Europe, most dangerously and treacherously exercised in the name of the so-called liberal ideas, until at last not even that cover was regarded as necessary and sheer force, without a veil, presented itself to be worshipped by a world cowering in the dust.[1]

If all this has shown us the result of the experiment to construct, as far as that is possible, the entire social nexus, as if it were an ordinary compact between individuals, from which follows that it could also strictly speaking only be a transitory nexus between contemporaries (for every new generation could of course only become associated by means of a new compact) and that force would therefore necessarily soon be the only governing power in a state of affairs that by its very nature was inevitably volatile; then history has on the other hand also preserved for us examples of the predominance of the opposite principle, which treats society as an original, natural arrangement, the conditions of which are given once and for all. – That applies in itself primarily to the simplest society, to the family or household. Relationships such as those between spouses, between parents and children, and the closely related one between master and servant (in so far as the former must always possess an essentially paternal authority over his servants), are of all such cases those that nature itself has most closely determined and least allowed human arbitrariness to be able to change. Wherever the family has thus become the model for the state, we also find the rule

134

of the abovementioned principle. That reveals itself by the fact that such states as little as possible recognise any *acquired* right and therefore as far as possible treat every right as given by nature itself, that is to say as *innate*. That would of necessity, however, lead to a quite different result than the equality that more recent theories have wished to derive from the doctrine of rights that are innate and common to all. The first society or the family does not know that equality but on the contrary implies an original *difference*.[2] That very difference, transferred to civil society and there expressed on a far larger scale, became, through the concept of the transmission of rights through birth, or their hereditary nature, which is natural to such states, once and for all fixed and confined within certain limits. – That is the origin of the hereditary estates, of the division into strictly separated castes, which in Asia appears to be as old as civilisation itself, institutions that, however unnatural they may seem to us, nevertheless have a quite natural basis and are nothing but a strict ordering of the entire state by family or kin relationships.

The republican principle – and by that I mean the one that bases society on compacts between equals – has probably for ages been too prevalent among the Europeans (and that constitutes their essential distinguishing trait) for us to be able to find among them equally perfect examples of all that is the very opposite of that principle. Nonetheless, even the history of Europe does offer one such example, that is to say of a specifically European kind. That is the *feudal system*, more discussed than understood, the source of which one already finds in the oldest constitution of the Germanic group of peoples.

Within that nation three classes have of old been distinguished: the *nobility*, the *free* and the *unfree*,[3] although one cannot apply to any of these the term *estate* in the later sense of that word as a class of citizens specifically defined by rights of its own. For the *free* people were indeed distinguished by definite as well as strictly hereditary rights from the *unfree*. But the term estate can strictly speaking only be applied to a subdivision of society in which there are *several* other estates. A single estate is still *no* estate. But the *free*, embracing those who in all circumstances answered for themselves or were *their own men* and therefore also had a vote and influence in national affairs, did not constitute a particular *section* of the people defined by special rights but, on the contrary, the entirety of the *actual* people, among whom the unfree, on the other hand, could not be reckoned, as they were *below* every form of estate. A *nobility* (nobiles, principes) is already mentioned by Tacitus among the Germanic peoples, although apparently lacking any other preferential rights than that the people elected their kings from among it.[4] The earliest nobility was thus a *royal family* or restricted to the ruling kindreds, though their reputation, hallowed by tradition, did not give them a superior power until *actual* authority was assigned to them on the part of the people. The *title* of chieftain or king was not, however, restricted to actually ruling individuals, though it was given only to those who by descent were entitled to it.[5] In Scandinavia the royal families were regarded as descended from the gods, whose priests the kings also were. As such they appear in the most ancient times among us to have borne the names of the very deities over whose cult they presided,[6] by which conjuncture the ancestry of the ruling families all the sooner blended into the superhuman. A royal family was thus also a divine family and a nobility, defined by descent.Alongside that nobility the people led a free existence; for even the power of those who governed was, in itself, extremely limited. Kingship involved three things: the highest priestly function, supreme judicial power and command in war. The national priestly function was exercised at the great sacrificial festivals, which were also national assemblies. The priestly dignity represented both the sanctity of and a danger to the king; the first through the higher respect provided by the communion with the gods; the second because the people made him responsible for the favour and benefits of the latter, for instance for good annual harvests, and if one of those failed to occur for a long time it would occasionally demand his life as a propitiatory sacrifice. Two kings of the Yngling dynasty in Sweden suffered that fate. Furthermore, it seems that the king could impose punishments only by virtue of his priestly dignity.[7] The right to punish did not belong to him as a judge, as no judge really possessed it in relation to free men. All legal relations between the latter consisted of *peace*, a mutual agreement regarding the security of persons and property, and violations of that peace were atoned for by means of damages and fines, according to a tariff set by equals. The judgement amounted to conciliation, not punishment, that is to say it could not extend to life and limb, for with regard to those the free man recognised no lord and could therefore not be condemned to life and limb without having first lost his status as a free man or, what amounted to the same, his honour.[8] If every judgement between free men was conciliation – and it was so all the more certainly as each party was free, if the judgement did not reconcile them, to decide their dispute in a straightforward feud – then nor was the king's judgement anything else. The king did not act as the highest conciliator nor judge the free man in the absence of his equals, for all judgements were given with the people or, what is the same thing, with an elected *jury*. – In war the king was the commander, though the people did not follow him unconditionally in anything except what it had itself taken part in deciding or which the presence of the enemy in the land made necessary.[9] All other warfare was not a national war but merely a feud, in which the king could also *freely* engage with *his* men, that is those who owed him particular allegiance (fideles) or allied themselves temporarily with him.[10] For no free man, even if subject to a king, was the king's man, but his own. To be called the former required a specific relationship.

That relationship again depended on a preferential right personal to the rulers, more important for their power than the very limited rights given to them as heads of government, as we have seen, namely the right to accept into their following and their service free men, without that dependence being demeaning for the latter[11] or associated with the loss or diminution of freedom, which otherwise in public opinion accompanied any form of dependence on someone else. For only he was regarded as free who was in every respect his own man or, as the ancients expressed themselves, a *man for himself*. Public opinion had made an exception for royal service, though originally only in so far as that service was war service, as war was exclusively the occupation of the free as well as being the most honourable undertaking by the king. Those warriors who were attached to a king by a particular obligation formed his court – the *retinue* (comitatus) that Tacitus describes among the Germanic peoples so vividly and in such close correspondence with the records of ancient Scandinavia. That Germanic royal retinue was the *second* source of the nobility and the first of feudalism in Europe and deserves a closer consideration of its original character. – It was based on a personal commitment between the king and the man who entered his retinue, whereby the entrant became the king's man, in the same way that the servant was generally that of his master, although here with the difference that royal service, when it was military, did not prejudice his freedom and that honour made the bond between king and follower more sacred.[12] Every royal retinue was a *private*, more or less numerous *warrior band* with the king as its leader.[13] Every free man was also a warrior and the people itself an alliance for war – the same as the national army – so that it was among us in ancient times also called the *peasant host* or the *land host*[14] and was in its overall division into hundreds and regional units military. The difference between the national warrior and the warrior in the royal retinue was that the latter was a professional warrior and was therefore also described among us as a *fighter*, until that name was later replaced by that of a man of the king's bodyguard ('hird'), court or following. The king's retinue was above all a permanent war-band.[15] That war-band was more mobile than the land host and war was the most royal activity, from which – as the kings depended on the good will of the people with regard to the national army – competition arose among them as to who would surround himself with the most renowned fighters, the most numerous and bravest retinue of warriors, dependent on their leader and knowing no other occupation than warfare.[16] Nor was that competition limited to those who actually ruled; it was the object of the ambition of every descendant of a king. He who lacked a kingdom became *'king of a host'*. With royal descent went, if not land, necessarily a retinue, and the latter was the means to obtain the former. – No less did that competition express itself between the warriors themselves, to attain a higher position in the retinue[17] and generally among all free youths to be admitted to a prestigious royal retinue. Royal favour and acquired renown in such a position resulted in *nobility* or the title of 'thignar'. – That warrior nobility was a nobility of service and of the court and for a long time did not, and only with the expansion of royal power, gain any preferential rights with regard to the people. Nor were any of the advantages that accompanied it hereditary or even permanent in respect of a given person. For he could quit his service[18] and immediately rejoined the free community or free-holding peasantry, unless he attached himself to another retinue. Advantages connected with the service were *military command* and *land grants*. The former was exercised by the royal companion within the retinue itself, if he occupied a senior position there, and in national wars probably also over the free community (although that also had its own national war-leaders). With regard to the latter, or the land grants, in order to discover their probable initial nature one has to consider what the kings originally possessed to give away. First from enemies plunder, which was thus *one* source of the generosity of the king,[19] then from their own people not taxes (for none such properly speaking were, of old, raised from *allodial land* or free property) but voluntary contributions in kind.[20] In Scandinavia that was called *veitsla*. The retinue shared in the king's veitsla or were together with him or on his behalf guests among the people, and Tacitus expressly refers to that as its only reward.[21] As the original custom was such, it does not surprise us to find in the ancient Norwegian 'King's Mirror'[22] that one part of the king's retinue was called *guests*, a name that properly belonged to the entire court, which ate the king's bread. Veitsla or free maintenance was thus the first fief,[23] in the oldest sense of the latter word as a gift, enfeoffment in general.[24] Later the ordinary, more restricted sense arose, according to which enfeoffment is a right of use in exchange for service, what is properly expressed by the barbarian term *feodum* or *feudum*, though that is wrongly restricted to land or fixed property, for any kind of alienable right could be given or received as feodum. Finally, it may be noted that land given in fief must from the beginning have come from the king's private property, the royal domains, where such existed,[25] and that every fief, in so far as it is distinct from veitsla or maintenance, was a voluntary gift on the part of the donor, an act of generosity and not a duty: for which reason it was expressed in Latin by *beneficium*. The way in which that warrior nobility and the privileges associated with it, military command and fief, changed from a personal to an hereditary feudal nobility constitutes the first stage in the history of feudalism. How that nobility, having had the relationship *above itself* or to the king determined, by the same principle ordered the people *below itself* into numerous degrees of hereditary dependence, by which the old national freedom was lost, constitutes the second. Only in a few nations of Germanic origin did feudalism not even entirely pass through the first stage – in Scandinavia itself, for instance, the fiefs never became hereditary, even less was serfdom introduced among the people, which remained closer to its old freedom among us, as among the Swedes of the Alps, the Swiss.[26] – Among most of the others feudalism expanded, namely among all those who, migrating and making conquests in the former Roman provinces, founded new realms. But that development of feudalism occurred above all among and through the Franks, the greatest land-gainers of them all. The actual conquest itself would already of necessity mainly increase the power of the professional warrior class or royal retinue, as the kings, with regard to the entire mass of former Roman subjects, at once acquired all the rights of the Roman emperors and thus had vastly more to give away, which primarily benefitted their own men after the retinue. The free German did share with his king – to whom for a long time he also preserved the same independent relationship as before – and took his portion of land and property, though that of the king was naturally the most extensive, in and of itself and because he presumably seized land at the same time both for himself and for his following and finally because all the private imperial property (the former res privatae principis) in the province fell to him. The power of the retinue[27] thus soon increased by land grants among the Franks all the more as the constant redivision of the realm among the kings continually gave rise to wars, which they generally conducted with their own followers and were therefore obliged to attach them to themselves by ever greater privileges and to expand their numbers. In that way the system of enfeoffment was extended; thus the fiefs were first confirmed to the possessor for his lifetime, then made hereditary; thus the well-established renown of the retinue gradually became so great that its leaders – the *maiores domus regiae*, the earls – had more influence than the kings themselves and finally replaced them, even in name, having long since held the power. That was the first change of dynasty in the realm of the Franks. Out of the old royal retinue a territorial nobility had already been formed, though it was at first disappointed in its hopes, if it had entertained them, of gaining advantages for itself by the elevation of its leader to the throne. The earls, now kings, being forceful as usurpers generally are, had also learnt a lesson from the fate of their former overlords. They therefore rallied the still numerous *free men* as a countervailing force to the nobility, thereby associated the former more closely with their own interests and, in addition, engaged both people and nobility in constant wars. That was the policy of Charlemagne – by and large a policy of conquest, based on temporary objectives – for which reason his state structure – that reflection of the old national constitution, which he appears in many respects to have revived, though mostly for military purposes, by redesignating the land host or the people as a national army – also fell into decay and disappeared when his personal vision and hand no longer directed it. On the development of the feudal system he had, even if unintentionally, a powerful influence – firstly, by the extent of his conquests, which would after his time multiply and complicate the feudal relationships; secondly, and chiefly, by restoring the imperial dignity, whereby feudalism, which is always associated only with a power derived, delegated or granted from elsewhere, finally obtained a highest, sanctified point, from which it could proceed by means of its emanatory system. Even the importance that Charlemagne sought to restore to the people became disadvanta-

143

geous for the latter and everywhere opened up new ways for the downward extension of the system. The land host was depleted by the constant wars and became ever more dependent on its own officers, previously elected by itself but now appointed by the emperor, who under his feeble successors were able to make their positions hereditary and the former communal contributions in times of war into permanent ones, to their own advantage.[28] But with the introduction of taxes the old allodial freedom was gone and soon not even the agreement of the people was required for raising them but only that of the feudal nobility. The subsequent incessant hostilities and the territorial divisions between the Carolingian princes themselves would inevitably increase the power and independence of the nobility, while the general insecurity, aggravated by the contemporaneous attacks by Norsemen, Hungarians and Saracens – waves of devastation that almost converged from the north, east and south in the heart of Europe – delivered the mass of the people and the remaining free men ever more into the hands of the nearest protector, that is to say the nearest powerful vassal. As the more expensive cavalry service, which was primarily that of the warriors of the court, gradually displaced the old national infantry, the more affluent entered his military retinue. The poor man paid him for his protection, but along with his weapons he also lost the rights and honour of the free man, which they symbolised, and sank ever deeper into servitude. Thus, when the Carolingian dynasty ceased to govern, as far as Frankish rule and influence extended, that is to say across the larger part of the Germanic or germanicised Europe, the entire social order became more or less, though everywhere in its basic forms, distinctly feudalistic.

We have presented these most general characteristics of the history of feudalism simply in order to elucidate the principle of the system and for that purpose summarise the results here. I. Historically, the principle first reveals itself in the ancient Germanic royal retinue. From that already follows that all feudal relationships arose from a familial relationship and that that basic relationship was certainly the one between the master and his household, for the king's men were part of his household and designated accordingly.[29] The feudal terminology, during every phase of the system, recalls that original sense.[30] II. The only difference was that the master of the household was here a *king* and his household was *military*,[31] and that difference also explains how the entire social structure could under favourable circumstances be formed on the pattern of an otherwise private relationship. III. Being a professional warrior preserved the status of a free man for whoever had surrendered his personal independence in the service of a king, or at least caused that dependence not to be regarded as dishonourable, although a member of a king's household, according to the rule, left the company of the free. The expansion of royal power *ennobled* that same dependence. *All nobility is* thus *derived from the king's household*.[32] The first nobility arose from royal kinship, the second nobility from a personal relationship with a king. One was originally a nobility by descent, the other a service, but which with the heritability of the services or military commands as well as that of the fiefs, itself became hereditary. IV. The more independent, the latter, thereby

became of the kings, the more it established its own right
to maintain a court with fiefs and services, which eventually became hereditary in the same way as the royal ones.
The insecurity of the times favoured that endeavour of the
nobility to make the free men dependent on itself. Thus
vassals were created below vassals at various levels and
in many different forms of dependence, until the whole
of society consisted of feudal relationships. V. Regarding
these generally, we merely wish to add that all court service, higher or lower, out of which the feudal relationship
originally arose,[33] was by its nature military service and
remained so (with the personal exception of the religious
professions, though that was not always observed either).
The feudal system thus in effect embraced every element
that remained under arms and that retained its martial
honour; the rest of the people were divested of arms and
freedom and became commoners. Furthermore, all feudal
relationships emanated from the king, as from its source,
so that in the proper order of things the vassal, too, could
only himself have vassals as a vassal of the king.[34]

If we should now wish to express the principle of this
entire constitution in a single proposition, it would be the
following: *All right and power in society comes from above – it
emanates from something higher, as a gift and a grant* – a principle that derives directly from the family itself and expresses its original structure under the rule of a master of
a household. No less does the very manner in which that
principle manifested itself recall the same origin, namely through the prevailing inclination to make all *rights*,
though in terms of acquisition *granted*, nonetheless in that
of possession *hereditary* – the tendency towards the heritability of rights that we have already noted as the distin-

guishing mark of those social constitutions in which the familial element is predominant. We have thus completed our task, which was to show that the feudal system is a constitution of that kind: a truth that is by no means new but has hitherto, so far as I know, neither been adequately defined nor seen in its overall connection with the theory of the state in general. The principle forms part of that theory chiefly, however, in the sense that it has contributed to the formation of society throughout the world. The feudal constitution is merely a particular European instance of that.

This principle has had its dénouement as well, which in historical terms presents itself to us in – the *crusades*. In order to show the connection of that world event with feudalism, we need only adduce the following here. It was inherent in its nature that the principle underlying the system; that every right and form of power emanates from a *higher* one – when adopted by the church, would be defined as from the *highest*, and, as the highest is invisible – from its visible representative on earth, who called himself Christ's viceregent. That hierarchy grew entirely out of feudalistic soil and merely gave the system a strict consistency. When the pope, therefore, whose very title (papa, father) implied a familial power over Christendom, at last openly stated the principle that all worldly power is granted by the church, those claims were already so well prepared in every mind that the emperor, by no power other than that of public opinion, succumbed in the conflict. The most exceptional proofs of the predominance of that outlook are exactly contemporary with the epoch of the internal conflicts of the religious and secular power – the crusades, undertaken by millions in the name of the church and in its interest. Even in its ultimate perfect hierarchical form the system did not disavow its martial character. The latter was merely given a new direction. For each crusade, which set the forces of a whole continent in motion, the pope was the presumptive commander, every participant, including the king, being a soldier of the church. And what consequences were not inherent, according to feudalist notions, in that circumstance! – We have seen that the feudal relationships were essentially military. The model of the church and its requirements now completed the evolution of the military estate by creating an order, closed within itself, with obligations to defend the spiritual power. That was the *knighthood* – an actual profession or guild with grades of novices and masters (armigeri et milites) for those who devoted themselves exclusively to the military life, which had now acquired a holy purpose in the battle against the enemies of the faith.[35] In that knighthood – the highest flowering of feudalism – a nobility of *merit* arose within the nobility, also remarkable because the latter only now turned from a territorial or service nobility into a familial nobility in the strict sense and thus needed a specific symbol of merit. For the territorial nobility had also been a familial nobility, in so far as its fiefs had become hereditary, but it was nonetheless by its nature a nobility of service, which through the potential forfeiture of its fief would be lost. With the appearance of *family names* and *coats of arms* at a time when the territorial nobility had in addition made itself virtually independent of its overlords, the nobility first became in reality and by name a nobility of descent. And that this change first occurred during the crusades, which by intermingling warriors of all nations made such distinctive marks necessary, is well known.[36] The nobility was thereby fully formed as an hereditary estate – the real *fruit* of feudalism – also in the sense that the fruit of every plant detaches itself from its stem and contains the seed of new formations. That change had the most decisive influence on the state of society; for precisely with the ripening of that fruit did the feudal system also cease to be the *only* system in society, namely in the following way. It is obvious – something that we have postponed remarking upon until now – that with the evolution of the feudal system the kings abandoned and lost the old national kingship for a territorial overlordship, the real basis of which lay in a private relationship. They could regard that as a means of expanding their power as long as the old popular freedom stood in their way. When that had disappeared and feudal relations formed the whole of society, even when the servants began to become lords, they could still be satisfied with their position, in that it was the most elevated within the system, that there was nothing *beyond* it, and therefore also no ground for comparison. But as soon as the former territorial nobility closed ranks and shut itself off as a familial nobility and became a separate caste, it necessarily no longer presented itself as the whole but as a part, an estate within society, and the king, if he continued in his former relationship, was no longer the leader of the people but leader of a nobility that had moreover made itself virtually independent of him. If he did not wish to become *merely* the first among private individuals in his kingdom he must seek to restore the old kingship. That, in turn, could not happen except with support from the *people* and, as that was now definitely detached from the estate of the nobles, by rallying the *people* in *opposition* to it. And thus the interest of the third estate began to coincide with the royal interest. In addition, by the intervention of the religious hierarchy, the entire feudal system had with regard to its underlying principle seen a transfer of authority elsewhere, which would inevitably separate the interest of the system from that of the rulers.

Thus the period of the crusades displays a general disruption of the social structure, the full development of the feudal system but also the emergence of a countervailing system, which, once the ferment to which it had given rise during the final centuries of the Middle Ages was over, first enabled the kings to establish sovereignty (according to the ancient maxim of rulers, *divide et impera*!), until that countervailing system in our own time itself gained the upper hand and ventured the attempt to actually expel the feudalist element that had remained within the state, which took the royal authority along with it. That happened through the French *Revolution*, the principle of which we have theoretically indicated as being that which based society exclusively on compacts but have not yet explained in historical terms. Until that is done, however, we may take it as settled, by the voluble affirmation of the revolution itself, that it was diametrically opposed to feudalism. The *epoch of the crusades* and the *revolution* are thus the two extremes in the history of the European constitution and, as such, with regard to the inner nature of the social order itself, the most illuminating ones of all. For one needs to know the extremes in order to find the middle.

But before we continue with the historical discourse, this would be the place to show how the feudal system is related to the concepts regarding *compacts*. The above-mentioned opposition also reveals itself in the fact that feudalism, even if it also gave rise to compacts, nevertheless in its essence embodied a relationship that could never be fully expressed by means of compacts. That already follows from the fact that it had adopted a primordial relationship, namely that of the family, as its pattern. But the primordial relationships also differ in that regard from others, and they are entirely *personal* even with regard to their content and purpose, that they not only carry an obligation to perform certain specific activities but also involve the entire personalities of the parties in all possible circumstances. They can therefore also, like everything primordial, never be fully defined in words. – Or who can determine and enumerate all the duties that mutually connect spouses, parents and children? Unless in the sense that all owe each other everything, namely not this or that particular duty but *personal loyalty* (loyalty towards a *person*) in its widest extent. Consequently it is also not merely out of a certain reverence, which is found in the customs of all peoples, but out of sheer necessity, from a lack of *ability* to determine matters, that civil laws refrain from intruding into the innermost family relationships and that domestic rules throughout the world have their own sacrosanct sphere. – But primordial relationships are not only those provided by nature itself, such as the bond between parents and children as well as family relationships in general. Others may in the same sense also be adopted through agreements but are always characterised by the fact that they can never be fully analysed conceptually, so that the agreement itself denotes more than words are able to express about them. Of such a kind is *marriage* – in general, under conditions of equality between individuals, *friendship*, which national customs often present to us in the form of agreements[37] – or again under unequal conditions, the relationship of *servants* to their *masters*. All are typified by the fact that they involve personal loyalty in general, for even the servant's duty to have regard in everything to the good of his master no law is able to define. In the feudal relationship both of the cases referred to here were combined – the relation between master and servant – the relation between warrior and leader, a friendly relationship of comradeship in war, generally reminiscent of that of the ancient Norse sworn brotherhood.[38] In neither regard could their mutual duties be fully determined by law. It is therefore characteristic that the advantages provided by the leader to his followers were not originally referred to as an obligation, such as wages and rewards, but as a *good deed* (beneficium) and that the duties owed to him by the latter could only be expressed to their full extent by the general notion of what *honour* required. By the requirements of honour we still really mean duties the fulfilment of which no law can compel;[39] for which reason, when the nobility emerged from the royal retinue, that became its peculiar possession. That such honour was also based on a personal all-embracing loyalty is shown by the fact that both *trust* and *honour* linguistically denote the same virtue and that every *trusty* servant and *liege man* of the king has at once entered the sphere of aristocratic honour or has a legally recognised honour, not only juridically but morally.[40] – Thus Montesquieu is right to make *honour* the active principle of monarchy, namely provided that he thereby means the feudalist monarchy, of which the chief element is the nobility. More accurately, under monarchy it (honour) is above all the principle of the nobility. But then one also sees the seed of dissolution that

the feudal system carried within itself – how all attempts
to define obligations within it by law would never entirely
succeed, as, although with the transformation of the ben-
efices into fiefs, with the heritability of the latter and the
absence of the nobility from the court, the feudal duties
had to be more precisely defined, thereby giving rise to
a separate feudal law, the mutual relationship between
vassal and feudal lord was nonetheless in its origin and
nature unlimited and embraced the entire personality of
both – how the entire dependence of the former, if he was
powerful, would soon consist only in submitting himself
to the symbolic ceremonies that were customary when
fiefs were granted or confirmed – how the whole system
could easily be transformed into utter *lawlessness* and that
this would not only be a preferential right for the powerful
but could also in some degree extend to the humblest, as
personal loyalty was the basis for the *entire* social structure.
Thus that same constitution – despotic in so far as it was
formed on the pattern of the family and in reality alien to
civic freedom – would be dissolved for precisely the reason
that it left excessive scope for *natural freedom*, to do what
one *can* and is *able* to do,[41] and thus allowed arbitrariness,
with all its attendant disorders, to become its natural outcome, an outcome that is plainly observable in the history
of the Middle Ages.

We have already mentioned a *countervailing system*
that arose in particular during the crusading era, due to
which feudalism was no longer the only one in society
or at least the clearly predominant one. It remains to us
to characterise in historical terms that other system, of
which one would already, owing to its antithetical nature, presuppose that it would pose a civic liberty based

153

on agreements against feudalism, which only knew a (by its very nature indeterminable) personal relationship and dependence. That is indeed the case. For the origins of that system, however, one has to go as far back as with the former, namely to the primeval Germanic constitution, in which it once occupied a distinct sphere before the *royal* war-band gained predominance with the Germanic conquests, from which the entire feudal system gradually arose. – That earliest Germanic constitution was presumably a constitution of tribe and kindred, so that those natural ties were deeply venerated, the actual national union even initially being based on them, as the kindreds expanded and separated into tribes and the tribes combined into peoples. The first indications of the creation of a nation were three, *common cult*, *war service* and a *judicial system*, on the model of the family, united in a *single* cult and a *single* defence under a *single* set of domestic rules. Among a warlike and freedom-loving people, however, the pattern of family rule could only be followed closely with regard to the first. For the family implies an original *inequality* due to the power placed by natural and divine right in the hands of the father. That inequality was expressed in the national union by the privileges granted to the often mentioned royal nobility, whose members, owing to their heroic ancestors tracing their descent from the gods, had an innate claim to represent the latter and by their superintendence of the communal sacrifices continually reminded the people that it constituted a single large family, all the more so as a national god is generally only a personification of the people itself and therefore so often bears its own name. The original kingship or government was undoubtedly *priesthood*,[42] although that period in the

154

history of the Germanic nations has been virtually oblit-
erated, for which reason the Scandinavian one, though not
in time, is older in character, which is also due to the fact
that it is not derived from foreign sources but emerged
from its own traditions. In Scandinavia we know the original government to have been rule by priests, in which
even the title of king appears to have been unknown. The
first 'Odinic' rulers, whose family possessions consisted of
the estates known as 'Upsala öd'[43], set aside for the maintenance of the national sacrificial festivals, and of the national priesthood associated with them, bore the title of
drott. But drott referred not only to the deity itself and the
priest who represented it but also to the master of a household generally as the owner of the property; drott could
likewise designate the people of the heathen temple itself
as well as the *entire* population (or kindred).[44] Everything
thus points here to a familial rule based on divine, that is
to say, priestly authority.[45]

For the fact that this [priestly authority] did not already give rise to an actual hierocracy, without the detour
through feudalism, such as one finds, from the same origins of the state, to have occurred in several places in the
East, one cause possibly lay in the ancient Nordic religion
itself, which had too few positive precepts with which to
fetter the minds of people and was also, like the character
of the people, wholly warlike. For that reason it happened
that the warrior displaced the priest among the rulers,
which already appears to have taken place in the time of
Tacitus within the German branch of the Germanic peoples,[46] or, if both of those identities were combined, that of
the warrior became predominant, which seems to have occurred among us as soon as the title of drott was exchanged

for that of king.[47] That title itself is derived, according to the opinion of some, from the ancient military subdivision of the people into groups of a hundred (hundari, the territorial hundred) and has changed from meaning the leader of a certain number of people to designate leaders in general.[48] It therefore no longer surprises us to hear of many kings among us in the most ancient times, from the overking or as he was also called in that capacity, the 'sole-ruling king' in Upsala, to the kings of hundreds, who emerged as a result of the constant subdivision of the kingdom as the royal kindreds branched out.[49] But it is also apparent that such a military status would not carry with it the same paternal authority that all priesthoods find it so easy to acquire. Military comradeship is, despite the subordination, a relationship of *equality* and family rule could no longer serve as a model. For the master of a household does indeed have the right, for offensive or defensive purposes, to demand obedience from the members of his household. But also from those of his neighbour? Not without voluntary agreement. That extended even to the king. The people followed him only in such a war as it had itself decided upon together with him, unless self-defence made the war unavoidable. Should he want to go to war of his own desire he had to do so like everyone else with the people of his own household, which provided the reason for the expansion of his warrior household, his court or the royal retinue. The abandonment of the priestly status for the military one would affect the king's relationship to the people even more, as *judge*. For only as a priest did he possess the right to impose penalties; as a warrior only in war, in peace time only over his household, but none over that of the free householder. The indi-

2. FEUDALISM AND REPUBLICANISM

vidual households, within which each master was the natural judge, stood to each other in a perfect relationship of
equality. But all judgements between equals amounted to
conciliation, and the conditions under which injuries were
to be reconciled and atoned for, or the conciliation tariff
– for there could be no question of penalties of life and
limb between equals[50] – were established through common agreement by the masters of households themselves
and constituted the *law*. Such a law presupposed and implied an intention to maintain a mutual *peace* guaranteed
by collective force, and that peace formed the first society
based on an explicit compact between equals. If one looks
for the simplest example of that, it is the *hundred* (hundar-
it). We already know of that as an alliance based on military comradeship and probably also on kinship,[51] but it
was also or became, through the extension of common
defence from times of war to those of peace, a civilian alliance. It still retains that character in many respects, although a more advanced form of government has shown it
little favour and has neglected to make of it all that it
could become, preferring other such subdivisions of the
people, which represent a bureaucratic power, to that
original one, which rests entirely on the foundation of the
old popular freedom. – The hundred, I maintain, still in
many respects preserves the character of a separate society
through communal duties of cooperation (for example in
building a road or bridge) – in a number of places through
communal land (hundred commons) and everywhere
through a communal district court. Most remarkable in
that regard, familiar in Swedish law, is the share of the
hundred in fines (in cases of manslaughter and wounding). Why now, in cases of breaches of the *peace*, should

not only the injured person and his relatives but also the hundred be conciliated, unless it regarded itself as injured by the injury of any of its members, unless it had thus actually been a civil alliance? But that share of the hundred in compensation fees is not only as old among us as the earliest concepts of justice in general; it is already recorded as a Germanic custom in Tacitus.[52] Equally clear evidence of the original character of the hundred as a separate republic is provided by the old Nordic rule that a violator of the peace at first became an outlaw within the hundred and not further afield.[53] Only if he did not respond to a charge at the hundred assembly would he have to be prosecuted at the *provincial assembly* and became an outlaw throughout its jurisdiction. – For just as the hundred was the alliance of the free masters of households, the *provincial jurisdiction* was such an alliance of the hundreds and the *kingdom* in turn an alliance between the provinces, so that the actual national union consisted of those three associations in conjunction. But each of the first two kinds was already a national union on a smaller scale and its distinctive features, common justice, war service and cult, apply to all of them. They all had general gatherings of the people to decide on those public matters, the common name of which was 'thing' or *assembly* (hundred assembly, provincial assembly, national assembly or 'allshärjar-thing'); and at the head of all those alliances from the hundred to the kingdom stood persons elected by the people itself. One should remember that even the kingship, although heritable within the kindred, was in respect of the individual elective and that, even if the eldest son generally followed his father on the throne, the people nevertheless formally always exercised their right to vote. In the beginning, as we have seen, all national leadership was presumably kingship and we find kings of hundreds and of provinces ('fylken' or 'land') as heads of the lesser alliances, as the overking was of the whole. It would not remain so, as we know. The overkings sought to eliminate the minor ones, but that served so little to extend their power that the lesser alliances, on the contrary, appointed community leaders in place of the petty kings and that the entire social constitution – under the drotts *priestly*, under the kings *military* – now began to develop the actual *civil* or communal element more independently and to become republican. Also in accordance with that was the fact that those new community leaders did not adopt a name from any precedence based on descent, as the kings did, but from the law, as an expression of the general will, whose agents they were only intended to be. They were called *lawmen* (lagmän) and were the public servants not of the king but of the people, by and from which they were elected,[54] whom they represented before the king and the national assembly and in whose name they voted in the election of kings. Just as the lawman replaced the provincial king, so the hundred king was replaced by the *district judge*, likewise originally elected by the people themselves. The latter presided at the district assembly, the former at the provincial assembly, all of which goes to show that, even if their position was essentially juridical, they were nonetheless generally the chief spokesmen on the public matters that could arise in such a popular assembly and were thus the heads of the lesser alliances.[55] They could not exercise authority without the people, any more than they could judge. Their living law code was the memory of all free men, their entire power the assent and decisions of the people. All of that also applied with regard to the royal authority. Allegiance was not sworn to the king, once he was elected, until he had expressly confirmed the laws of the alliances, both sides among us regarding themselves as so insecure before that had been done that they mutually exchanged hostages.[56] Once allegiance had been sworn to him and he was in power, he did not rule without, much less against, but in every sense jointly with the people, whose decisions taken together with him at the national assembly set the limits to his authority,[57] while outside those limits every free man could interact with him as man to man, or no longer stood in any relationship of legal subordination towards him.[58] It is obvious that under that social constitution one only needs to delete the title of king to recognise it as purely republican, and it does appear as such in Iceland, which was settled from Scandinavia, where the lawman held the highest office.

In tracing this development we have referred in particular to the Nordic countries and to our own country, as it is only in the oldest Scandinavian records that the stages in the evolution of the national constitution that we have noted here have been preserved, albeit dimly, yet so that one can follow them. It seems certain that it was mostly during the period immediately preceding the introduction of Christianity in Sweden, that the republican spirit of the constitution evolved and was then embodied in the national laws, which were only written down later, and that was surely also the case among the Germanic peoples a mere few centuries earlier, before the conquest of the Roman provinces laid the basis for the superiority of the royal war-band over the free population and, simultaneously, with the adoption of a new religion prepared the way for a new social order. With that we have also explained our expression that, with regard to the original form of the Germanic constitution, the history of Scandinavia, though not chronologically older, is more archaic in character. Everything that we know about the constitution of the other Germanic peoples, from the Romans *before* the period of conquest and *after* it from the laws of the nations, agrees very exactly with what we know best and most recently of the ancient Nordic one. The correspondence between the oldest written laws of those nations[59] and the Scandinavian ones, not only in their general spirit but even in the most specific details, in formulations and expressions, even in the barbarised Latin in which the greater part of the former have come down to us, is astounding. The division into hundreds was general (the hundred was called *centena* in the barbaro-Latin laws – among the Anglo-Saxons *hundrede*) or, where that term itself is not found,[60] another appears (Markgenossenschaften), corresponding to it in nature. The hundreds were again combined into larger alliances of the same kind. One such is called *judiciaria* (the jurisdictional area, as among us) in the Langobardic laws – among others the hundreds were called *pagi* (Gauen). Both of these associations had their gatherings to decide public matters by common agreement, their *assemblies* and their spokesmen, which, like the alliances themselves, being both in name and in their originally entirely popular authority, not derived from the king, are reminiscent of the Nordic ones. Corresponding to the district judge is the *centenarius*, to the lawman the *grafio* (der Graf – among the Langobards he was also called *iudex*).[61] However, these subdivisions among the people with their spokesmen may have been more numerous or fewer, more

161

or less subordinated to each other; what interests us here is only the general nature of that constitution, common to all Germanic peoples, and it consists in the following. I. The subdivisions were everywhere at the same time military and civilian. II. Every larger or smaller division was above all an alliance between the free householders for common peace and reconciliation in cases of violation of that peace, the conditions of that reconciliation constituting the law of that society.[62] III. All power within such an alliance – and even the national assembly was merely such a one on a larger scale – emanated from the members themselves through election and delegation and was in its nature entirely a *mediatory power*, which otherwise, except during wartime, did not include a right either to compel or to punish free men.

Such were the basic features – still recognisable in the ancient laws of the nations, despite all later additions – of the Germanic constitution, or more precisely of the constitution of the free class, the free warriors and landowners (the allodial peasants). With regard to its principle, it is the following: *all power and justice emanates from below, through delegation by the people* – from which proposition this second one is inseparable: *society is an association formed by an explicit compact between equals.* But that is what we call the *republican* principle in society, which is thus, just as much as the opposite *feudalistic* one, based on the oldest social organisation. We have seen that the latter evolved out of a familial relationship. In the most general sense, therefore, the feudalistic principle – covering relationships that no compact could either fully express or establish and the nature of which is to derive all authority and justice from a higher one – that, I maintain, belonged to

2. FEUDALISM AND REPUBLICANISM

the sphere of the family, the republican one, on the other
hand, to that of the mutual relationships of families that
were independent of one another – one in an original relationship of *inequality*, the other in an original relationship
of *equality*. But the familial principle as the principle of a
state is in reality feudalism and as such we find it, along
with the republican one, acknowledged by the following
principle, namely that every man should be bound either
by a *hundred* or a *pledge* (in hundredo aut plegio).[63] In the
former case he was entitled to his own peace, assured to
him by the hundred, in the latter case that of his protector, who answered for him. – In the absence of either, he
had not given the community any surety. That rule necessarily had to be general under a constitution of which
the essential nature lay in a surety given for peace. The
principle could also be expressed as follows: everyone shall
be subject either to the *law of the land* or *curial justice* (hof-
rätt).[64] It is still required in law that everyone shall either
act in his own defence or under that of another. Here two
systems appear to us in society, their point of convergence
being the king; for monarchy, as both hereditary and elective, was also simultaneously both feudal and republican.
We would therefore expect that both systems, which at a
lower level by their nature excluded each other so that for
example no one could simultaneously be his own man and
someone else's, the higher up one goes and in the vicinity
of the king should increasingly converge. And so it is. For
to be subject to the king's pledge was specifically to be
subject to a free pledge (in plegio liberali), or did not deprive one of the status of a free man, and that, as applied
to the king's warrior household or retinue, an institution
common to all Germanic societies, from which the entire

feudal system then evolved, places the *king's men* from the beginning at the pinnacle of that system. They were, with their freedom unimpaired, associated with a lord by personal duty and loyalty and as it was a preferential right of the royal nobility, which also ennobled the dependence, and as nobility later also arose from that more noble dependence, one can see that the feudal principle in society was in reality that of the *nobility*, just as the republican one was the principle of the *free estate*. Yet, although the law of the latter estate or the law of the land in general did not equate those who belonged to the *king's* household with other persons who were subject to domestic rules, so that for instance in Nordic law the manslaughter of a king's man was compensated for or settled at as high a level as for a free man, except for the special fine for the king's honour (tuckabot) that was due in such cases,[65] the provincial law among us nonetheless retained certain rules which indicate that it no longer fully acknowledged a king's man as belonging to the association of the free. Thus the Västergötland law [province of Västergötland law code] decrees that no official may be a juryman unless, it adds, that is done by the will of both the peasant and the district judge.[66] But to be a juryman was only an exercise of the right of every free man to be eligible to be a judge or arbitrator.[67] That the law according to that rule excluded the official (the king's or anyone else's) from that exercise of a right common to all free men is evidence that the latter no longer regarded him as their *equal*. He was not their equal in that he was subject to another law, that of the royal court, which both in domain and spirit differed from the law of the land – in domain, as it really only included those who belonged to the king's court – in spirit, as the law of the land was based on *conciliation* but the curial law on *punishment*: the one agreed to by equals, the other decreed by a lord.[68] Such a strictness is also part of the nature of martial law and the curial law was at the same time the first *martial law*. That they were not merely different but entirely opposite in character, together with the circumstance that the curial law was closest to the highest authority, also explains why with the passage of time and the growth of royal power, though incorporated together with the law of the people into the same governmental system, it must nevertheless always relate to the latter law as an exception or as a *privilege*, a privilege that, by freeing one from the obligations and burdens of the general law, with regard to the people eventually more than compensated for the strictness which, on the other hand, or with regard to the ruler, was the original principle of the privilege.[69]

The conflict between the systems, barely noticeable under the old conditions, when the social bonds were generally so loose, was at once decided by the importance that the Germanic conquests gave to the royal warrior estate, from which it then naturally followed that feudalism became predominant in society among those peoples and finally its ruling system. But as if it were necessary for the opposites to evoke each other and most certain when each had reached its ultimate development, no sooner had that happened than the republican principle again came to life and, although in a different form, occupied its place in society, following which the real conflict with feudalism began. That happened because of the power of the *towns*, which also makes the period of the crusades so remarkable. It is known that towns were for the Germanic peoples not only at first unfamiliar but odious[70] and the obscurity into which the towns everywhere sank and in which they remained for centuries after the conquests best demonstrates that the antipathy lasted for a long time. One can and must then ask: from where did that urban republicanism come among peoples who had known nothing but rural freedom and among whom the majority had already long since also lost it? It is acknowledged that this new spirit of freedom came from the south. There, in Italy, the free constitution of the towns is commonly seen to suddenly arise at a certain point in time, as if out of the rubble.[71] That change, already remarkable in itself, becomes even more so when one considers more closely the forms in which that spirit of freedom expressed itself. For one recognises everywhere the old *Roman municipal constitution*, not only in its nature, namely an internal self-governance under locally elected officials, but in its entire organisation with people, senate and magistrates.[72] Those forms could not have been transmitted until that period by tradition if one presupposes, as is usually done, all that would make such a tradition impossible, namely a complete destruction of the constitutions of the towns in the Roman provinces at the time of the conquests. Even less can one ascribe such a great influence to a renewed acquaintance with the ancient literature, as that occurred later and everything moreover indicates that the case in that regard was the opposite and that the revival of the old social forms was precisely the living soil from which the love of the culture of the ancients was born and had such a great impact in Europe. All would be explained if one could assume that the Roman municipal constitution in the towns had in fact never entirely ceased, only to emerge again after an interruption of several centuries, but had

166

continued in its essential features until particular circumstances in the 12th century revived it. But that this is not a groundless supposition but an historical fact has been fully demonstrated by ingenious and thorough recent research.[73] When Goths, Burgundians, Franks and Langobards established new kingdoms on the ruins of the Roman empire one generally imagines a total destruction of all the old conditions. – Wrong. – The destruction was indeed great. Innumerable Romans were killed, driven away or enslaved. But one can and must nevertheless assume two facts of the greatest importance. I. The old nation was generally by no means extirpated by those peoples. The conquest of Britain by the Anglo-Saxons is the only exception. The latter conducted an actual war of extermination against the old inhabitants. And the reason for that exception is also clear. They were still pagans. The other Germanic peoples who founded kingdoms in Roman provinces were, on the other hand, already Christians, just like the peoples that they subjugated. That the Latin element in the Romance languages that developed through the admixture became the dominant one is also incontrovertible evidence that everywhere else, even after the conquest, the Romans formed the majority of the population. II. Nor were they, as a nation, turned into slaves, however many individuals may have suffered that fate as prisoners of war. They retained that property as their own which was left to them after the partition with the conquering people. They retained their law and in many respects their constitution. – All of this can be historically proven. Firstly, with regard to the property of the Romans, what has been said already followed from the nature of the partition that the Germanic peoples undertook in the conquered lands. For they did not simply divide the land up among themselves, with the Romans themselves accompanying it as slaves, but they shared the land and property with the Romans. That was the general principle, the application of which nevertheless differed among the various peoples in its extent and manner. The Burgundians and Visigoths took two thirds of all cultivated land, with the Romans thus keeping the remaining part, which appears in the laws under the same name (sors, lot) as that of the Germanic peoples. Both the German and the Roman with whom he shared property were in that relationship called each other's guests (hospites) and the Burgundian law stipulates that if a German wished to sell his lot his Roman host should have the first right of purchase. The Ostrogoths and after them the Langobards took a third of the Roman lands in Italy, although in different ways. – The Ostrogoths methodically and universally, so that even from such Roman property as had not in fact been individually subdivided they nevertheless demanded a third of its revenue, which in that case went to the royal treasury, the Langobards, on the other hand, less methodically and in a simpler manner, so that every German was assigned one or more Romans as his hosts, from whose property he took one third of all produce.[74] Among the Franks one finds no mention of a partition, but among them, on the other hand, as among the abovementioned peoples, another firm proof that civic rights were granted to the former Roman subjects after the conquest. For they retained their law, the Roman one.[75] We know that according to ancient Germanic concepts all law was *personal*, related to kindred and descent, not to territorial boundaries, so that in one and the same land and under the same king, for example in the Frankish realm, Franks, Burgundians, Goths, etc., lived together, each under their inherited national law.[76] In cases of mutual conflict the basic principle followed was that in civil cases the descent of the accused but in criminal cases that of the accuser determined the law by which the case should be judged. All of that was also extended to the Romans. They were left in possession of their law, all the more because the *clergy* everywhere lived by Roman law, which had already for that reason gained an accepted place among the other legal codes and generally a wide influence. That acceptance of the validity of Roman law for the former Roman subjects involved a solemn recognition of those civic rights in themselves and particularly by Germanic notions. For according to them law, being a personal possession, was one of the distinctive attributes of free people. Only the slave was not born into any legal system but everywhere followed that of his master. The Romans, though otherwise in various respects not on an equal footing with their Germanic conquerors, for instance in their liability to pay tax, being more strictly subordinated to king and officials and with their personal surety less highly valued (by the Germanic laws), in all of which the Roman differed from the Germanic rulers, yet in that regard did have recognised civic rights. With that retention of the law the continuation of the ancient Roman constitution was also still necessarily associated, at least to some degree, namely in certain lesser matters, for all higher administration would of necessity change with the ruling people. After the initial destruction, however, *only* the most essential changes were generally made, especially because the simple-mindedness and ignorance of the conquerors made them inclined to leave things as they were among their new subjects. Being little acquainted with the forms of a developed civic order, they did not understand either how to use them systematically for oppression, which is eminently practicable. Nor could the expenses of a simple government be great. And those circumstances undoubtedly provide the reason why the Roman subjects, despite all the individual cases of violence that they had to suffer at the hands of their new rulers, nonetheless on the whole clearly preferred the rule of the Germanic peoples to that of the corrupt, despotic Roman court. – Thus even in rural areas the Roman constitution, Roman minor officials and Roman legal procedure undoubtedly survived long after the conquest. That constitution would necessarily also change and come to an end first in the countryside, yet in such a way that that change proceeded in parallel with the transformation of the Germanic peoples' own ancient national constitution. Here, in the countryside, Germans and Romans were most intermingled with each other. Through the amalgamation of the two a new people eventually developed, to which the former ethnic differences in constitutions and laws no longer applied. The system of personal laws came to an end and the feudal system arose instead, soon embracing all social relations and absorbing into itself in various respects more or less of both Germanic and Roman law. Specific circumstances could even in advance suggest that all of this did not apply equally to the towns. Originally alien to the Germanic peoples, they ought to have retained a more unmixed Roman population and along with that Roman institutions. But that the Roman constitution really did continue in the towns has been placed beyond doubt by von Savigny.

Since the days of the Roman republic that constitution of the towns in Italy was republican and the sovereign power was exercised as in Rome by the people, which passed laws and elected officials in its assemblies. As early as the beginning of the imperial period the citizenry mostly lost that power, the constitution became aristocratic and the rights of the popular assembly were transferred to the senate, which within itself elected the magistrates, who together with the council conducted the internal administration, for which reason the term *municipes*, which originally designated all the citizens and their rights, was subsequently applied primarily to the council. Magistrates elected in that manner and with their own jurisdiction were really the distinguishing feature in the Italian Roman towns. In the provinces, except in the towns that possessed *ius italicum*, the situation was different, in that one does find a council, a curia or ordo decurionum, which with its leader (principalis) conducted the internal administration in the towns, but not magistrates with their own jurisdiction. That was exercised by the Roman governors or their legates. The provinces later received a substitute for the absent magistrates in the so-called defenders (defensores civitatis), elected by the entire citizen body, who from the time of Justinian possessed the rights of magistracy, so that the citizenry, the council and internally elected magistrates with their own more or less extensive jurisdiction are generally the constituent elements in the Roman municipal constitution. But those very elements, in particular the main one, a curia with its own jurisdiction, are found in the towns, in some places (as in southern France, for example) with more extensive freedoms after the conquest than before, both in Gaul under the rule of Franks and

Visigoths and in Italy under that of the Langobards, and can be followed historically, if only often by dim traces, through all the centuries, until specific events at a particular point in time in Italy gave new life to the towns.[77] Before we proceed to look at that time, we would merely add a few remarks. The Germanic peoples, although the urban institutions were from the beginning alien to them and long remained so, generally, as we just stated, left them intact. Those institutions would nevertheless have to in some way be fitted into the new regime, to which they were now subject. How was that done? What place could they be given in a Germanic constitution? The answer is simple. The principle of the Germanic national constitution was freedom under an internally elected authority. But the principle of the municipal constitution was exactly the same. On that common ground both could coexist, rural freedom with urban freedom, and have long coexisted with each other. The similarity of principle brought with it similarity of forms (even if different laws applied in country and town), and that is particularly noticeable with regard to judicial matters. According to Germanic law no judgement was given without a *jury*, that jury originally representing in the court the people or the assembly of the free men. For the ability to become a judge or mediator in settling disputes was a right that belonged to every free man. Just as the law belonged to the people, judgements were also delivered in the assembly with the assent of the people. With increasing complexity of social conditions and an increased number of trials, the presence of the free men in the assembly turned from an honour into a burden, which one sought to evade. From the time of Charlemagne a certain number of free men were therefore jointly elected by judges and people to be assessors in the court. They are called scabini (Schöffen, echevins) and corresponded exactly to our jury. But roughly the same situation appears in the municipal constitution. There, too, the citizenry had vested the exercise of the judicial power that belonged to them collectively in a certain number of men, namely the council, together with the judge or magistrate. And those urban councillors were so close in their position to the jurymen of the people that they appear not infrequently in the medieval records under the name of the latter, just as the municipal constitution generally is often found disguised under Germanic names. Thus one hears, for example, of Roman scabini in the towns, which undoubtedly referred merely to the councillors (decuriones, curiales) of the municipal constitution, who are also often quite simply called *good men* (boni homines, prud'hommes). According to Germanic social forms the leader of a hundred (tunginus, schuldais, centenarius) was placed with a more restricted jurisdiction under the count (grafio, comes), the highest local authority. But the magistrates of the towns also had such a limited jurisdiction. Both thus simply needed to be subordinated to the count as the common authority for Romans and Germans. In the old Germanic national constitution the towns could therefore easily be accommodated, although the German himself had an aversion to urban life, which only time would overcome. – On the other hand, the feudal system was by its whole nature directly contrary to the municipal constitution based on civic freedom and in that system – we have to admit – the freedom of the towns could not find a place except as an alien, unauthorised and therefore subdued element. It may therefore be presumed as an historical axiom that the more strictly and more generally that system prevailed in a country, the more were the urban constitutions there destroyed and, on the contrary, the less power that feudalism had gained, the better did the municipal institutions maintain themselves. The former applies to northern France (though not without exceptions) as well as southern Italy, once the Normans had introduced feudalism there in all its severity. The latter again to southern France and northern Italy, in the second of which the new flourishing of the towns would indeed begin.

The time when that new power of the towns in Italy began was really the twelfth century and the change was brought about by both *external* and *internal* causes. Among the former we include the crusades, through the increased activity that they imparted to commerce. Those advantages were primarily gained by the Italian cities, among which Venice even during the darker centuries of the Middle Ages had maintained a free constitution and conducted a not insubstantial trade with Constantinople, a trade that through the crusades and the connection that they opened up with the east – especially after the capture of Constantinople by the crusaders with Venetian help – at once achieved a far greater extension and importance and gathered all the treasures of the Levant in the hands of those courageous and wise republicans. Genoa and Pisa competed with them, though they were mutual rivals. The wealthy burgher began to be aware of his importance in relation to emperors and princes. The consciousness of power gave rise to a spirit of independence that spread, and we soon see the cities in northern Italy emerge – in a successful struggle with a powerful feudal nobility, which was for the most part obliged to move inside the walls, to which a fierce sense of freedom gave invincible security against external attacks – as small republics, in which the old municipal forms now gained new power and greater importance. Such causes were active more or less everywhere among all the nations that took part in the crusades. Those immense armaments in an unsophisticated era, poor in financial facilities, at once created an enormous need for money in Europe. That was what really imparted a new life to commerce; for commerce alone creates money or, what is the same thing, makes wealth disposable. Of that need for money it was everywhere the towns that took advantage as, even before an expanded trade could substantially enrich them, they were nonetheless generally inhabited by an acquisitive class that could more easily than others keep its wealth in ready money. They bought themselves free from feudal dependence, thereby acquiring personal freedom and security from arbitrary imposts but above all the right to elect judges and magistrates among themselves, a right that, now as before, became the distinguishing mark of an urban community (communia, commune).[78] Such was in the main the origin of the communes both in France, where the kings themselves set an example in the granting of liberties within the crown lands, in Germany, where the clergy in particular appeared as the protectors of the towns, as well as in England, where the exceptional, unlimited power that the Norman conquest gave to the crown, created the odd situation in which nobility and townspeople at an early date used their strength *jointly* to secure themselves against the royal power: a circumstance that, together with the insular position of England, largely explains the peculiar aspects of its constitution. Apart from that, it goes without saying that the rights acquired by the towns, with regard to both extent and manner, may have varied considerably in different places. Spain, for instance, lies outside the region affected by the crusades. Here other circumstances had already had the same effect earlier and the need of the kings for the loyalty of the people in the fierce internal conflict with the Moors had at an early stage given the estates, and among them especially that of the burghers, greater power and influence than elsewhere.

If, on the other hand, we look at the internal causes of that emergence of the third estate they all combine into a single large and principal one, which we have already indicated, and that lies in the feudal system itself and its relationship to the organisation of society in general. For it was an internal necessity that this social system, once it had reached its highest and most extreme form, should bring forth its own antithesis in society. Remarkably enough, in this case it was the *church* that brought about the transition. We have already noted how it seized upon the principle of feudalism, founding upon it the rights of hierarchy and itself assuming the highest position in the system. That would not be achieved without a fierce conflict, however, as that highest position was already occupied by a secular authority, namely the imperial power restored by Charlemagne, which subsequently remained with the kings of Germany. The epoch of the crusades, which more than any other demonstrated the power of the church over the minds of men, was therefore also the epoch of a great intra-European conflict pursued at the same time: the conflict between the religious and secular power, between papal and imperial authority, initiated by the real founder of the hierocracy, Gregory VII, against the emperor Henry IV and then continued for 200 years, ending with the ruin and destruction of the heroic and imperial Hohenstaufen family, brought about by the popes. That conflict, already favourable for the emergence of a new social order in that it overcame the feudalism within itself, was not merely a general struggle for the highest position but also specifically a struggle for Italy and has in that respect had no less remarkable consequences. Rarely has a title, merely as such and only due to the concepts associated with it, become so historically important as the Roman imperial title during the Middle Ages. In the general opinion it gave universal power, similar to the Roman one, to those who with the title of the emperors were believed to be their actual successors. Thus the imperial dignity was regarded as involving a general power of protection over the Christian world and in particular a claim to supremacy over Rome and Italy. It was thus in itself an ideological power, like that of the papacy, though the outcome showed that the latter had established its foundations more firmly. The influence that general opinion had attached to the title of emperor was so great, however, that the emperors thereby became the only rulers who, lacking the royal sense for their own advantage, neglected to establish a *genuine* power base or else sought it where it could not be established, across the Alps in Italy. There, on the other hand, they were most dangerous for the popes, for which reason that land was to become the real battle-field. Everything in that conflict depended on which party was supported by the Italian cities, which throughout all of upper Italy were already the most powerful. The emperors chose their allies, not in accordance with the royal interest, which otherwise sought in the emergence of the towns a welcome counter-balance to an over-mighty feudal nobility; they chose them, as one might expect, on the basis of a power based entirely on feudal concepts, for which civic rights were alien. They took sides *against* the cities. That was already one reason for the popes to side *with* them. Italian patriotism was another and there was a third and more profound one, which will become clear below, when we consider the relationship of the church to society. At all events, the popes at the head of the Italian republics broke the imperial power and also became the protectors of civic freedom. In vain had the great emperor Frederick Barbarossa within 22 years (1154–1177) led seven large armies in succession from Germany to Italy and armed half a million people in his cause; in vain did he level heroic Milan with the ground and sow salt in the place where it had stood; in vain did he seize Rome by force of arms and fire and compel the head of the church to seek refuge in the Colosseum and to flee from there incognito through the countryside. The new spirit of freedom was invincible. It was during this period that one saw the citizens during the siege of Crema for the sake of defending the city sacrifice their own children, who having previously been delivered to the imperial forces as hostages, had then been tied to the outside of a mobile siege tower, from which the enemy with gruesome assurance attempted to approach and scale the walls. One saw the fathers from the wall, with large stones from mangonels, crush both tower and children with loud cries of lamentation, among which voices were heard to shout: fortunate are those who while still at a tender age may die for freedom and fatherland! It was during the same period that, during the siege of Ancona, all foodstuffs had been consumed, so that when, after the most careful search, scarcely six sacks of grain and barely a score of eggs were found in the entire city, an almost 100-year-old blind man, a former consul, rose in the popular assembly and raised everyone's courage, reminding them of the exploits of his youth. Ancona then fought simultaneously against hunger and the enemy. A young, beautiful and noble lady, carrying her child in her arms, saw a soldier fall to the ground fainting (with thirst). For fourteen days, she said, I have kept alive by eating boiled hides and I feel that the milk for my child is beginning to give out. But, if my breast can still give any nourishment, stand up, put your lips to it and recover your strength for the defence of your native city.[79] – Such traits need no elaboration. One senses that it is the republican virtues that are again visiting the earth. The Milanese rebuilt their walls and defeated Frederick utterly at Lignano, while the same pope, Alexander III, who had to flee his capital before the imperial arms, now head of the league of Lombard republics, signed a treaty with the emperor in Venice in which the free constitution and all the rights of the cities were recognised, although under imperial protective authority, and then made a ceremonial entry.[80]

Thus the church mediated the transition from feudal rule to civic freedom and made room for it in society. And that not only in Italy. It was largely responsible for the rise of the towns, particularly in the countries with a purely Germanic population that, originally unacquainted with urban institutions, lacked any heritage from the Romans in that respect, that is to say in Saxon Germany and throughout the Scandinavian north. The same methods that Charlemagne had used to pacify the Saxons were employed by the emperors against the Slavic tribes that had migrated into northern and eastern Germany, namely Christianity and warfare. The latter destroyed, but the former preserved and cultivated. Everywhere fortresses and episcopal sees were established on the borders. Around both of these inhabitants settled under the protection of the castle (or burgh) constructed there and were consequently called *burghers*. Henry I (who ruled 919-936) ordered that those localities should be surrounded by walls against the plundering raids of Hungarians and Slavs, that every ninth man should move there from the neighbouring hundreds and that the towns generally at times of enemy attacks should became both storehouses and places of refuge for the neighbouring inhabitants.[81] As those measures were adopted at a time when the old popular freedom had not yet been extinguished, the towns thereby received, in addition to the lord of the castle's own men and subordinates, a number of free inhabitants, who from the beginning, even after the move, were subject to national law but gradually withdrew from that and obtained one of their own. It is also clear that the feudal dependence could not become as strict in the towns, where it confronted a mass of people united by a common interest, as in the countryside, where the free people were overcome one by one. Even the common duty to defend the town would necessarily create a closer bond between the inhabitants who lived within the same walls and lead to common deliberation and executive action and add weight to the voice of the citizenry in all regulations relating to external security, so that such concerns could no longer be exclusively those of the lord of the castle and his retinue. There soon followed local measures with regard to internal security and order, likewise enacted by common consent. In all of this a principle showed itself to be active in a particular manner that was directly derived from the old national constitution, by which I mean the *covenanting spirit*, so powerful among all Germanic peoples, which in the form of the guild spirit now became in effect the Germanic element in the constitution of the towns. In a social order that itself offered inadequate protection and cared little for the concerns of individuals, the latter were free to and needed to form associations, fraternities or guilds and to agree on internal rules for them. The term *guild* denotes the regulations for such an association or fraternity and, in the nature of things, a multitude of such associations would arise in the towns, where a division of labour spontaneously comes into being and many different professions exclusively employ and combine a certain number of persons; all the more so as such associations were also allowed among unfree people (which all craftsmen originally were) and precisely they felt the greatest need, at least within themselves, to experience the happiness provided by civic rights and relationships. That covenanting spirit, which in so many ways showed itself to be active during the Middle Ages, in the old constitution, in the feudal relationships, in knighthood, in the religious orders and finally in the towns, with regard to the last of these sought its principal protection from the church, which is already apparent from the fact that every such guild and fraternity stood under the protection of a certain saint. The church could also give the desired protection only to associations of which all the members were engaged in peaceful occupations. In a violent era it was the only power that possessed weapons other than those used to set force against force and is always the only one that can *sanctify* peace. For that reason, where social institutions are underdeveloped, all peaceful professions have everywhere sought the protection of religion. Thus the trade routes of Asia are the same as those of the great pilgrimages and the greatest market places – the goals of the caravans – those places that reverence has hallowed and protected. The same causes had the same effects during the Middle Ages, and what better proof of that is there than the fact that *mässa* (mass) – a devotional act – has also become the Swedish term for a *market*? Why? – if not because religious services in such places gave sanctity to the peace that trade and social intercourse require. Another reason why peaceful livelihoods attached themselves to the church and its servants and flourished chiefly in proximity to them lay in the fact that of all forms of feudal dependence that of the church was the mildest, for it exempted its property and its dependents from the multiplicity of secular burdens. That explains why in Northern Germany and the Scandinavian north we see towns developing in particular from episcopal sees.

A lively commerce first made those towns that were well-situated for it independent of the need for that spiritual protection and gave them powers of their own. That new life of commerce appeared in Germany a century later than in Italy and only displays its effects in the 13th century. In a constitutional regard, they manifested themselves in an autonomous internal administration with municipal forms,[82] partly based on the examples of the Rhenish towns, in which they [such administrative forms] had survived ever since the Roman period (especially in Cologne, the constitution of which now became a common model),[83] partly arising from the intrinsic nature of the matter. For the greater volume and importance of affairs would place the management of them in the hands of a smaller number, a committee of the citizenry, necessitate a council and magistrates and introduce a collegial administration. For the institutions of all the Nordic towns the German ones again served as a model.

That same covenanting spirit which had shown itself so active in the creation of the constitution of the towns revealed an even greater power, as urban industries and commerce increased, in alliances between the towns themselves. They were aware that there was no place for their rights in a social order based on feudal concepts and that the only guarantee for their survival had to be sought in their own, combined forces. – Thus we see not only in Italy the powerful league of the free *Lombardic* cities arise in the 12th century, challenging the rule of the greatest emperors; we see from the middle of the following century their example followed in Germany: the extensive *Rhenish* city league combine against the violence of the rulers and the nobility; the even greater and longer-lasting *Hanseatic* one within a century encompassing seventy-seven towns, from the borders of Flanders to Russia, and expanding into a power that could dictate laws to kings – in England, France, Spain, everywhere the cities made common cause. Commerce, conducted on a larger scale with common consideration and under common protection, increased along the already familiar routes, or sought out new ones, and generally expanded in Italy and Germany to a level and a significance that it has never again attained in those countries. With Genoa, but in particular with Venice, both Augsburg and Nuremberg had a lively intercourse in the 14th and 15th centuries, bringing Levantine and Indian commodities from there and distributing them in the rest of Germany through Erfurt, Mainz and Cologne. In the north that trade with the products of the south was encountered and taken up by the Nordic commerce, conducted for 300 years exclusively by the Hanseatic league, with staples and exceptional privileges in Flanders, England and Russia, from where it extended by way of Novgorod into Asia. In the Scandinavian kingdoms Hanseatic merchants were in control not only of the external but also of the internal trade. As intermediaries between the Italian cities in the south and the Hanseatic ones in the north and as entrepôts for the exchange of commodities from both the Low Country cities of Bruges, Ghent, Antwerp and Brussels emerged, surpassing others in an early craft activity in a wonderful land, which had freer and wealthier farmers than any other part of Europe. – England and France were still inferior in the arts of peace, but not Spain in an era when Toledo alone employed a large number of people in the weaving of silk and wool.[84]

The need of protection for freedom and enterprise had created the leagues of cities in an era when the powerful had little respect for either. The Lombardic cities exacted the recognition of their rights by force of arms and only after the most bloody battles. In Germany, too, that recognition was given only when the power of the cities was so firmly established that it could no longer be denied. In the same period, when the treaty between Lübeck and Hamburg founded the Hanseatic league (1241) and the Rhenish and Swabian towns established their association (1247), the emperor Frederick II had banned all leagues

184

between the towns and all associations and fraternities of any description whatever among burghers and had declared null and void all the municipal communes that had been established without the consent of the lords of castles or the bishops.[85] The more the power of the towns increased, despite such decrees, the more strained would the relationship become between them and the prevailing feudal order, which not only obstructed all peaceful community between peoples and countries by means of particular hateful practices, such as the horrors of riparian rights,[86] the oppressive decrees regarding the persons and property of foreigners and the exorbitant tolls and customs duties, but made it impossible by the constant feuds of the nobility. It was against those nuisances that the city leagues were formed, not only in Germany and Italy but also in Spain, where the Castilian and Aragonese towns founded the association known by the name of *the sacred brotherhood* (Santa Hermandad) in order to maintain peace in the country.[87] The towns became particularly odious to the nobility because they attracted and liberated its dependents, for which reason one respected medieval author even calls them cursed institutions.[88] For, just as in feudal terms even the air made one a *serf*, so that a foreigner after a certain time became the possession of the landowner on whose estate he resided, in the towns, on the other hand, it was said that the air makes one *free*, so that everyone who took refuge in a town and stayed there for a certain time, for instance a night and a year, at once escaped the bonds of feudal dependence and came under the protection of the townspeople.[89] One can easily see how that is connected with the old Germanic principle that every man should have protection, either his own within an association or that of a lord. When, after the destruction of the ancient freedom of the hundred, there were only now again *free associations* in the towns, though of a different kind, one can without difficulty imagine which form of protection would be preferred by the oppressed multitude and how many dissatisfied people from the countryside must have been driven to the towns, within whose walls freedom beckoned. And that right to freedom would in that respect have all the more important effects as the towns extended it to the surrounding countryside by the acceptance of extramural citizens (Pfahlbürger)[90], who, although they lived outside the town, were nonetheless subject to municipal law. All of that provoked violence and made individual force most prevalent during the very same centuries when civic freedom was created by the rise of the towns. – Those external occasions for animosity between nobles and burghers merely indicate a mainly internal difference, which manifested itself not only in those symptoms but in laws and customs, in the constitution, in property, in working practices, in entertainments,[91] in everything, revealing that antithetical social principles were at work within those two estates and were in conflict with each other. Of that hostile relationship we merely wish to note here one important consequence, namely that the freedom of the towns necessarily, although peaceful in its aims, had to become an *arme*d freedom. But nothing consolidates alliances so much as a common prolonged and active defence and nothing contributes so much to equalise the rights among the allies. One finds from the beginning a great dissimilarity in that regard within the towns. Everywhere we see patricians – families of which the members alone had full civic rights, exclusive claims to membership of the council and the government and who for a long time (as in Rome) regarded all admixture through marriage impermissible between themselves and the rest of the citizenry, which consisted of lesser merchants and craftsmen who, originally unfree, had subsequently acquired freedom, though not therewith the same rights as those possessed by the former. The latter, associated among themselves in particular guilds, formed the actual people (plebs), without whose agreement new laws, binding on the entire community, could not be passed, nor taxes be imposed or other particularly significant general matters be decided – for all of which the consent of the popular assemblies was required – but who were nonetheless excluded from the council and government. It was the republican wars, together with a growing population and prosperity, that in these new republics, as in the old ones, raised the self-awareness of the less well-off burghers, gave the masses experience of their own importance and the courage to demand equality with the patrician families in the rights that they had jointly defended. Thus, no sooner had the Lombardic towns won recognition for their freedom than the plebeians restricted the rights of the patricians and progressively democratised the constitution.[92] A century later the German ones display the same progression, through the increased influence of the guilds and their participation in the council, which was not generally achieved without internal disturbances and most often bloody upheavals.[93] No towns had taken in so many noblemen from the countryside as the Italian ones. The defiant territorial lords had, with the increasing power of the towns, been obliged to request to be admitted as burghers for their own safety. For that reason it was also in those republics, after the glorious victory over the imperial power and when the internal democratic ferment in the constitution subsequently began, that factional strife was most intense. With tremendous speed those societies passed through all the degrees on the republican scale, which are the same wherever history records them – simple habits and an aristocracy of virtue while the growing freedom defends itself against external force, after victory popular freedom, equality of rights, then demagogues and finally tyrants. It cannot be denied that equality is the flower of republics and that as soon as it becomes part of the constitution an entire springtime array of exuberant forces appear and inevitably recall all that is beautiful and wonderful in nature's seasons of flowering. On the other hand, the period of flowering is immediately followed by that of decay and dissolution. The only means of preempting that fate would have been – either to hold back a premature development through a strict aristocracy based on morals and virtues (as one destroys the flowers on young fruit trees to prevent them from bearing fruit) – that was the policy of the ancient Roman senate which managed to conquer the world before the constitution was overthrown – or to completely prevent the real flowering of republican freedom by means of the preferential rights attached to noble descent. That freedom was therefore lacking. On the other hand, where the aristocrats themselves did not lose their game by incompetence, they developed a stability, tenacity and durability that defied time; for aristocracy is generally and without exceptions the sustaining, preservative element in all republics. The best example in that last regard is Venice, which not only survived Italy's internal republican storms during the middle ages but in more recent times held out against the power of the kings and only in these last, all-destroying times saw a constitution perish that had had time to become the oldest in Europe. Warned by the party struggles that emerged in the other Italian republics from the womb of freedom – struggles that took on an all the more cruel character because the hatred between the defenders of imperial and papal authority (Ghibellines and Guelphs) intervened in them and drove them to the most inhuman savagery – Venice restricted its council and government to a certain number of families (Serratura del Consiglio of 1297), which, with inherited principles of government, were to ensure the continued existence of the society.

In monarchies where the towns had not, as in Italy and Germany, along with freedom acquired sufficient independence to undergo those storms, their democratic aims nonetheless revealed themselves in other ways: partly, in this period so full of internal conflicts, directed by the kings against the feudal nobility, partly by the latter against the kings and partly again by individual heads of factions, who used the burghers, eager for political influence, as means for their own purposes. Thus in England Simon de Montfort, earl of Leicester (1258-1265), made use in particular of the restless spirit of the burghers of London to almost annihilate the power of his king. The attempt led to his own downfall, but what the burghers of the city had gained through a rebellion was later legally confirmed to them – the right to send delegates to the national assembly. In France they were indebted to the kings themselves for the same privilege, from the time of Philip the Handsome. Later their influence grew along with their pretensions and during the English wars (after the imprisonment of king John in 1356) France saw the burghers, the most powerful of the estates, not only appoint a royal minister, themselves select the controllers of the public revenues and all at once dismiss a number of senior officials but also in Paris, incited by a faction calling itself the friends of the people, force their way into the royal palace and kill two marshals by the side of the dauphin, who, spattered with their blood, was himself saved only by the circumstance that one of the leaders placed a red and blue cap (the distinguishing mark of the faction) on his head.[94] Here, too, the ambition of powerful individuals directed these movements, which are reminiscent of later scenes of the same kind and of the proverb that there is nothing new under the sun. In Spain, where the Castilian Cortes, in which the towns played an important part, dared to publicly throw down an image of their king (Henry IV) from an open stage, constructed for the purpose, and thereby declare the throne vacant (1465), while those of Aragon, under a confirmed privilege to form a mutual alliance against their own king, had as it were gained the legal right to rebel, a privilege that one king (Peter IV, 1347) annulled by wounding himself in the arm in the assembly of the towns and letting his blood pour over the parchment – while the Catalans, wealthier and more independent than all others due to their industriousness and commerce, by withdrawing their allegiance from the Aragonese kings, had contemplated establishing a republican regime (1462) – in Spain, I say, the powerful cities, combining in a league of their own (the sacred Junta), separated their cause entirely from that of the nobility in the civil unrest during the first years of the reign of the emperor Charles V, attacked the feudal rights under

2. FEUDALISM AND REPUBLICANISM

audacious popular leaders and formulated principles in which one imagines oneself hearing the language of the 18th century.[95]

The same tendency was unmistakably revealed everywhere among the lower classes of society. Evidence of that was the great *peasant revolts* in almost every country of western Europe: in France (1358), in England during the reign of Richard II (1381), in Germany during the 1520's, all directed against the nobility, all distinguished by the cruel acts of violence to which an unrestrained mass of people so easily gives way, all ending by more firmly re-imposing the yoke that they were intended to remove, so that generally by the beginning of the modern historical era, since all the freedom of the lower estate had taken refuge within the walls of the towns, leaving the oppression to continue in the countryside, since both the tax system of the rulers and the feudal rights then weighed heavily on the labouring class, the condition of the latter was certainly no better than previously during the Middle Ages but rather the opposite. Among those unsuccessful attempts at revolution emanating from the people itself, history does nevertheless record two remarkable exceptions. One was the *Swiss* revolution, which in the 14th century removed the Alpine region from the threatening autocracy of Austria, the other the *Swedish* one that broke the Union of Kalmar, along with the aristocratic bonds by which it was held together, and moreover made Sweden independent. I mean the great movement among the Swedish people that began with Engelbrekt, sustained the Sture family and brought Gustavus Vasa to the throne. In neither case do I underrate the immortal merits of the leaders, but both of those revolutions were after all, in terms of their origins, power and resources, brought about by the peasantry. And the reason why they were the only ones that succeeded is also clear. In both countries, in Switzerland as in Sweden, a free allodial peasantry had maintained itself. The farmers of the Alpine region gave themselves, or rather simply retained, a democratic constitution, which one recognises even in the old Germanic hundred association, under internally elected authorities. Under simple, restricted conditions such a constitution could be durable and moreover gained strength through alliances with the neighbouring free cities in the struggle for a common cause. In Sweden – as all the towns and burghers' power that have existed or still exist on the Scandinavian peninsula are relatively insignificant – the ancient popular freedom allied itself with the power of the crown. We thus see here, along with independence, the old monarchy, a national one in ancient times among all the Germanic peoples, restored over a free people. No monarchical state in Europe incorporated so much democracy as the Swedish one. Both Gustavus Vasa, who established the new order of things, and Charles IX, who secured it, were therefore also as much leaders of the people as kings; and that quality has continually reappeared from time to time among Swedish kings. The consequence of all that, together with the fact that in Sweden a powerful nobility[96] had emerged during the Middle Ages, was firstly that the Swedish monarchy became distinctly *warlike* and in addition that the two opposite aspects of the social constitution, with their extreme positions and lacking the temperament that an estate of burghers, solidly based, significant and consequently with an interest in peace, might have provided, have always been internally in conflict with one

another among us and have brought about more constitutional upheavals than the history of any other monarchy
can show during the same period.

Thus a general conflict reveals itself during the Middle
Ages between the various elements in society, each individually striving to assert its independence. The results of
that ferment were, in their later fixed relationships, the *estates* – states within the state – but each of which represents
a power in the state that had once sought to dominate the
whole of society. If there were no historical record, or if
it had been lost, even the contemplation of the positions
adopted and the mutual relations between those social
formations, such as they still appear to the scholar, could
partially recreate it, just as the geologist in the strata of the
mountains, dumb witnesses to ancient upheavals, reads
the history of the earth. They cannot be fully observed
here until we examine the relationship of the church to
secular society further on in this essay. So much is clear in
advance, that the conflict to which we have referred and
the main events of which we have just traced was basically
a conflict between the feudal principle in society and the
republican one. During the final phase of the Middle Ages
the disorder that it caused finally increased to such a level
that it almost threatened to dissolve all social bonds. But
at the same time no greater forces have emerged from any
conflict than from this one. Or does history, as far as its
gaze reaches, know of any epoch that is richer in that regard than the one that forms the end of the Middle Ages
and the beginning of the modern historical period, imperishable due to the greatest discoveries of human genius, on
the oceans, in the heavens, in the depths and most of all
within itself, in the immeasurable realm of thought? One

may audaciously say that history can adduce no other epoch – is unable to name its equal. All those immortal discoveries, all that power and brilliant activity of genius is
again most closely connected with the great social conflict
to which we have referred, in particular the emergence of
the third estate and civil freedom, which might easily be
substantiated in each individual case if it did not now take
us too far from our subject. The conflict ended, once the
parties had sufficiently weakened each other, by placing a
far more extensive power in the hands of the kings at the
expense of both. With that expanded royal power, which
at the same time gave the European states an internal unity and greater reciprocal cohesion, modern history begins.
That the royal power in itself, however, could not produce
the required unity, that it had rather repressed than har-
monised the contradictory forces that we have noted in
society, has been confirmed by experience. Our aim in
what follows will therefore be first to briefly show how, in
what circumstances and by what means the kings pursued
their objective, to unify the state in the hands of a single ruler, as well as how the two opposed social principles
were related to that external unity – and then to examine
whether an internal, genuine synthesis of the opposites is
possible, whether history and theory have any lessons to
teach us about that synthesis and what those lessons are.

It is the genesis of royal absolutism that we now wish
to consider.

Feudalism, though originating in a familial power,
knew of no *absolute* dominion, which was generally alien
to the entire constitution of medieval society. That could
not arise within feudalism; partly because the household
from which it developed was a royal warrior household of

free men, whose sense of honour did not tolerate humiliation and oppression, partly because all subordinate relationships within the system were associated with property (fiefs) and became hereditary and thereby gained a
security and stability that set them above the individual
arbitrariness of a lord. It is also sufficiently well know how
little that constitution favoured the royal power. But the
same applied to the power of the vassals themselves over
their subordinates, as long as martial honour and hereditary property were maintained in that chain of subordination, that is to say throughout the system in its more
restricted sense. For everyone who was not a warrior or
enfeoffed in some other way in reality stood outside it. Beyond that border-line, it would seem, there remains only
an unlimited paternal power over those who were themselves in their persons hereditary property and moreover
excluded from the companionship and honour of arms,
namely the serfs. But it is firstly incorrect to imagine that
even during the period when feudalism was most dominant the entire mass of the people belonged to that class
in the strict sense; secondly such a class was not created by
the feudal institutions but passed over into them from the
old Germanic constitution, while it is undeniable that the
feudal system, formed under the influence of Christianity,
ameliorated the conditions of the serfs compared to what
they had been previously. The merits of the church in that
regard are known, as, openly declaring that all human beings were free, as Christ had redeemed all equally, it partly encouraged the freeing of serfs as a pious deed, partly
ensured that the labourer could at least not be personally
sold as a slave but went along with the estate and partly
set a good example itself by a mild and reasonable treat-

ment of its dependents.[97] The chief contributory factor in the amelioration of serfdom was the feudalistic concept of *property* itself.

That a human being is owned like a thing is what arouses all human feelings against slavery. And that condition is in itself so unnatural that one would not be able to explain how it has arisen if *slave* had not initially been the same as *prisoner of war* – a subjugated enemy over whom the right of the stronger was exercised to its full extent. The very name of slavery among a number of nations also points to such a primordial origin,[98] while it is also most insufferable and harshest in those countries where a ruling nation causes the land to be cultivated by another, subjugated one.[99] From such slavery another form of dependent relationship, differing from it in origin and character, should be distinguished, one that does not concern human but political rights and ought really to be called *unfreedom*. Among our ancestors freedom was a precisely defined positive concept – (contrary to what it is in modern political theory, where freedom is merely a negative concept, namely to be allowed to do that which is not forbidden, whereas that which is prohibited or the unfreedom is the positive part). In the old sense he was *free* who in all possible situations answered for himself or was his own man – unfree was everyone to whom that did not apply but who stood under the defence and protection of another. Unfreedom was thus only a negative concept here and as such very extensive and indeterminate, for in the absence of complete freedom numerous degrees of unfreedom, or a greater or lesser dependence on another's protection and will, could exist and indeed did exist in the Middle Ages, so that nothing is more erroneous with regard to the constitution of that epoch than to heap together every kind of unfreedom and make of that one large mass of slavery. – The positive unfreedom or slavery arose among human beings from the dreadful power of violence in war; the merely negative or political form, on the other hand, emerged from a familial dependence, for as far as the protection of a master of a household extended, so far, according to the old concept, did his family also extend, for which he and no one else was responsible under the law.

It is all the more necessary to distinguish from the outset these two different conditions, as the boundaries between them everywhere, precisely due to the numerous intermediate degrees that were developing during the Middle Ages, merged into each other, so that it is almost impossible to define exactly the difference between slavery and unfreedom and again between that and freedom itself. There are many intermediate stages everywhere. It is the feudal system itself that everywhere mediates those transitions, that is itself that incessant modulation between freedom and unfreedom. That derives in particular from two of its characteristics, basing the entire social structure on a personal relationship and dependence that is by its nature unlimited and yet possessing only a *single* concept for its manifold degrees, namely the concept of *property*, which was applied to persons as well as things, indeed more early to the former than to the latter. The highest vassal was the king's man, the humblest serf was his master's man; both were in a personal and hereditary relationship of subservience and yet, what an enormous difference! – It seems to follow of its own accord that a property right in persons cannot be anything but restricted, or must involve a mutuality of obligations; the feudal system does also display an endless gradation of such restrictions, until they appear to end with the slave and an absolute property right commences. The only clearer limit that can be determined in that gradation is the one we have already mentioned, namely the right to bear arms and perform military service, which was the most common distinguishing mark of freedom within the system. But that not even that distinctive feature is entirely certain will be admitted by everyone who is familiar with the constitution of that epoch.

It remains to examine whether in even the most complete right of property according to feudal notions there were not some restrictions that we do not generally associate with it. Such limitations did indeed exist, for an absolute right in private property was in the feudal system, if not unknown, by no means the dominant one. Most property was conveyed through personal relationships or was granted in good faith (fidei commissum) and that in more than one respect. Firstly with regard to a protector or a feudal lord, by whom the property had either been granted as a fief from the outset or was subject to his protection and defence by the acceptance of a feudal duty (feudum oblatum); then with regard to family and descendants, for whom the fief became hereditary and for whose collective rights the current possessor was the trustee; finally with regard to the property itself, which consisted of hereditary relations of subordination on the part of various dependents and fellow-protégés. From whatever perspective one thus looks at the feudal property, the pure, unlimited proprietary right, as over some arbitrarily usable thing, everywhere disappears. That which is owned is, as it were, surrounded on all sides by a nexus of personal relationships, which transform all *property law* into *personal law* and at the same time the bond between possessor and property into a reciprocal and essentially moral bond. For who can deny that a hereditary, inalienable family property linked by personal relationships to the state possesses a more noble intrinsic value, which is not attached to the merely private property? If one examines the source of that intrinsic value, it really arises from a moral bond between the owner and the property, which means that he must *safeguard* a collective or even public right in it and which, as it restricts his arbitrary dominion, associates him with his property by motives other than self-interest and enhances it into a moral object. – And we now arrive at the conclusion: precisely because in feudalism even *things* were owned in a personal capacity, *persons* could also be owned in it under property law, without that necessarily giving rise to all the terrible human degradation that is quite inseparable from the modern mercantile notions of property if they are applied to persons. – Thus every epoch must be judged in accordance with its notions.

When, with the emergence of the estate of burghers the antithesis of feudalism appeared in society and became active, that also expressed itself in a changed notion of property, in which pure property law now prevailed, just as the personal relationship had been the predominant aspect of feudal property. The very genesis of bourgeois property explains that difference. All feudal property was above all associated with the land, but the first and simplest form of production by agriculture is characterised by the fact that it preserves the *wholeness* of human beings, separating neither their powers not their needs, requires a real man and preserves him as a man, without the activity itself ever transforming him into a mere tool. For that reason all agriculture is apt to involve personal difficulties and liabilities, as the occupation itself demands an undivided personality. It is a different matter with the secondary form of production, which involves the transformation of the primary products – the factory, craftsmanship. An endless variety of activities here take the place of the original simplicity and whoever chooses to engage in one of those activities (and one can hardly select more, as each activity in that sphere becomes a separate craft) must be able to depend for that craft of his not only on acquiring from the primary production what is necessary for his basic needs but also of the other artificial products what is required for the satisfaction of other needs, whether natural or generated by the crafts themselves. In a word: the *division of labour* arises. As such labour by means of the craft skill really first adds value to the material or at least immeasurably increases it, while the value in the primary production really lies in the production of the raw material or natural product, so this secondary production, or processing, is necessarily associated with a more unrestricted right of disposal over its material and similarly over property in general. Therefore, when we see in the feudal half of society all property assume a kind of personal nature, whereby the strict right to property is toned down and subjected to various restrictions, all property in the bourgeois half, on the contrary, naturally assumes the character of absolute private property and pure property law prevails. But what the right of ownership has thus gained in force it has lost in scope. Everyone in the first place owns their own production, but when that has here been distributed among many due to the division of labour into various kinds, the production of each individual needs to be supplemented by that of all the others if the individual is to be able to exist, and precisely because he has absolute ownership of the thing that he knows how to make, he has at the same time become dependent on all the other things that he needs but cannot make. An exchange thus becomes necessary and for the sake of that exchange one thing, above all, that represents all the other things, for which they can be acquired and by means of which the abovementioned indispensable exchange can occur. Such a thing is *money*, let it otherwise be whatever you like. For it is really generated and acquires its value, as money, from the necessary exchange between forms of production that it mediates, that is to say, without its circulation it is not money. The bourgeois half of society is primarily the sphere of money, not as if the primary production can altogether do without it, yet it is nevertheless conceivable without money – the other, on the contrary, is not.

When we have now seen how in the sphere of the division of labour things complement each other to fulfil needs by means of money, the same question nonetheless remains at a higher level: how are human beings themselves under these conditions made complete? – how are the elements of the complete human being, which are split apart as it were by the division of labour, again reunited in the case of each individual? It is easy to realise that the question is not superfluous. For the same disparity that exists between the individual craft product and the totality of the needs of a human being also applies to the particular preferentially developed craft skill in relation to the entirety of the human faculties, yet it is as a whole, complete human being that everyone wishes to be regarded, to know oneself in the full capacity of one's humanity and personality, and therefore also demands a complementing in that regard, if one has been obliged to develop only a certain portion of that capacity. The answer is that every individual capacity can only achieve that complementarity in so far as it *is aware of itself within the whole*. But that sense, which, in permeating every individual, makes him even in the most reduced condition a participant in the wealth and security of the whole, is what we call *public spirit*. That therefore represents the role of money at a higher level or is indeed itself the highest, invisible money in society, by means of which even the material aspect first becomes assured and can fulfil its purpose.[100]

It is also due to those two representative relationships, which emerge especially through a free estate of burghers, that the constitution of that estate and thus that of the third estate in general is essentially representative, as no one here counts in and for himself but in and through the whole and by being himself, through property, public spirit and the trust that they engender, a representative of it [the whole]. – It was therefore natural that the middle classes, when they first began to participate in legislation, should exercise that right of theirs through delegates, as it was likewise natural that the same institution could not be used in the feudal sphere. For here property itself, as we have seen, was not representative and of a general nature (as money was) but personal; the entire formation was moreover, due to the military character of the feudal system, intended to develop personal prerogatives and without the need of the third estate's system of complementarity in that regard, so that feudalism in effect knew no other civic designation than that of *man*, in the undivided sense of that word. But personality can only be represented by the persons themselves. – Thus our reflections on the history of the constitution can teach us why the representative system, having emerged from the estate of the burghers, has therefore become the system peculiar to the third estate, why that again could not happen within the social class that is based on political personality and why in general the nobleman counted *for the state* in and through his person – the burgher, on the other hand, only as part of a mass and as a representative of the latter.

And here lay the key to absolutist rule, as soon as the class in society that was defined by personality ceased to act as a counterweight to it and the opposition to the nobility that had sustained the republican spirit of the burghers thereby also lost its meaning and force. A direct relationship evolved between the third estate and the power of the crown, the most favourable of all for the extension of that power beyond every limit. For with the extinction of the active public spirit that brought the burgher and his equals together into a republican whole, with the weakening of the independent corporations, he was both as a private individual and as a subject delivered into the hands of the royal power. But no royal power respected the burgher as a person, as he in himself lacked a political personality. For the highest power he became a kind of abstraction,[101] a monetary value, a certain sum of industry or mechanical power and skill, in a word: a tool, a means. – Thus the entire theory of despotism is fulfilled only in the naked relationship between a king and a third estate. And here the concealed necessity reveals itself that has made the demand for a kind of mediating class, an aristocratic, feudalistic element in the state, characterised by having a political personality, into a principle of practical politics, to which it has constantly been obliged to return.

It was not because that principle had been infringed but because it had not yet been formulated, not because a social class such as the one referred to was lacking, but because in its arrogance and brutality it had transgressed all order, all legal bounds, that an exceptional power was placed in the hands of the kings after the great social conflicts of the Middle Ages. When feudalism prevailed the feudal nobility had been *all* and did not wish to be *less*. Already drawn by its military nature and its personal rights into high-handedness, it was further provoked into that by the opposition of the rising free cities and deteriorated to a level of violence and anarchy that made it intolerable to itself and others. A large part of that titanic race destroyed itself in the fiercest internal conflicts before a more stable social order could emerge. One may recall the Anglo-French wars (1338-1450), which were also internal factional wars in France and made that glorious land a scene of disorder and devastation for a hundred years; in England the conflict between the houses of Lancaster and York or the red and white rose (1452-1487), which raged with so much bitterness, cost the lives of 80 princes of the blood on the battlefield or by the executioner's hand and destroyed the flower of the English nobility; the situation in Spain before Ferdinand the Catholic, in Scandinavia during the Union of Kalmar – in Germany, in Italy during the 15th century. The disorder, insecurity and misery had reached such a level that all means seemed permissible that could restore a calmer situation. For that reason those rulers who established or attempted to establish the foundations for royal power in that violent age – some of them rulers of exceptional genius – all more or less bore the features of tyranny: Louis XI in France, Henry VII in England, Ferdinand in Spain, Christian the Tyrant, Cesare Borgia (the last-named – the Prince of Machiavelli|). The policy of all of them was on the one hand force and cunning, on the other security and order, applied according to the following maxim: "destroy the mighty, protect the humble!"[102]

That principle of royalty, together with a common enemy, namely the feudal nobility, would of necessity create a common cause between the rulers and the estates – at least for a time. The association could hardly remain sincere for very long. For just as the feudal system, although it was centred on the king and in actual fact represents a large royal household, nonetheless, due to the indeterminacy that was its essence, favoured the development of individual independence bordering on self-indulgence, so the bourgeois system in the city leagues reveals itself from the beginning as a pure republicanism, striving in a different way for independence. Neither would therefore promote unlimited royal power. The nobility saw in it merely a loose and indeterminate feudal overlordship, the burgher merely a highest defensive power, the protection of which was purchased by certain fees and duties, whereas he demanded to be allowed, in association with his equals, to determine his own affairs and those of his city and community as he wished. There was a great, even unruly spirit of independence among the people of that era in general, which makes the prospect of society as a whole confused and incoherent, precisely because it displays an almost limitless profusion of separate forces struggling against each other. Great mutual destruction was the immediate consequence – mostly among the class that had to fight simultaneously with the king, with the burghers and with their own unruliness, namely the old feudal nobility. Its remnants then attached themselves for their own survival to the kings, and with those allies the monarchs now turned against their former ones, oppressed the burghers, broke up their alliances, curtailed their privileges and stifled their spirit of independence, which, after the victory over the nobility won jointly with the kings, in vain led to fierce revolts in several places. – And only now could it be seen clearly that the two instruments of absolute rule had in reality passed from the estate of burghers into the control of the kings. What were those instruments? The answer is money and soldiers.

In the feudal system every kind of duty was *personal*, every burden and obligation a *service*. Tax became due only if one could not pay by personal service and we know what personal payment applied generally throughout the system, namely military service. Liability to taxation was thus a concept that only affected those who did not, like the warrior, pay in their own person and as the ancient national infantry or militia had ceased to exist, along with the old national freedom, and all feudal military service was primarily courtly or equestrian (for which reason in Scandinavia 'courtier' and horseman were synonymous),[103] so the more expensive equipment needed all the sooner to be subsidised through charges on all those who could not personally participate in it. That was the historical basis for liability to and freedom from taxation, the reason why the nobility, as a military estate, and its dependents were in that respect *exempted*, while the remaining part of the people (the commoners) were *non-exempt*.[104] Nonetheless, a settled system of taxation was entirely unknown to feudalism. First and foremost, no such system formed part of the maintenance of the rulers. The kings drew their revenues from their domains – from a number of more or less extensive crown properties in various places (mints, mines and salt-works, forests, hunting-grounds, fisheries etc.) – from the royal share in fines and the contributions for the maintenance of the court on campaigns and journeys – from the income raised from the vassals when fiefs were granted, confirmed and transferred. And one sees that none of those revenues was based on taxation as such. Secondly, where such taxation was levied it had, on the one hand, from the outset the *exceptional* character of a war levy, though subsequently also demanded for other requirements; on the other hand, when that was in time transformed into permanent imposts, they nevertheless did not for that reason immediately have the character of a *public* burden and obligation but were a private income for the feudal lord from his tenants and were received by the kings in no other capacity than as feudal lords; finally, those charges were mostly paid in kind and were therefore necessarily tied to local circumstances and requirements, which would already in itself prevent them from being imposed according to any generally adopted and settled criterion.[105] In a word, the entire finance system of the Middle Ages bears the character of a private household, with all the differences that particular circumstances within different households entail, and is consistent only in the fact that *personal* duties were the main source of all revenue and of those the *military service* was almost the only one that was at the same time a public duty.

2. FEUDALISM AND REPUBLICANISM

All of that would be transformed by the emergence of bourgeois property and the greater influence of money associated with that. For money is the supreme medium of exchange in society, with which people everywhere can interact with each other without having to pay with their own personal service. Representing the labour by which those things that are needed are produced, money enables its possessor to transfer his labour as *labour value* and thereby at his own discretion, as it were, detach part of his capability (wealth) without all of it disappearing at once each time, unlike the case of personal service, where the labour involves the arm and the arm the entire person. It is thus only by the use of money that the partial, *abstract* agreements that do not embrace the entire personal capability but a specific proportion of it, leaving all the rest unencumbered and free, become possible to any larger extent. In society they are as necessary as their opposite, or the original, living, *personal* connections. It is nonetheless precisely the main fault of modern political theory that it has been inclined to view the totality of social relations as such an abstract, partial contract, from which it has of course followed that the state is ostensibly only an external mechanism, not a system with an inner life.

Yet to create such a living system within itself was the obvious aim of the estate of burghers in the first flush of its power, as long as the higher currency, the totally committed republican social spirit was alive in the city leagues. But from the state as a whole they regarded themselves as in a manner alienated and merely desired to purchase its protection or at least toleration, in return for the right to determine their internal affairs themselves and to freely engage in their business. The kings accommodated them

in that regard all the more willingly as the monetary resources of the entire society began to be found mainly
among the burghers and the rulers wanted above all to
make use of that new powerful instrument, in addition
to which they saw with satisfaction from the beginning
in every free commune, in every city league that had
freed itself from the bonds of feudal dependency *unmed-
iated* subjects.[106] The purchase of protection was effected
through *taxes* (in which the customs duties in particular
gave the kings a considerable income), once they had succeeded, with the weakening of the nobility, in making
them a royal monopoly and through *grants of supply*, initially by agreement, which first gave the burghers a role
in representation or indeed first created it, as the right of
representation had formerly been personal to the nobility; later on, when internal conflicts had curbed both the
power of the nobility and the spirit of independence of
the burghers and had also made the overall protection of
the kings more necessary, there remained as a result of the
increased circulation of money and its influence among all
classes a more general, permanent system of taxation, for
which the agreement of the subjects was in part no longer
required, in part obtained merely as an almost superfluous
formality.

But nothing contributed more to the development of
the system of taxation than the altered condition of military service and that change likewise emanated from the
burghers, from the armed freedom of the city. We have
seen that all military service in the feudal sense was a personal duty, even a preferential right, that one therefore
neither wanted to nor could transfer to someone else.[107]
It is the burgher who first introduced a representative re-

lationship, a delegated authority, into warfare as well. –
However, one must also draw a distinction in this matter
between the period of the first, healthy republicanism and
the later docility – between a period when the communal
spirit and another when money was for the burgher the
highest representative of the overall system. During the
former, when the cities strove towards republican autono-
my, the difference from feudalism immediately manifests
itself in the fact that military service was no longer a personal but a *civic* duty and could therefore also be assigned
to someone else, as long as it was generally fulfilled. Such
assignment was no doubt rare, however, during the early,
strongly libertarian period. The right to bear arms, acquired by autonomous action together with freedom, constituted the honour of the burgher, which he was proud
to display to knights and noblemen. The immediate consequence, however, was a change in the character of warfare. In war, as everywhere, the burgher counted only en
masse and he therefore also at first deployed military mass
formations against individual knightly valour, against the
feudal cavalry based on personal strength and skill. With
that the *infantry* began to recover its importance in war.
Moreover: the burgher lived within walls, by day and by
night his shields against hostile attack; within their safe
protection he managed his workshop, his occupation,
his own and the communal affairs, secure even if outside
them the violence of the knights prevailed on the roads
or trampled down the crops. To make those walls secure
would soon become a separate matter of the greatest importance. The art of fortification and the related one of
siege-craft first emerged from the towns and was a towns-
man's art. Both for defending and besieging walls, as in

battles on open ground, the burghers were also the first to make use of the terrible new means that would gradually create a new art of war, namely gunpowder. The first cannon, initially of an immense calibre, were constructed and used in the towns, just as handguns first came into use through the marksmen's guilds of the burghers.[108] The old aristocratic valour defended itself with blazing indignation against these pernicious novelties, which destroyed all hitherto existing military tactics. In vain. The fortified walls were the despair of the knight inexperienced in the art of siege warfare, the infantry massed in great depth broke his cavalry charges and the gunpowder which he cursed as a godless, diabolical invention, spread a form of destruction against which he had no weapon, as it appeared to equalise the outcome in battle for the brave and the cowardly.

But all these incipient changes would only be developed by the kings once the use of *mercenary* soldiers had become common and even in that regard the towns had been their precursors. A representative relationship even in war has shown itself to be an aspect of the nature of the estate of burghers. That military representation, for which in the initial periods of freedom every burgher enthusiastically volunteered, proud to live and to die for the community, subsequently, when the patriotic spirit declined and the material money along with individual interests began to replace it, also became a representative relationship of and for money. War became the business of the mercenary (the soldier). That was so contrary, however, to all previously valid social norms that the profession was at first regarded as dishonourable and that those who engaged in it for money were recruited from *outside* society.

The first soldiers were *vagabonds*, people without law and homes, strangers, the dregs of various nations, which the great civil wars during the final period of the Middle Ages had discarded and who sold their lives and their services to the highest bidder. That the vagrant is liable to military service in the newer states instead of that service as before being a preferential right, in both the feudal and the republican system, still remains as evidence of the inglorious origins of standing armies. – Just as the Italian cities had preceded the others in the gaining and defence of freedom, so they were also the first among which the use of mercenaries became signs of the decay of freedom and of the republican virtues. One finds that practice already from the beginning of the 14th century in Italy. Bands of military adventurers then came across there from Sicily, mostly Spaniards or Almogavars (as the descendants of Christian and Saracen parents were called), who had been raised in that profession during the Spanish-Moorish wars, remained together under their leaders after the conclusion of a peace between Sicily and Naples (1302), sold their services to the highest bidder, equally dangerous to friend and foe, sometimes plundered on their own behalf and lived as enemies of the human race. With such bands the republic of Florence already defended itself against the emperor Henry VII of Luxemburg (d. 1313). One already heard the wealthy Florentines say that valour was not a civic virtue; it might be suitable for Germans, Frenchmen and others, who were in their eyes barbarians.[109] With such attitudes, which spread increasingly in the Italian republics and from that time onward, together with the lack of a national context, have been the reason why valour as a national virtue is still largely absent among the Italians or else appears only in the earliest and still best preserved nurseries for soldiers in Italy (namely the robber bands), it was natural that the mercenary groups, which treated war as a means of livelihood, would increase. Soon all feuds were decided only by the use of such groups (the practice of hiring bandits is in Italy merely the old custom preserved on a smaller scale), decided, I say, with little bloodshed on the side of the combatants; for all of those bands spared each other like comrades and one saw fierce battles in which only a single man was injured – and he by a fall from his horse – but all the more destructive for the country, which they jointly plundered. The leaders of such bands, the so-called *condottieri*, more than once decided the fate of Italy in that period, formed as it were a training school for the many petty tyrants of the country and the cities, acquiring power and princely headgear, and the peasant from Cottignuola who had thrown away the hoe to enter the military trade could under the name of Sforza leave his son a power that made the latter duke of Milan (1450). From Italy the custom of using hired soldiers spread further afield. In France such troops were created in particular by the misery of the English wars. The so-called great companies (les grandes compagnies) emerged, conducting warfare for pay and plunder, "the sons of Belial, warriors of various nations, without names," says the author who first mentions them (in the year 1360).[110] They then appear under many designations, of which several – for instance Ribalds and Skinners – reflect their trade. They were long a national scourge in France, to which war constantly gave rise and then left behind. We find them in the Netherlands, in Spain and in the fifteenth century in Germany, where they were called *lancers* from their weaponry and were feared and in demand for their bravery throughout Europe. Particular renown was acquired by the association of mercenaries known by the name of the great or the black guard (*Legio Nigra*, *Les Bandes noires*), originally German but soon composed of soldiers of every nation,[111] which, serving by turns different powers in various parts of Europe (also in Sweden under king Hans against Sten Sture the elder), maintained itself for more than half a century until it was destroyed in the defeat of Francis I at Pavia (1525).[112] France was the first state in which an attempt was made to transform such roving bands into permanent soldiery. That happened after the conclusion of the truce with England (1444). In order to simultaneously occupy the bands of soldiers (*les Armagnacs*) who flooded the country after that truce as well as his own restless son (the later Louis XI) king Charles VII turned them loose on the Swiss republics, "those sworn enemies of all power instituted by God and all nobility," as the French manifesto stated.[113] There the battle of St Jakob an der Birs (the Swiss Thermopyle) – for Louis bloodier as well as more costly than many a victory – annihilated a large part of them; dreadful excesses[114] and the despair and rage of friend and foe destroyed others. The rest were disbanded with a strict prohibition against forming bands of their own again or else were absorbed into the so-called companies of orderlies (1445) and free archers (*les francs archers* 1448), by which in France first of all states the foundation was laid of a *standing army*, paid for by the king and dependent on him. The change coincided with the introduction of *permanent taxation* (*taille perpetuelle* in France from 1445), and the two institutions are so naturally connected that they have everywhere been coeval. Louis XI already more than doubled both the expenditure[115] and the standing army, which he strengthened by taking into his service (from 1479) a number of Swiss soldiers.[116] The peasant tactic of fighting for freedom and fatherland had during more than a century of battles against emperors, princes and nobility turned those republicans into the finest infantry in Europe. From then on they began to sell themselves, especially for French money, and have since then always done so. In a simultaneously poor and warlike people the custom may seem largely excusable. Nonetheless, its introduction was already a sign that the old reputation of the Swiss for invincibility was about to come to an end. It did indeed come to an end after the battle of Marignano (1515). But France had set an example for all states, which would be imitated all the more because it had everywhere been prepared for by the same causes. Since then the systems of taxation and the development of standing armies have always kept in step with each other in Europe. Thus the originally republican representation in war, which had now become a *salaried* representation, a military power, had placed the mightiest weapon in the hands of the kings. However, the fiscal and military systems, the two instruments of absolute rule, were still difficult to manage, only incompletely understood – and that would continue until, with economic growth, commerce and the activity of the third estate, money had permeated all of society sufficiently to make the powers of the state easily extendable in all directions. The effect of that general solvent was still too limited. Too much was still associated with the land, with the old, inconvenient state of affairs, with the old personal obligations. The income of the kings had indeed increased con-

215

siderably and in order to keep their budget under better control their ministers had learnt from the burghers, for all government accounts evolved from the departmental and fiscal systems of the towns and from the book-keeping of the trading companies.[117] For a long time, however, the revenues of the states were still too irregular, too heterogeneous and generally too inconsiderable to be able to meet the enormous expenditure that a war in the new manner required. The main strength of the armies still consisted for a long time of temporarily hired men, who in the absence of pay were immediately ready to rebel and whose payment in cash was more difficult when there was a great lack of money and the interest on loans was exorbitant.[118] No wonder, therefore, if during this infancy period of European princely policy one sees the greatest enterprises hastily brought to a standstill or have a trifling, negligible or even ridiculous outcome due simply to a temporary financial embarrassment; sees the success of the French armies in the Italian wars often depend on the daily pay of the Swiss; sees the emperor Maximilian, unable to pay his lancers, obliged to serve himself as a volunteer in the army of his ally (Henry VIII) and Charles V, master of the treasures of Mexico and Peru, often stand more embarrassed before his soldiers than before the enemy. The fault lay as much with the princes themselves as with the shortcomings of the state institutions. Having recently been struggling with so many powerful individual demands within society and barely able to overcome those, they had not yet learnt to see the interest of the state as their own but most frequently allowed themselves to be swayed by individual or even private considerations. – Such things created inconstancy in planning, at the same time as the sense of newly-acquired power produced an inclination to bold and hazardous ventures and arbitrariness in all forms of government. All of that therefore distinguishes not only the first stern founders of royal power but especially the princely generation that followed them and enjoyed what the former had prepared. I recall – in order to justify that judgement – the French-Italian wars at the beginning of the modern period, conducted for hazardous or absurd ends, with so much bloodshed, so little forethought, so many changes of alliances and counter-alliances, as easily dissolved as concluded; I recall Henry VIII of England, with tyrannical puerility tasting all the fruits of autocracy; the emperor Maximilian's diverse plans, among them to become pope himself; that of Francis I to become German emperor; that of Charles V to partition France, and so on. – Even when the immense power that fortune had brought together and concentrated in the hands of Charles V would appear to give politics a wider scope and greater purpose, as it gave rise to the rivalry between the Austrian dynasty and France, which has since then pervaded all of modern history, with what little reason does one attach to the beginning of that struggle all the implications of a later statecraft! Or who can deny that the conflict between Charles V and Francis I, so protracted and so famous, was begun more for personal and incidental than for political reasons, continued due to personal rancour and ended without even bringing about a solution with regard to the relatively insignificant Milan, although it was the chief object of a struggle that lasted more than twenty years? One may observe that human enterprises often have the most profound consequences, though those consequences are not the ones that the originators envisaged but often quite different ones. But that abundance of consequences, even if the immediate purpose fails, applies in particular to the external changes that also constitute *internal* changes in the outlook, beliefs and customs of nations as well as to those events in which a great human or national interest is likewise involved and is the invisible force that elevates them above all individual calculation. Wherever such an interest is lacking (and it is almost entirely lacking in the preludes of European politics, among which the conflicts of Charles and his rivals also belong), wherever only the princes and not also the nations are concerned, there all conflict is in itself unremarkable and has since the beginning of time merely given new occasions to apply the proverb that what the kings bring about, the peoples have to pay for. (*Quidquid delirant reges, plectuntur Achivi.*)

From the greater power of the princes, however it was employed, there followed of its own accord a greater connection between the states. That great interconnection between states, however, which already began to show its effects, opened up to politics, still guided mostly by individual incidental aims, what was an immensely larger field than before and it is from that contradiction – great forces guided by small interests – that the first European politics acquired its own character. However, the contradiction, which could not be resolved, had to be *veiled*; a minister, who in reality had to work for his master's personal inclinations, nonetheless had to speak and act in the name of the benefits to the state. That is the reason for the great importance that would be attached to *the forms* – beneficial whenever the forms are real, however inconvenient as *juridical* forms – without which they merely lead to the art

218

2. FEUDALISM AND REPUBLICANISM

of *deception* under *respectable* forms. Such an art on a large scale is what politics now became and the teachers of the princes in that regard had become – the *clergy*.

No power in Europe ought to find itself in a position of greater embarrassment between what it was and what it should represent, between appearance and reality, than the *papal* one at the beginning of modern history. Ever since the great schism, ever since the councils, following which the Transalpine and Nordic nations already lost all hope of a reformation emanating from the head of the church, which had for so long already been demanded, the popes became Italian princes with regard to their real interests, concerned mainly with the maintenance or expansion of their worldly power. They had thereby in fact changed their relationship to Christendom, without being able or willing to admit it, as Rome never takes a step back and as their spiritual authority always remained the principal means of achieving their worldly aims. There was a falseness in the relationship itself, which always breeds duplicity and falseness in conduct. In Italy the head of the church was moreover surrounded by a number of smaller restless states for which, precisely because of their proximity, the pope of old counted least of all as pope and against which he had to use the weapons of cunning and sagacity, for which reason it was really also the popes who, exploiting their great European influence, for their own purposes drew foreign powers into the affairs of Italy – sometimes using them against the Italians, sometimes the latter against the foreign barbarians – themselves as a priestly, that is to say by its nature a peaceful power, always in need of assistance that was obtained, negotiated for, acquired by all kinds of expedients. Add to this that every priesthood, due to the spiritual and secular demands that are difficult to combine and the intelligence that is incessantly sharpened by that antithesis, is by its nature the most political of all estates, or can at least only avoid being so through the purest, most Christian simplicity, and one can imagine or rather one cannot without the help of history imagine all the means that an old corrupted hierocracy, placed in that relationship to Europe generally and Italy in particular, has used and needed to use for its purposes. Here is the school that Machiavelli himself attended. Thus Italy was the centre and seat of learning for a policy, in its essence Machiavellianism, which with Italians and priests, with Italian princesses (one remembers Catherine of Medici), with cardinals serving as ministers (which is why we find so many of those from the clerical estate during a long period), with Jesuits as confessors spread and ruled in Europe, in so far as human affairs can be ruled by cunning and force.

It never works for long. It has only been possible during certain intervals in history, as if while the human genius has slumbered, to rule by the petty means (all the *great* ones are those of justice), and that policy is all the more risky as it is not even capable itself, with all its sophistication, of conceiving who its real enemy is and therefore, as soon as the latter makes a move, merely fences in the air. Based on the calculations of egoism, it is also only armed against them. Its principal art and power is to *divide*, to set every person against every other one, to weaken, dissolve all the great natural and moral bonds between people, to transform everything into a mass of individual interests and – as human nature always requires *some* unity – to locate that unity in the individual interest of the *ruler*, in the cleverest and strongest egoism. The system coheres as long as its precondition is valid and collapses together with the latter, that is to say it falls as soon as the *higher commonality* in humankind comes to life and rouses the peoples – and one can almost be certain that the more the process of dissolution in society by the egoistic policy appears to have succeeded, the closer is the eruption of the inner flame of the souls, which, suddenly annihilating, dissolving and merging the individual interests into a higher common one, as it were recasts the image of mankind in the flames into a new splendour. And how could the adherents of Machiavellianism be prepared for such a change. When it not only lies outside their calculations but also outside the *basis* of all those calculations, namely individual interest, and the very possibility of which it is thus their first principle to deny! Moreover, such a change never approaches when they do not, as if by some secret influence, lose their reason, become unbalanced and through some great folly and absurdity themselves usually destroy their dominion. It is the peculiar air of a thunderstorm that precedes revolutions and confuses the minds of the mighty on earth. (*Quos Jupiter vult perdere dementat.*) I have never been able to observe that particular phenomenon in history without recalling the awesomely beautiful and sublime passage in the Odyssey about the mad laughter of the princes, the wooers of Penelope, before Minerva left them as victims in the hands of Odysseus. The poets are prophets. Thus a kind of insanity (the vindictive penalty of one's own guilt, often that of ancestors) is also found on the threshold of all great social ruptures and if one listens to its voice it is in distorted, confused sounds the old voice from the Underworld: "Pay heed, o mortal, to justice – and despise not the gods!" (*Discite justitiam moniti et non temnere divos!*)

The Reformation and its Legacy*

These remarks, generally applicable to all great revolutions that emerge from the inner nature of the human being, may be particularly apposite here when we proceed to reflections on the remarkable change of that kind that confronts us in the first phases of modern history in the *reformation*. It is only its political aspect that falls within the purview of our examination, its religious one only in so far as it is inseparable from the former. It is therefore also from the political point of view that we have reflected on the corruption of the hierarchy, which revealed itself in the priestly Machiavellianism of which the principal centre was Rome and which from there poisoned the whole of Europe. By our reflections on that Machiavellianism and its relationship to the higher interests of humanity, to the power and effects of which it (otherwise so perspicacious) is blind, we have also characterised papal policy during the period that immediately preceded the beginning of the reformation or coincided with it. And if one wants examples of the giddiness and madness (of crime or folly, or both) that seizes the corrupted powers in the revolutionary atmosphere, one should recall the Neronian debauchery of Alexander VI, the indomitable desire

* inserted by the editor

for war of Julius II, the profligacy and immorality of Leo X, the blinded nepotism of Clement VII, Paul III and IV, combined with the most extreme, immoderate zeal for the rights of the Roman See – all of them popes who ruled just before, during or after the outbreak of the reformation – all (as the popes generally were) men of excellent qualities – all of whom, however, partly refusing to recognise, partly despising, partly by unskilful means tackling the danger that threatened or was already at hand and by the most uninhibited hunger for revenues and worldly power giving Christendom of every party continuous offence, while the changing outlook undermined the very foundations of their rule. Thus an attack on indulgences could light a wildfire that raged through Europe and confused, scattered and destroyed the entire edifice of the hitherto existing religious as well as secular policy.

The essence of the reformation from a religious perspective is very simple and is expressed by the following principle: everyone is in the first place personally responsible for their salvation – no human being, no church, even if it calls itself the one and only saving one, no external and no spiritual authority can assume that responsibility. But that principle, which directs human beings towards self-improvement, is the eternal principle of practical Christianity. That the reformation brought it back, restored it to life again in the minds of human beings, is to its imperishable credit and that is why it had such an irresistible and permanent effect. For all change that does not redirect the attention of human beings to the eternal, to certain simple basic principles, is itself and in its effects perishable. The reformation was such a redirection towards the essential, practical, living aspects of Christianity, and with regard to its innermost nature it was, though necessarily beginning with a protest against the old, dead ceremonial worship and all lip-serving Christendom, in itself nonetheless independent of the theological system of one or other of the parties, remains so today and has in its beneficial effects by no means been confined to any particular creed or church. It is important to draw attention to that universality in its essential nature (though it was often confused and made unrecognisable by party bitterness) in order to be able to understand the likewise general and unrestricted nature of its political effects, which have also usually been perceived only in a one-sided manner. Thus one commonly hears it remarked that the reformation gave the princes greater power. – True. – The internal religious disturbances in all countries would of necessity (like everything in a state that overturns the usual order) place exceptional power in the hands of the already powerful rulers, when two antithetical parties hoped for everything from them and in a certain sense laid their own fate in their hands, willing to purchase the victory of their faith by the sacrifice of many other rights. Thus the Spanish zeal for catholicism made the Spanish monarchs autocratic and the consolidation of catholicism in France and Austria their rulers, just as the victory of protestantism in England, in northern Germany, in Sweden likewise strengthened and extended the power of the rulers. Apart from those advantages that were dependent on the conflict itself, the reformation, by its own nature, restricted the authority of the clergy. With regard to its income, its political influence, its dependence on the Roman See, that estate ceased to form a state within the state independent of the secular power and even if that primarily applied to the protestant countries, the same effect, due to the general weakening of the papal power, also extended to some extent to the catholic ones. All of that is true and it is undeniable that the reformation, both by its immediate and its indirect consequences, strongly contributed to the consolidation of monarchical power. Nonetheless, that is only one side of the matter and for exactly the same reasons one could on the other hand argue that the reformation elevated, strengthened and consolidated the freedom and power of the peoples. – Certainly the hierarchy had ceased to be a counterweight against secular autocracy and what remained of it, on the contrary, attached itself for its own survival to the rulers, sanctified and defended their power and directed it towards religious persecution. Through the power of religious conviction, on the other hand, an absolute limit had been set to all arbitrary rule. There was at least one point at which the violence, cunning and even the cruellest persecution mania, having exhausted all their means and despairing of success, had to admit: this is the end. That was in regard to faith. There was at least one point at which every person was prepared to say: here one must obey God more than human beings – at least one single point, where superior power had won nothing whatsoever by depriving people of happiness, property and life, as they sacrificed all of that for their conviction. And with regard to freedom a single such point is *everything*; for arbitrary power exists only by virtue of the absence of any fixed limit; a single such limit nullifies it. An invisible power of conviction and outlook had arisen, which, whether it united the rulers more closely with the peoples or separated them or divided the latter internally, would nonetheless always *end* by being acknowledged and asserting itself not

only in a religious but also in a civil context. I recall the
results of the great wars of religion, the independence of
the Netherlands, the constitution of England, the renown
and power acquired by the poor Swedish nation through
the struggle for religious freedom. Thus the reformation
had simultaneously increased the power of the monarchy
and that of the people.

And this is the place to draw attention to a great truth,
testified to by all of history but little heeded. Every single change that generally gives new life to the religious
principle in human beings at the same time increases the
activity of the *entire* society, injecting renewed energy into
all the elements of society.[119] That is due both to the divine innocence of religion with regard to worldly advantages and interests, which also makes it simply indifferent
to the form etc. of one social system or another, and to
its all-embracing, invigorating nature, which makes it the
root of all social being; for no community between human
beings is conceivable without the highest: one God, one
hope, one faith. In that regard it resembles light, which
enlivens all of nature but, depending on the objects that
it encounters, blazes with different colours, without itself
ever ceasing to be the same pure light. So, too, religion,
the light of the moral world. It animates everything but
varies in its colours according to the different minds that
receive its rays and can in the impure ones even light the
fire of every passion; and yet it pervades the world – *innocent*. The fury of human beings has shed streams of blood
in the name of religion, without their being able to leave a
stain on its garment. Woe therefore to those who use it for
worldly purposes, who use it as a political means for one
purpose or another! It will itself indeed escape their brutal

assault; it can no more be grasped by human hands than the lights of heaven. But it is *their* spirit that from its rays ignite in confused souls the flame of all passions and transform the light of the world into a conflagration. Leave it therefore in its eternal peace – ye statesmen – and out of your selfish calculations! It is worthy only of *adoration*. Do not think yourselves able to lease the light, ye priests! The slightest spark that you are able to separate from its heavenly source for mundane purposes will become a flame that will close over your heads. – And no one should dare to play with fire!

With what more apposite reflection could we indicate both the horrors of the wars of religion and the great beneficial effects of the reinvigorated religion in general!

We said that the reformation, like every single change that involves invigorating the religious principle among human beings, gave more energy to *all* the elements of society, on the one hand strengthening the powers and rights of the kings and on the other those of the peoples. Just as we have also seen the Catholic Church during the epoch of its full activity simultaneously develop the feudal system and likewise under its protection give rise to the civic, republican estate. With that we have also described the relationship of the reformation to the two opposed social systems, the emergence of which during the Middle Ages we have observed and following the internal conflicts of which at the beginning of the modern period the kings established their more absolute power. For everything that still remained of feudalism had gathered around the royal authority. The nobility had in that regard rather returned to its original form and function, such as it was before it made itself almost independent of the kings by the heritability of the fiefs. It had again become a *military* and *court nobility*, within which the chivalric spirit turned in a new direction. The transformed nature of warfare no longer exclusively favoured the development of individual strength. One had to identify oneself with the whole and become part of it. The same was the case with regard to the state in general, which had become more unified, due to which the significance and wilfulness of the individual increasingly disappeared. The nobility, however, as we have seen, was in its origin and nature an estate distinguished above the others by political personality, that is to say it demanded personal honour and standing in the state. Such a demand is necessarily based on the principle that the state itself is not a general, abstract entity but embodies personality. And what makes that so, if not the king's person? The king is the personal society; and the royal words *'I am the state'*, which have sometimes caused widespread offence,[120] can contain both a quite permissible and a very objectionable meaning, depending on how they are understood. The former – if it implies that the king embraces all the interests of the state as his personal ones; the latter – if the case is the opposite one, in which the king recognises no other interest of the state than his own. The former sense is, especially in a hereditary monarchy, the natural one – so natural that the policy guided by private aims that we have initially criticised in the kings could be excused primarily by the fact that the nations, exhausted by the great social conflicts of the Middle Ages, still counted for nothing, that no great general national interests appeared to be involved and that the individual ones of the rulers therefore had free scope and lacked a nobler direction. That deficiency was remedied by

228

the reformation and the great forces that it set in motion among the peoples for and against it. It was impossible not to acknowledge that in the general way of thinking a force had thereby emerged that obliged the rulers to act in a wider sense, according to what public opinion indicated to be to the benefit of the whole and thus to expand, elevate and refine their personal aims to coincide with those of the state itself. That refined personality of the kings determined the new spirit of the nobility or was at least the idea by which that spirit was activated. For the king was himself in that sense an idea, an ideal personality, the personified state; or *ought* at least to be so in his own eyes and those of others, even if reality did not correspond to that necessary requirement. And as, once one has found the clue in the labyrinth of civil society, even the smallest matters gain significance from the whole and in a natural way fit into the overall context, it was undoubtedly that requirement for an idealistic, higher, refined personality in the kings (a requirement that would already of necessity arise with the expansion of royal authority) that at the beginning of the modern historical period gave them the new title of *majesty* – a word that denotes a particular blend of power, justice and mercy and which one may perhaps most suitably translate as *personal justice*. For that is what the monarch should represent within the state, that is to say not merely the abstract law and its implementation, as if by an official, but the living justice, which is the spirit of the law and which can adjust, modify and mitigate the severity of its literal meaning in the many cases where the highest justice would be the highest injustice. The right to exercise mercy is therefore such an essential right of majesty that without it the majesty itself ceases to exist; so that it was also quite consistent of the *legislative assembly* in France to deny the king the title of majesty once the *constituent assembly* had previously deprived him of the right to grant mercy and thereby abolished all that was personally noble in the justice of the state.

So, if the nobility denotes the personal system in society, the king's majesty, in itself as an idea the highest and noblest personality, appears as the brilliant centre and sun of that system, to which everything relates. Personal loyalty to the king in life and death became the highest honour for the nobility, which it sought above all to display in self-sacrifice and warlike exploits. Once the old religious spirit of chivalry had become extinct, along with the life of the ancient constitution and the old church, and the nobility had for a time degenerated through the violence of the law of the strongest to the most terrible savagery, with the restoration of internal order within the states the *royal spirit of chivalry* became the ennobling principle that again raised that estate to great splendour and excellence. – What was not the Spanish nobility before Philip and fanaticism inhibited and cast a gloom over the powers of the noblest of peoples? And what was it not even for a long time after that? What was not the English nobility under Elisabeth – the French under Henry IV and at the beginning of the era of Louis XIV – the Swedish under the great Gustavus Adolphus – the Portuguese earlier, during the short but exuberant heroic age of that kingdom, the great discoveries, and in the lustre of the days extolled by Camoëns? – One could call it the aristocratic era of the history of Europe.

If such a lustre did not extend equally to the nobility of the Germans and of Italy, it was due to the fact that those countries largely lacked both a national and monarchical unity for the abundance of their individual energies. They alone had fallen behind in that regard and would necessarily remain so. Both had namely been the focal points of the entire political system of the Middle Ages, one the centre of the papal, the other of the imperial authority. When a new system arose, based on a more powerful royal authority, creating a stronger political connection between the states, Germany and Italy, remained like the ruins of the old system without national unity and retaining of their former political importance only the destructive precedence of thenceforth being the battlefield and arena where the feuds of the European powers would be fought out. The old political notions, of hierocracy and imperial authority were outdated and had lost their significance. And even if it cannot be denied that the thought had occurred to Charles V (and was the only great one in his policy) to restore the old imperial authority, which the Middle Ages at least knew conceptually as a European principate, yet such a notion was no longer sustained by the spirit and conditions of the age, would therefore only lead to war and could never, especially due to the obstacles created by the reformation,[121] have been realised without leading, instead of to the desired principate in the old imperial sense, to a despoticising universal monarchy, an ambiguity that rightly or wrongly caused the Austrian dynasty to be accused of such plans. Only that ambiguity can also explain the very peculiar position of the popes. One sees them continually wavering, now supporting the emperor, in order to check the reformation by means of his authority, then again suddenly retreating or allying themselves with his opponents, seized by the old envy of the imperial authority and fearing that that authority, once consolidated, would overwhelm their own. Thus those two powers would pass the time, half in support and half in enmity, until the reformation by its both religious and political effects introduced a new order of things. – Such events sometimes provide the most instructive spectacles in history. That reiterates the important doctrine *that an old, corrupted power can only fail*, wherever it turns and however it acts, with the greatest wisdom and cunning, and even most surely if for a change it sometimes employs the weapons of sincerity;[122] for *that* is its incurable disease, that even the *good* has become a poison for it. It is everywhere caught in its own nets. Therein lies the explanation of the *awful* truth of history, that the misdeeds of the fathers are avenged on their children. Every misdeed spins a thread in that destructive net of furies, which persists down the ages. Every instance of guilt becomes a weight attached to it until the spinning is completed and ensnares in its toils for their destruction both the personally guilty and the guiltless. May the unfortunate one who bears the sins of ancestors hope for mercy from God. History feels none. Away therefore with the pernicious doctrine and political art that instructs every existing generation to think only of its own advantage, without regard for its successors! Each of them holds in trust the common inheritance of all and is therefore responsible to all. And precisely for that reason there is a memory, a posterity, a history and a judgement of the ages. (*Die Weltgeschichte ist das Weltgericht.* Schiller.)

In a new way Germany continued to be the focus of European affairs, by giving rise to the reformation and thus in a different sense renewing the old opposition under its emperors to Rome, which was naturally the principal centre of the reaction against the new opinions, a reaction that after the initial consternation adopted a regular form, as a system, through the Jesuits. – There followed the 80 years of religious wars, first (after the earliest outbreak and the subsequent precarious settlement in Germany) conducted mainly with regard to the freedom of the Netherlands, with dreadful internal disturbances in France and with Philip of Spain on the one hand and Elisabeth of England on the other, the mightiest catholic and the most energetic protestant power, representing the chief combatants – then continuing and blazing up into a general European war after the reconciliation of the two Habsburg dynasties, the Spanish and the Austrian, the danger arising from that to the protestant cause and finally the decisive participation in the struggle of the hitherto for Europe virtually alien Nordic countries. What would ultimately be able to mediate in that conflict? The strife of the two religious parties could not now be resolved according to any hitherto accepted principle, since all the efforts of popes, emperors and church councils had only increased the disunity. There remained necessity, which finally terminates all conflicts that cannot be decided in any other way. But that necessity would, owing to the equal strength of the parties, lead to the *recognition of reciprocal rights*, all the sooner as, due to the participation of a major catholic power, France, on the side of the protestants in the war, that had itself ceased to take the bitter form of a war merely of religion but had acquired more political aims, to which general legal principles are more easily applied. In that respect the Peace of Westphalia instituted a *European international law*, not only because it determined by explicit treaties Germany's internal relations and those of a large part of the European states to each other (for many of them still remained unsettled, such as the conflict between France and Spain, between that power and Portugal, and the relationship of the entire East to the European state system) but in particular due to the principles on which it rested, for in such a novel case as the settlement of the claims of two great religious parties one had to resort to the general rules for mutual justice and fairness. Europe had not entirely lacked a practical system of international law before then and during the Middle Ages. The pope had exercised a mediating, conciliating authority as the recognised head of Christendom. Such an authority was likewise often exercised by the emperors as the highest secular protectors of Christendom. But both of those powers had taken sides in the present conflict, which was to destroy their former authority. One does indeed still see the pope, with a residue of his former prestige, appear as a mediator (though not acknowledged by the protestants) in the Westphalian peace negotiations. But what political influence could a power retain that, like that of the papacy, did not recognise and even today does not recognise that great peace treaty, which in so many respects established and defined the European state system? The imperial power had also as a result of that peace treaty, even in Germany, by the rights that it conceded to the rulers, been entirely transformed into a title without authority. Not even the shadow thus remained of any particular European power judging or actively mediating at the highest level and, as that which had existed during the Middle Ages in theory rather than reality had been confined within the Catholic Church (for *outside* it, there was as little justice as salvation), with the breaking of that constraint and the recognition of rights for heretics as well, the sanctity of rights, simply as such and from a general human point of view, would also be recognised. But that is what first in a genuine sense deserves the name of *international law*, which generally signifies a justice that is independent of any particular state and for that very reason is also applicable to the relations between the great independent entities that are called states and nations. That justice knows no positive court of law, as little as any executive power. It derives its sanctity and its authority, as well as its source, solely from the *justice of public opinion*.

Thus a *writer*, that is to say someone who for his genius and knowledge possessed a vote in the republic of public opinion, could already by the great effect he had on the elaboration of the idea of international law gain a greater historical importance than many rulers. That was the Dutchman Hugo Grotius, through his renowned work 'De jure belli ac pacis'. During the fiercest war of religion, raging across the whole of Europe, with a partisan rancour, even between those of differing opinions within the same church, that exceeds all conceptions and to which he almost fell victim within his own native country,[123] he wrote that book, as an exile, pointing a ruined world, agitated by passions, above itself to the gentle light of the divine justice that is applicable to all human conditions. And so great was the need to find some common point of convergence in conflicts that appeared to exclude every notion of reconciliation that few books have had a greater, a more beneficent effect. It gained a wide readership[124] and its great value was soon acknowledged even among the senior and ruling members of both parties; although, written by a sincere but fair and moderate protestant, it can with good reason be reckoned among the truest products of the reformation. It therefore also won the highest approval of the hero of the reformation (alongside Luther, the greatest one), the immortal Gustavus Adolphus, as a result of which Grotius, a friend of Oxenstierna, was himself later associated with Sweden, which, as it commanded his loyalty for 11 years in the most important place (as Swedish ambassador in France 1634-45), may not unreasonably share in some part of his honour. But during the same period the respect accorded to him was also great within the Catholic Church. Even in Rome his work was cited with praise[125] and gradually acquired a kind of classic status with regard to all the issues of international law with which it deals. The scientific flaws of the book itself were combined with positive aspects that gave it a more general impact. For one seeks in vain in this famous work for a strictly scientific coherence. Grotius does not scruple in the least to adopt for his international law a multiplicity of principles, as he derives them partly from the social nature of human beings under the guidance of reason, partly from agreements between peoples and finally partly from the will of God.[126] He considers his subject more as a statesman than as a philosopher, which is already apparent from the reason, derived from the needs of the time, that caused him to produce the work.[127] An elevated political and practical spirit give it a coherence that it lacks from a theoretical aspect. It presents the idea of a *Christian European republic* or a system of independent but, through the mild justice of Christianity, mutually associated states and therefore both within and outside themselves practising that Christian justice. How deeply that age needed such a redeeming idea, with what practical significance it was therefore also imbued, not merely as a theoretical doctrine, can best be seen by the fact that a king such as Henry IV of France could, even before the last great conflict of the thirty years' war erupted, not only grasp that idea from the greatness of his own soul but also negotiate and prepare for its realisation, when the dagger of Ravaillac brought his life to an end.

And who can deny that this glorious, elevated idea had a great influence on European politics after the Peace of Westphalia? One should perhaps hasten to note the exceptions, in order to prove that not justice but violence and interest have always governed the world; and it may willingly be conceded that on this occasion, too, those exceptions were all too numerous. Yet I maintain that a state system in which, as in the European one as now constituted, even the weaker enjoyed respect and security, a state system under the protection of which a simply innocent, no longer powerful freedom, such as that of the Swiss – small republics, such as the Italian ones, extending to San Marino – the small but for the history of the European outlook so important Geneva – the German free imperial cities – so many smaller states in Germany and Italy – could exist independently alongside the most powerful monarchies, that such a system was not possible without the respect for divine justice also being a power among the powers. Examples such as the ones adduced therefore to my mind represent the triumph of European history, greatly surpassing all the victories and conquests and everything else that makes it so remarkable and spectacular. For if you want a measure of the real benefits of a state system, as of the individual state, do not ask the powerful, the wealthy! Ask the humble, the poor man, if his cottage, his plot of land, his mite are as protected and secure as the palace and possessions of the powerful one! And if you have found that in a single state system, in a single state, there is respect for something as sacred as *the right of the weaker*, then boldly say or praise with tears that justice has not yet fled the earth! – For that reason this is also the place to briefly mention the famous European system of political equilibrium; for that is inconceivable without international law, inconceivable as merely a balance of power without at the same time being a balance of justice. As such, the Peace of Westphalia had first established it, as such it was consolidated (following the near-universal reaction against Louis XIV's plans of conquest) by the Peace of Utrecht, as such it still remained, at least formally, though with an ever more weakened and fugitive spirit, until the most heinous partition of Poland (the burning infamy of which every honourable man should, as long as a memory or record survives, perpetuate until the end of time) would reveal a corruption among the mighty of the earth, for which the heavenly or infernal nemesis has had the well-merited penalty of vengeance in preparation in the destructive events of our time.

One can generally also imagine that European system of equilibrium as an equilibrium based on equal justice between the stricter monarchies, which have also retained most of the old feudalism, and the states tempered by a stronger spirit of freedom and republican principles. As the former remained loyal to the old church and the latter, on the other hand, developed largely under the influence of the reformation, the great conflict of religion was also a conflict between the principles of those two constitutions, and the peace, if not a reconciliation, nonetheless a mitigation of the opposition between them through respect for their reciprocal rights. In that respect it is not without significance that a republic that had itself originated in a catholic environment and was already as old as the Swiss Confederation only had its independence explicitly recognised in the Peace of Westphalia. And what an immense influence did not the freedom of the republic of the Netherlands have, being recognised after such protracted struggles! Did not that republic afterwards become for a long time the focus of European politics as a whole? – But what we just observed about the political tendency of one religious party or the other applies only to its *predominant* aim, for it is not otherwise difficult to show traces of the activity of both of the opposed principles on either side and also within the old church, though one has to ascribe even that to the reformation, against the silent, powerful effects of which and the new life, both religious and political, that was generally awakened thereby, it could not entirely defend itself. – Of all the states, Spain kept most strictly to the old in all respects, most implacably stifled every breath of new vitality but with that eventually also in the slumber of despotism its own powers. In vain did the golden streams of Mexico flow through the stiffened body-politic; they animated it as little as (after the conquest of Portugal) the treasures of the *Indies*. They were, on the contrary, drawn to the magnet of freedom and poured all their wealth precisely into the country that, by the power generated by the reformation, was torn away

from the Spanish monarchy – namely the united Netherlands. What the strict unity brought about in Spain occurred in another way in the divided Italy by its dissolution following the similarly excluded influence of the
reformation. It sank into insignificance and only gave the
appearance of an ever more fading religious and political
life. Nearest to Spain in its principles came the Austrian
monarchy, though fortunately without being able, despite
the persecutions of Ferdinand II and Leopold I, to achieve
the same deadly uniformity with regard to the so dissimi-
lar components of that monarchy. On the other hand, we
see in France, during and after the fierce internal wars of
religion, alongside the *strict* catholics, who were here as
almost everywhere also a Spanish faction, likewise a significant party of *moderates* who, though devoted to the old
church, were more tolerant towards the new religious
opinions and also, if not entirely, shared with their adherents the republican principles, to which they would already be driven by their continual struggle both with the
religious hierarchy and the royal authority in France, or at
least a tendency to demand and protect civic rights. That
party pursued the middle way between the strictly catholic one of the Guises and the republican-minded Huguenots and is adequately denoted as well as honoured by the
name of the noble chancellor *de l'Hopital*[128] and by the fact
that it was the humane and more just principles of that
party which became the ruling ones with the accession of
Henry IV and put an end to the terrible misery of the 30-
year civil wars. Richelieu later broke the Huguenots as a
political party; the revocation of the Edict of Nantes
(1685) and the dragooning methods of Louis XIV destroyed it as a religious party in France. But the above-

mentioned opposition between the strict and moderate catholics did not therefore, or any the less, cease to be active both in the religious and political sphere. It expressed itself in the protracted fierce struggle between the *Jesuits* and the *Jansenists*, of which the former by every possible means unceasingly endeavoured to evoke the fanatical spirit of the strict catholicism in support of the authority of the Roman hierarchy and were only too successful in that regard with the rulers, while their moral casuistry aroused loathing among all right-thinking people and their aversion to all light ridicule; the latter, on the contrary, in demanding a more practical devotional Christianity and generally far surpassing their opponents in intelligence as well as culture, were a reminder, both by their gentler religious and freer political opinions, that they, though sincere catholics, had nevertheless warmed themselves by the candle that the great reformers had lit.[129] Even with regard to civil affairs that opposition between Jesuits and Jansenists became remarkable. For it is obvious that Jansenism formed and maintained a political opposition in France, which expressed itself particularly in the parlements – from the era of Richelieu the only, feeble counterweights to an arbitrary royal power – and it is well known that those conflicts continued until the portents of the latest overturning of all things already began to appear in France. That that terrible revolution followed, that the two opposed parties, which as we shall soon see appeared even among the protestants and far more honestly and more powerfully among them, did not arrive at any constitutional equilibrium within the old church, as they did in several places within the new, proves better than anything else that the spirit of the reformation was the truly formative and creative factor among the peoples with regard to the constitution of the state; consequently, moreover, where that spirit was not accommodated the result was a progressive decline in social vitality, either contracted into harsh forms or stagnating in dissolution; where again it was stifled and not allowed to act in the right way, it necessarily sought a revolutionary outcome. The cause of that in France was that the French state, more than any other European one, had abandoned every religious standpoint. In the protestant countries religion entered more than ever into the state constitutions or, in effect, provided their basis. That closer, more intimate connection between church and state was one of the most important effects of the reformation. Even in the catholic states that connection became stronger and more intimate after the reformation than before. The French state, on the other hand, in reality lacked any religious warrant: I say in reality, for it is well known that the freedoms of the so-called Gallican church, which were supposed to be what distinguished French catholicism, only had political and not spiritual aims and with regard to religion itself France excluded all genuine attention to it from its policy or used it merely as a political means. Francis I and Henry II (who did not even reject alliances with the Turks at a time when the fanatical power of the latter made them a great and genuine threat to all of Christendom) persecuted and burned the protestants within France at the same time as they sought and established political relationships with them outside France. Once Richelieu, by subjugating them, had consolidated the autocracy within the realm, he established the supremacy of France in European affairs, following the support given to the protestant cause in

Germany, and prepared the way for that brilliant era of Louis XIV, which was nonetheless sullied by the at once cruellest and most unreasonable persecutions of the last remnants of religious protestantism in France. In a word, from the reformation the French rulers generally wished to arrogate to themselves solely the political and external advantages, while they rejected and persecuted all that was essential and interior to it; one could even call their entire statecraft a merely political protestantism. That complete divorce between religion and politics (or rather that subordination of the former to the latter) is commonly cited as particular evidence of freedom from prejudice and as a great step forward in a genuine statecraft. That only furnishes us with the occasion for the to our mind extremely important observation that no relationship that is false and ambiguous *in the matter itself* will exist and continue, of which the injurious effects can be annulled through any *personal* skill. That is due to the great *truthfulness of things*, which is older than that of humanity and belongs to nature itself. Consequently everything exacts a penalty in history. For that same, merely political protestantism, without any religious essence, in which the rulers had set an example, subsequently became in the minds of the people the main outcome of all the religious and civil disturbances in France; it was embittered by the rapidly increasing corruption of the royal authority after Louis XIV, was fomented by a constant inflow of the political opinions of the reformed republicans from the same locality from which formerly the religious ones had mostly penetrated into France (namely from Geneva),[130] increasingly took hold on public opinion after the expulsion of the Jesuits (1764), became dominant after the participation of France in the American War of Independence and thus prepared the way for a revolution, the lessons of which are historically inexplicable unless one also regards them as a translation in a *merely political* sense of the principles of the most republican party, *without* the religion that was the very life and inner essence of those principles. The very atrocity (there is no equivalent Swedish word) that briefly appeared in the revolutionary scenes of bloodshed, having apparently slumbered ever since the dreadful Huguenot wars,[131] was a gruesome feature engraved by the French statecraft on the character of a naturally amiable, happy, brave and good-hearted nation, the offspring of that unprincipled intercourse between politics and religion that has for centuries, ever since the time of Philip the Handsome, characterised French government. – Fanaticism, even when overt and viewed by itself, is terrible, but pour into its veins the poison of intrigue and you face the tiger. The purely religious kind destroys but may possibly bring its own cure with it; that which is mixed with a false and insidious policy or, since all religious motives have dried up, purely political fanaticism is the bitterest fruit that the human soul can produce.

We said that the opposition, both religious and political, of which we also find traces in the old church expressed itself even more actively and powerfully within the realm of protestantism itself and there gave rise to free constitutions, built on foundations of justice, and it is that assertion which we now intend to justify. The two protestant churches, the Lutheran and the Reformed, already form such an opposition in relation to each other. Their different political tendencies, with the reformed doctrine, having originated in republics, also developing especially in such polities, in Switzerland, in the Netherlands and in the republicanised England, whereas the Lutheran one was more favourable to monarchical authority, point to a deeper difference in character between them than one would suppose at first sight. It is also remarkable that almost all of the particular sects that protestantism generated have sprung from the womb of the Reformed Church, in which from the beginning a principle of mutability and progression turned out to be far more active than in the Lutheran one. An astute writer remarks[132] that the very source of that difference already lies in the initial divergence between the doctrines of the two parties, as insignificant as that divergence may appear to the eye of the superficial observer. The Lutheran doctrine on the sacrament is important in that it recognises as it were a mysterious core in religion that is never entirely penetrable by rational enquiry, as religion is directed at once to *all* of the human faculties and therefore cannot be fathomed by reason *alone*. But everything in the sacrament that is a mystery according to that view disappears almost entirely according to the reformed explanation, which turns it into merely an image, a sign. I would add: the difference lies even deeper. For if one considers of what that core of religion of which we have spoken really consists, that imperishable inner quality that can never be attained by any analytical process of reason or be exhausted, it is nothing but *the personality of God*. That is the first and only mystery of religion, encompassing all the others, on which all mysteries (such as the sacraments) rest, as they presuppose a *personal* relationship of the divinity to the human individual. That notion, according to which God is not merely a concept, a law, an order or an abstract essence

245

but is in nature and effects a *living, personal being* is surely so common to all Christianity, representing its distinguishing feature so much, that it is not omitted from or unacknowledged by any Christian confession. – On the other hand, it may be more or less prevalent, and the Reformed Church in that respect undeniably manifests itself more than the Lutheran as a merely rational religion, that is to say, it proceeds from a more abstract, impersonal notion of the deity, although it does not in the least differ in word and doctrine from the former in that supreme part of theology. It is above all noticeable, apart from what has been said about the sacrament, in the stern doctrine of the Calvinists of the unconditional election to grace (predestination), which introduces into the gentle and loving Christianity an obscure and bitter *fatalism*. But fatalism in one form or another, that is to say, the highest inexorable rule of a blind law or whim is precisely the outcome at which every theology constructed from mere concepts will necessarily arrive if it is consistent; for love and compassion can only be imagined in the personal, living God. We are certainly not unfamiliar with the fact that the abovementioned stern doctrine of Calvin never became general among the reformed churches, as they could never, in any case, like the Lutherans, unite around a certain system but at an early date split into several parties, but that the same spirit as the one revealed in that proposition prevailed from the beginning is shown by the sort of dismal fanaticism for the abstract that disclosed itself in hatred and destructive zeal against everything in the divine service that appealed to the emotions, all images, all decoration: a hatred that went so far that it also banished music from the bare churches as a worldly abomination

246

and generally expressed hostility towards all the innocent
joy of life; whereas Luther, on the contrary, once he had
preserved the essential thing, that is to say, had again un-
covered the fountain of eternal truth that wells up from
the living word of God, in accordance with his more amiable and humane character, he no longer differentiated
himself from the old church more than was necessary in
the external arrangement of a church building and matters
that appealed to the senses.

In that regard, among the reformed groups, the English
Episcopal Church was in accord with the older Lutherans
in a remarkable manner. The reason for that divergence
is presumably to be sought above all in the way in which
the reformation began in England, namely with the king's
declaration that he was the head of the church, from which
followed that almost all of the old ecclesiastical structure
and the religious offices, despite the subsequent doctrinal
changes, became a monarchical heritage, which was regarded as inseparable from the royal authority. That gave
rise to the political character that the church in England
acquired, more than in other countries, and has preserved
ever since, so that the Episcopal Church and the adherents
of the strictly reformed party, which soon likewise became
very powerful, generally also clearly denote two opposed
political parties, a circumstance that, given that the difference between the two seemed to mainly lie simply in
the external forms of worship and church administration,
shows that in regard to religion even minor divergences
often indicate a deeper difference in spirit than one might
have assumed. That is why the theological systems have
spilled so much blood in the world.[133] As the new energy provided by the reformation both to the monarchical

aspect of society (and the feudal element associated with it) and to the republican one expressed itself in no other country in greater conflicts or had more important consequences than in England, we wish to dwell principally on a consideration of that example, as being the most perfect one that history has so far been able to present both with regard to the antitheses and to their final arrival at a balance of rights, if not their complete spiritual union.

Nothing is more striking than a comparison between the rule of the Tudor and Stuart dynasties in England. The rulers of the former exercised the most unrestricted authority, those of the latter did not exercise it so much as lay claim to it in a general way. The mere claims to it, however, were the undoing of the latter, whereas the actual exercise of it had not involved the slightest danger for the former. The reason may be found not only in the personal qualities in which the Tudor rulers surpassed their successors. The former were by nature despotic; one can apply to all of them the words of the dying Wolsey about Henry VIII: "he hath a princely heart," reluctant to "either miss or want any part of his will." The Stuart ones (where fanaticism did not, as with James II, have the contrary effect) were rather characterised by mild inclinations. Their misfortune was brought about by the fact that they, with that less energetic character, nonetheless *proclaimed* absolute royal authority as an article of faith. But prerogatives theoretically expressed by those in power are far more dangerous than those actually exercised in practice. One does not notice the connection between the latter, which occur one by one. Only when they are insisted upon according to a principle does that connection become clear and makes the prerogative, in the smallest as in the greatest matters, *equally* insufferable for those of a different outlook. The system is now understood and that also makes the significance and weight of the whole felt in every least part of it. The conflict is soon transferred to the great, stormy area of public opinion. Among the rulers it is therefore often the successors who have suffered for despotic concepts rather than their predecessors for despotic acts.

Within the Stuart dynasty a certain monarchical theory was hereditary, all the more suited to stir people's minds, for and against, as it rested on a theological foundation, in accordance with the spirit of the age. That James I was himself a theologian and an author contributed to that. He borrowed the principle from the doctrine of the Anglican Church concerning the king being the head of the church, by which the royal authority was explicitly sanctified or even associated with heaven. The opposition and trouble he had already experienced from the fanatical puritans in Scotland strengthened his attachment to the principles of absolute authority and, having ascended from a foreign throne to that of England, he began and continued to tell his parliament that all of its rights and those of the nation were a gift of royal grace and could be revoked in the same way as they were given, that the royal authority was of divine origin, absolute by divine right and above all law, [134] although he admitted that a good king would adjust his actions to the law of his own free pleasure and to set a good example. That monarchical principle was also a hierarchical one and the absolute monarchy was regarded as so inseparable from the high church that they could only stand or fall together, from which the proposition 'no bishop, no king' became a kind of motto for the house of

Stuart. Such was the religious political system that James I was content to present openly, without any tyrannical intentions, it is true, but also without any understanding of how to enforce such high pretensions. Of the practical means of absolute power he possessed and developed none. Not money – his ridiculous, spendthrift favouritism placed him, during a never interrupted period of peace, in constant need of and dependence on the same parliament to which he preached the doctrine of passive obedience. Not soldiers – as England still lacked a standing army and he himself feared an unsheathed sword. Not even a brilliant court – his own conduct lacked dignity and he also had the royal foolishness to dissuade the eminent from court life instead of thereby making them dependent.[135] In a word, of absolute power James only had the theory and was merely a despot in so far as he was a pedant. The doctrine would all the sooner act only as a doctrine, be thrown out as an apple of discord for public opinion and serve only as a whetstone on which a party of an entirely opposite way of thinking sharpened its weapons.

That party was the strictly reformed or puritan one, which gained the upper hand first in Scotland and then also in England. They, too, opposed the former party on theological grounds. If the theory of the Episcopal Church and the earlier Tudor dynasty's practical principles of government represented the royal party, this latter one was, on the contrary, represented by a democratic theory with regard to the constitution of the church, the greatest loathing for everything resembling hierarchy, even in the slightest external symbols, and not least the actual troubles and persecutions to which all non-conformists, that is to say all who disagreed with the dominant Episcopal

Church, especially if they were clergymen, were so often subjected. – If the former invoked the divine right of the king, the latter similarly invoked their divine right not to be coerced in their convictions, and that they did not restrict that right only to such matters was demonstrated as soon as they (as earlier in Scotland) became the more powerful. For it turned out that the Presbyterian clergy had only abolished hierarchy *within* itself in order to practice it with so much greater force on a mass level. The state, the government, customs, all were placed under the most absolute religious censorship, the harsh nature of which one can already discover from the regime in Geneva of the founder Calvin and his consistory, an example that John Knox and the Scottish reformers ardently followed. That is most clearly shown in their treatment of the unhappy Mary, even before her vivacity, rebelling against the deadly boredom and the mental anguish with which a dismal, rancorous zeal surrounded her on every side, had driven her to crime. Those men possessed everything except the spirit of the Gospel. It can be said with such good reason of no other Christian sect that it was *under the law*, in the theological sense of that expression. That also explains its remarkable preference for the *Old Testament*, the examples and teachings of which, in particular the severe and vindictive ones, were constantly cited. From the yoke of the law they escaped only by seeking refuge in an even higher, gloomier law, namely the fatalism of the stern doctrine of predestination. And if one reads the theological statements of that era about the rights of the *elect* to execute God's penal judgements,[136] one cannot fail to appreciate that it was above all *that doctrine* that contained the seed of all the fanaticism that was to have such terrible conse-

251

quences. It is worth noting that the main leaders in England of the opposite party, the Episcopal Church, with regard to the doctrine of predestination inclined towards the milder so-called Arminian[137] concept, which, having originated in the Netherlands, had first been a target there for the fanatical persecution of the strict Calvinists, who contributed to bringing Olden-Barneveld to the scaffold and caused the downfall of Grotius. In England that single divergence marked such a great difference that Arminians were placed by the puritanically minded parliament in the same category as papists – (both alike were declared to be traitors against the fatherland and enemies as early as 1629) – and that from this point in particular, as if from the inner core of discord its bitterness spread to the external. Without reference to that inner and only essential difference, one cannot understand how external actions and signs – the ring in marriage, the sign of the cross in baptism, obeisance at the mention of Jesus' name, this or that cut of the garments of clergymen etc. – could from the beginning become subjects of such a vehement or even violent controversy. It was a great inner antagonism that here disclosed itself in the most superficial matters, just as the finest point can be electrically charged by the deadly lightning. The harsher or milder interpretation of the doctrine of predestination was the main inner difference, which, proceeding from there, revealed itself on the one hand in a form of worship that appealed more to the emotions, in an inclination towards the outward splendour of the church, the religious dignitaries and the ceremonies, in toleration of all the innocent joy of life, on the other produced an abstract fanaticism, in the view of which not only every trace of hierarchy but also every image, all ceremony, everything that appealed to the senses was an abomination and every pleasure a sin – painting a form of idolatry – music a noise of dumb animals, not of human beings – dance so many steps to hell – theatres the chapels of the devil –popular festivals, Christmas games, harvest homes and may-poles amusements that led to eternal perdition.[138] While such a mood was progressively gaining ground in the nation, what would the effect not be of the unwise undertaking by Laud[139] to incrementally restore the hierarchy and ceremonies of the Church of England to those of the old church, supported by the unfortunate Charles I with the full weight of monarchical authority? Particularly as that was accompanied by persecutions directed at all non-conformists and demonstrates the great absurdity of attempting to impose milder principles by harsh measures. I scarcely know any stranger example of that than the decree by which Charles, in order to curb the gloomy disposition of the puritans, not so much permitted as commanded games and entertainments of all kinds for the people on Sunday afternoons after church service. To refuse to take part in them was already to incur suspicion of deviation from the ruling church, while the puritanically inclined clergymen who refused to read out and promote the decree were punished with dismissal or suspension.[140] Where, as in this case, happiness itself becomes a subject of bitter partisan dispute, there insanity in the state is not far away.

We have dwelt on these reflections in order to set the subsequent revolution in England in its true light. For it is undeniable that the conflict, the most violent eruption of which would show itself here, arose from a religious contradiction that developed out of protestantism

253

itself – undeniable that the theological significance of the conflict was the primary and chief one (which even Hume admitted) and that its political repercussions were merely consequences inseparable from that. In accordance with the more clear-cut, more revolutionary nature of the Reformed Church, which took everything to extremes, one sees here a struggle between an ultra-protestant party and another (though in a protestant sense) ultra-hierarchical party, the political principles of which flowed from their religious ones. The hierarchical one was of course, due to the king's supremacy over the church, also an ultra-royalist party, which preached to the subjects the divine, absolute right of and the duty of unlimited passive obedience towards the monarchy. The other, already compelled by its position in the state to urge the doctrine of resistance, found not only justification for such resistance in its religious principles but, as no power and right on earth exceeded that which belonged to the assembly of the elect (*the godly*, as they called themselves), but soon also in the same principles a claim to *govern*. And should not then the constitution that they found themselves justified in calling for in the secular context be designed on the pattern of their ecclesiastical constitution, inspired by a republican-democratic spirit? The abstract dominion of a law, a rule, would of necessity manifest itself in regard to both. Thus it was on the basis of a theological principle that the defence of civic freedom against an arbitrary authority first really became vigorous in England; the subsequent victory of republicanism was also at once the immediate victory of a theological system and the explanation both of that resistance and that victory is of a piece and cannot be expressed better than with the words used by a member of the Commons in the same remarkable parliament (1629) that in the *Petition of Right* demanded back the security of the subject as to person and property. "If a man meets a dog alone," said the speaker, "the dog is fearful. But if the dog has its master with him, he will set upon that man, from whom he fled before. This shows that lower natures, being backed by higher, increase in courage and strength; and certainly, man, being backed with Omnipotency, is a kind of omnipotent creature. All things are possible to him that believeth; and where all things are possible, there is a kind of omnipotency."[141]

These strange words convey an immense meaning, both of truth and delusion, as joyous in the former as most terrifying in the latter sense. They explain why, notwithstanding all the earlier ferment, the rebellion against Charles I only broke out after he, in the perilous attempt to introduce the constitution and liturgy of the Anglican Episcopal Church in Scotland (1637), had dared to attack the entire concept of religion of the puritans – explain why that rebellion spread to England and there, fought out in the civil war of the Long Parliament, ended with an action that had hitherto been regarded as impossible and lacked any precedent: the murder of a king under legal forms (1649). This was an example of the summary process of the *elect*, an example of what *he* may dare to do, even in delusion and crime, who believes himself to have his back protected by the Almighty.

Once one has found a certain coherence in human affairs (and does not all history depend on the presumption of such a thing?), there is nothing more interesting than to also observe the extremes that counterbalance each other, in which that coherence is broken up and yet in the very

255

act of breaking up reveals its essence, namely in that every extreme necessarily passes beyond itself and, promoted to its highest extent, immediately transforms itself in the hands of the promoter into its own direct opposite. The true sense of the old proverb 'extremes meet' (*les extrêmes se touchent*) lies deep, or even at the core of all things. – Why do they meet if not because even the extremes are bound by the measure of the living unit: you shall proceed thus far and no further!

They therefore inevitably produce their own antithesis and themselves rush towards it in blind desire. It is during such moments of rupture that the intrinsic power of things (*la force des choses*) can be felt most perceptibly – as the necessity of which the hidden power is otherwise feared at a distance sweeps so low that one feels oneself seized and carried along by its irresistible progress. That always happens when the natural order and equilibrium has been disturbed in some great and notable way and when the extremes are on the rampage and engaged in their destructive work. That explains a strange phenomenon during revolutions, which is confirmed by all of history. For if one observes those that really deserve the name one will always find that, once they have got under way, *a distinct minority has come to power in and through them*. In what did the secret of the power of that minority lie, in a situation when all the usual bonds have been loosened and the majority would thus appear to be expected to act with the right of the stronger? – It lies in the *extremity*, in the courage or frenzy that dares to call forth, let loose and expedite its terrible power. In a revolution only he rules securely for the time being who drives it incessantly forward with the greatest energy. He rules by the power of the events themselves – but must also be prepared to be crushed under the rushing wheel at any moment. For it is peculiar to all extreme measures that they become the masters of those who use them and, once they are set in motion, propel themselves forward, until that rupture occurs towards which they rush with a hidden force of attraction. – Thus, after the English revolution had been set in motion by the puritans, we also find a numerically far smaller party, a minority in a dominant position, as it had understood how to possess itself of the revolutionary power once it had been unleashed. It was that of the so-called *Independents* who first, with strict consistency, applied the doctrine of the puritans and immediately exaggerated it to a contrary effect. The former, who abhorred all hierarchy with regard to persons and ceremonies, promoted it all the more fiercely and with the most rancorous impatience in the wider sphere, as the absolute dominion of the church, the clerical estate, of a certain theological system; for, although they also included lay people (presbytery, elders) in the management of the congregation, they were nonetheless subject to the strictest clerical supervision.[142] The independents, on the other hand, went a step further and condemned not only the hierarchy but all clerical rule in the church, abolished all real difference between clergy and lay people, invoked an inner illumination and calling, generally denied every other difference between people than that which arose from their progress in grace and at the same time also rejected from a worldly point of view all government other than that of the *elect;* for in the strictness of the fatalism of the doctrine of predestination they, if possible, surpassed the puritans. That, together with a common hatred of hierarchy and popery,

257

was that on which both were in accord. The independents were otherwise necessarily led by their basic principles to *toleration* in articles of faith, as they relied more on direct inspiration than on any system or on the power of the written word itself and were thus in that regard the complete antithesis of the puritans – the most intolerant of people – although they themselves had emerged from that sect. One thus sees the most abstract fanaticism for a blind law and rule suddenly ignite at the opposite end as a fanaticism for the most uninhibited spiritual arbitrariness; that, turned against secular society as well, at first generated the entire display of power that accompanies every unleashed, irregular force and finally, divided and split, quickly matures from the depths of anarchy towards despotism. The sequence was the same that we have seen repeated in later times, the only difference being that the religious content of the English Revolution made the crisis here more sincere, briefer and more easily returning to health, to which the insular position of England, which concentrated its forces, also contributed. The sequence was, as we said, the same. The puritans, who only desired to lay the hard bridle of their discipline in the mouth of the monarchy or, if the more impetuous of them also had a republican constitution in mind, nonetheless envisaged it with the aristocratic element retained in parliament and the state, made use of the independents, whom they regarded as madmen, to be unleashed like some kind of *enfants perdus* against the royal authority. But these first made the breach between parliament and the king irreparable, then dominated by the power of the extreme principles created in their committees as many clubs for the dissemination of those principles and revolutionary

courts for the exercise of them, won over the soldiers by
the fanaticism for equality, led the king to the scaffold,
proclaimed the republic and subdued the parliament by
means of the army. – The army and England were subdued
by Cromwell, an emperor under republican forms. Only
the Christian-sectarian pattern is specific to his time.

"You have taken the whole machine of government in
pieces" – the unhappy Charles I told parliament – "a practice frequent with skilful artists, when they desire to clear
the wheels of any rust which may have grown upon them.
The engine may again be restored to its former use and
motions, provided it be put up entire; so as not a pin of it
be wanting." – Fortunate is the people that after a great
social upheaval still possesses the materials to restore the
edifice of the state! It was not impossible that that might
not have happened after the restoration of the House of
Stuart to the throne of England. Popular power, which
had developed during the revolution, retained sufficient
energy, even after the weakening of extremism, to provide
a necessary counterweight to an arbitrary regime. Cromwell's usurpation was too brief (he was fortunate enough
not to outlive himself) to have a destructive effect by making the habits of military despotism permanent and was,
in other respects, by its energy and glory entirely suited to
raising the national spirit. I shall make the English name
in the world as feared as that of Rome, he was heard to
say, and his deeds were not a bad match for such proud
remarks. All emperors are in their creed Romans. – On
the other hand, the royal party – namely the larger part
of the nobility, which had neither emigrated nor denied
their ways of thinking in their misfortune as well as the
majority of the people, whom old devotion, weariness of

the civil disorders and pity for an unheard-of fate had attached or returned to the royal cause – naturally gained new power through the restoration. The moment seemed to have arrived for both powers of the state represented by those parties to be able to assume the legitimate relationship to each other, that balance, which constitutes true freedom, once the doctrines of the time of troubles on both sides had removed the exaggerated features that are destructive. The reason why that did not happen may neither be sought in the negligence with which they failed in the initial joy to adopt a constitution – that could have been remedied – or in Charles II's contemptible or James II's narrow-minded character, which induced one of them to secretly undermine and the other to openly attack the freedom of the nation. Against both one and the other one could learn to defend oneself. – All of those were contributory factors, but the main cause of the subsequent denouement, which deprived the Stuart dynasty of the throne, was indubitably that sort of secret but soon openly declared devotion to catholicism, which made a sincere reconciliation impossible and would erect an insurmountable barrier between the royal house and the people. James I already had an inclination, derived from his monarchical theory, towards the old church, which he regarded as more favourable to royal authority, and he was led by that inclination into the most preposterous policy, namely to attach himself to Spain, the most catholic power in Europe, which England by combating under Elisabeth had first laid the foundations for its power and its honour and had occupied its important place in the European state system. The reformation had determined that place and had become the political guiding principle of England, and no monarch can offend against it with impunity or attempt with impunity to move a people away from the course that its spirit and position have determined for it. There is a grand natural policy, that is to say founded on the essence of things, and that is its first principle. James was really the one who prepared the ruin of his dynasty. He gave its entire policy a non-national, foreign direction. For that reason high-handed ventures, in internal matters, far more trivial than those Elisabeth had indulged in without hazard, could bring disaster upon his son. *She* acted on the same lines along which the nation was moving and that gave a sense of security, power and fortune to it all that far outweighed individual inconveniences. The Stuart rulers followed a different course, namely against the current; every contact between them and the nation was therefore painful. Charles I also had within himself an inclination towards catholicism, sustained by his political theory and by his French consort. His French alliance harmed him as much as the sought-after alliance with Spain had harmed his father. His delivery of a few ships to Louis XIII to be used in the siege of La Rochelle – all of whose crews immediately deserted, as they were to fight against their co-religionists, the Huguenots – was at the very beginning of his reign the cause of the first breach between him and his parliament (1625).[143] The suspicion, though entirely groundless, that he had caused the rebellion and terrible bloodbath by the catholics in Ireland (1641) was what brought about his downfall in England. The wretched Charles II was a secret catholic, a pensioner on the throne of England, and negotiated with Louis XIV, in return for a certain round sum together with Louis' assistance against his own parliament and the English nation, to officially

261

convert to the Catholic Church.[144] James II, who had done so from conviction (1671) and, not satisfied with that, relying on the French alliance, had sought to introduce catholicism into the realm with such a blind and stubborn zeal (at a time when the protestants expelled from France inundated the shores of England and filled the ears of the people with lamentations) that Spain and the pope himself in vain advised him to be cautious,[145] was impelled by that fanaticism, when church and constitution were intimately connected, to launch the most imprudent, violent and cruel assaults on everything associated with law and freedom or that is dear to humanity. – When William of Orange landed, summoned by the wishes of the whole nation, James, abandoned by the army, the navy, the clergy, the nobility, by officials, by the people, by his own children, separated from him even by religion[146] – when he, alone, without being detained, without being expelled, left to himself boarded a ship to follow his exiled consort and infant son to foreign lands, he *then*, I say, had to experience what it meant to have severed *all* ties between king and people. That is how far a non-national policy, by a sequence of continually aggravated errors, led the Stuart dynasty.

There is a similarity between the fate of that unfortunate royal dynasty and that which in Sweden befell the branch of the House of Vasa that converted to catholicism. And if one considers that John III, like James I and the kings of the House of Stuart, was himself a royal theologian, who was led by the hierarchical system peculiar to him to papism and the elevated notions of his royal authority – and that due to those principles his son, even if he had not become king of Poland, would necessarily be placed in a hostile relationship to the nation and thereby to Swedish law and freedom; if one considers that both father and son, like the House of Stuart (which Sigismund even in his character also entirely resembled), had a considerable amount of support among the higher nobility and the clergy and that duke Charles, the head of the protestant party, showed a marked inclination towards Calvinism, its doctrines and church government, while John with his liturgy drew closer to the high Anglican church, then the similarity is all the more striking. In Sweden, as in England, the consolidation of protestantism as the state religion and the establishment of a protestant succession removed from the throne that branch of the royal family which had deserted the most precious national interests. In Sweden, as in England, following those revolutions, which in both countries restored the peoples to themselves and put an end to protracted civil disorders, there began an unusual national manifestation of power that prepared the way for the most brilliant epoch in the history of Sweden and has subsequently done so for that of England. Thus far do the similarities extend – but no further. The difference is that, due to the less intense Nordic social outlook and situation, only the first rough drafts were made for an internal constitution in Sweden, which in the wealthy England, closed in upon itself – left for almost a century to the settlement of its own conflicts – was fully fought out, evolved and stabilised. Among us a period of conquests intervened. And to that period and the circumstances in which it entangled us, all our internal revolutions, up to the latest one, may primarily be traced. For a century we have paid the price for having briefly, with a population of two million, been the leading nation in Europe. We can draw comfort from the fact that no more honourable debt can be incurred. But it is precisely *that*, namely that our honour has gained the venerable sanctity of misfortune and should be preserved in the innermost sanctum of our heart with the appropriate reverence, ought to teach those who with empty boasting continually bring it up that they know neither what is divine nor what is pathetic about it. A Swede who boasts is undoubtedly the most insufferable person, when both an ancient honour and prolonged misfortunes ought to have implanted in him the nobility of mind that does not need to display itself, because it *exists*.

The revolution in England in the year 1688 is particularly notable in that it occurred after such a long political experience gained through internal disorders, so that even issues concerning the very nature of society, which in other political revolutions, where power and events determine everything in advance, cannot even arise or are suppressed, were here brought to a public conclusion. The two parties based on different principles, which had hitherto, governing by turns, divided society, had thereby finally acquired, even in the theoretical sense, a purely political significance. That had increasingly developed out of the religious difference with which they began. We again find both the former hierarchical party and the puritanical one after the restoration and during the reign of Charles II as a *court party* and a *country* one, later called the *Tories* and *Whigs* (from 1680), designations of which the origins nevertheless show that the difference in religious principles had never ceased to be regarded as a principal distinguishing feature.[147] Through the conflicts conducted between those parties under one name or another for more than half a century two opposed social systems had emerged in *practice* within the state, presenting one of the most interesting political phenomena. The main difference lay in the diverse notions concerning the nature and origin of legitimate government, on the one side derived from the divine right of the *king* and on the other from the people. The latter principle had already been publicly propounded in its full stringency by the independents during their short-lived republic, namely in the sense that the people should also govern, which was also immediately followed by the right of the stronger or the placing of society under military law and rule by the army. After the restoration it had been propagated, though in a milder sense, through the country party and had found fresh support within it, as Charles II was a dishonourable betrayer of the freedom, independence and every right of his people, in the necessary resistance to the pernicious plans of the government. That resistance expressed itself in particular in their repeated attempts to legally (through the Exclusion Bill) exclude the Duke of York, the later James II, as a catholic, from the succession to the throne, attempts that were naturally most intimately connected with the question: whether the nation had the right to determine the highest authority at its own discretion or not. The royalist party, which was also that of the high church, tenaciously opposed those attempts, until the sequence actually showed that the bigoted catholicism of James would lead to the inevitable destruction of the state. They then found themselves in the remarkable position of *being obliged to let the person go, while nonetheless retaining the royalist principle*, which has shown itself to be active in the policy of the Tory party until the most recent times in England. The revolution was therefore in its essential character a *compact* between the two different social principles or their representatives – but in order to justify and explain that statement it is first necessary to consider the political theories that evolved during and due to those conflicts.

It was natural that the great practical interest of such an issue in the present condition of the nation should not only make every question connected with it both publicly and privately the subject of lively debates[148] but also engage the writers for and against them. Among these we would first name Sir Robert Filmer and Algernon Sidney. The former had attempted to demonstrate in a now long forgotten tract,[149] though for a time regarded both by his own party and the opposite one as the best explanation of the purely royalist creed, the divine origin of royal authority. He invoked the Bible and the history of God's people. But as even among the latter monarchy was not primordial, he went back to the patriarchs, with the assertion that Abraham, Noah and above all Adam had already been kings. For royal authority was derived from the paternal one, so that the same unlimited authority was due to the kings over their subjects as to a father over his children. Just as children are already from birth subject to the paternal authority, so likewise are the subjects of course to the royal one, which is equally unlimited, so that no one is born free but all, both persons and property, are possessions, of which the king can make use at his pleasure, without the subjects under any circumstances being able to legitimately resist, least of all to depose their ruler. – One sees that it is the theological monarchism, driven to its most extreme rigour by party strife. No more noble representative of the opposite point of view can be found than the hero and martyr of freedom, Algernon Sidney,

266

and his *Discourses on Government* are an all the more touching witness in his favour precisely because those writings were used against him instead of witnesses in the unjust trial by which he was brought to the scaffold.[150] He was an ardent republican, of a stern and high-minded spirit. His life, so rich in exploits and vicissitudes and his motto

– *Manus haec inimica tyrannis*
*Ense petit placidam sub libertate quietem**

characterised him even better than his writings. They stand in opposition to Filmer's assertions about the divine origin of royal authority, contrary to which Sidney teaches that God originally left to human beings the choice of forms of government; that it is therefore in accordance with nature that the nations rule themselves or choose their own government; that all authority (magistratical power), in order to be lawful, must be based on a mandate from the people, its authority thus dependent on the laws that the latter gives itself and its form subject to alteration, restriction or abolition by the people. Although Sidney, according to those principles, also recognises monarchy as a lawful constitution, he does not hide the fact that he sees the republican one as preferable and seeks on many grounds to demonstrate its advantages. These two writers are more remarkable historically than philosophically and express the convictions formed in practice on both sides during the party conflicts rather than any cause or derivation for them, being opinions rather than doctrines. More remarkable in a scientific regard are two others: *Thomas*

* This hand, the enemy of tyrants, seeks with the sword the gentle tranquillity of peace.

Hobbes and *John Locke*.[151] The former, whose doctrine has in public opinion become synonymous with absolute despotism, is nonetheless remarkably enough the first to have theoretically based society on a *compact*. That is again most closely connected with another concept that he was likewise the first to introduce into science and made the foundation of social theory, namely the so-called *state of nature*, as the primordial one of humanity. With regard to such an ambiguous concept as that of the state of nature one would expect that it would have had to be based on some observation from experience, in the same way that one later sees the philosophers during a certain period, particularly in this regard, having turning their attention to the savages of America and the Pacific islands, whose natural state was enthusiastically analysed and admired, although, as one writer (Fr. Schlegel) remarks, the man-eating or cannibalism that is fairly widespread among those peoples involved something disturbing for that admiration, which needed to be overcome. But that is not the case. The idea of the state of nature is a civilised, purely European-philanthropical product, and when one later turned to experience it was in order to seek confirmation of an already accepted idea. If one considers from where Hobbes adopted it in the first place, the explanation that seems most likely to me is that it emerged from the doctrine of the independents, which by abolishing all differences that had arisen in society invoked the absolute equality of human beings. That was an upsurge of ideas beyond the limits of both civil and natural society that would be followed by the strangest overturning of things. The river was then dammed within its banks, but an abstract notion remained as a memory of that overspill and has played a most distinctive role among political theories. Born of the most abstract religious fanaticism exemplified in history, that concept in its treatment by the philosophers lost even the vitality that every *feeling*, perverted or healthy, always gives to opinions (thus, for example, the doctrine of the independents that the degrees of grace are the only order of precedence between people, even in the civil sphere, nonetheless thereby gave it a real inner emotional force); merely the framework, the bare concept remained and was arbitrarily filled with a content assembled in various ways, for which reason nothing is more diverse than the opinions of the philosophers about the actual condition of that natural state, although they agreed to counterpose it to the state. Our intention is not to deny that concept all reality and we shall explain ourselves further on the matter later in this essay. We deny the contradiction between state of nature and the state only in the sense that they exclude each other, whereas they are on the contrary always *simultaneous* antitheses, and the state, both within and outside itself, is perpetually dealing with a never entirely ceasing state of nature, despite all the progress of civilisation.* To conceive of the state of nature, on the contrary, as a merely external condition, preceding the state and entirely eradicated by its establishment, is a doctrine that nullifies itself by its results. The reason why Hobbes should understand and use that concept in such a manner lay in his philosophy. For he was an abstract em-

---

* In every state of nature there lies the seed of a state, in every state a state of nature continues.

piricist, that is to say one of the philosophers who from the *external*, superficial aspect of the human being would construct her *inner* being.

As such a procedure derives from the notion that *both* cannot arise from any common unity, that such a unity is therefore merely possible *unilaterally*, or that one aspect is all or at least the first and original one, the other merely something secondary and accidental, but if the *inner* aspect is not included from the start and one never arrives at it from the *external* one but by way of an absurd precondition (for example, the one by which empiricism from a bundle of *impressions*, produces a *concept*, from a bundle of senses a *soul*), then that doctrine, however much it refers to *experience*, is nonetheless in itself the most abstract doctrine and also the one that has most distinguished itself by groundless hypotheses.[152] Devoid of all soul and interiority, it can only explain one external aspect by another external one, one inessential aspect by another inessential one. Thus Hobbes was led to a merely external, inessential explanation of civil society and began with a condition in which he placed the abstract human being, such as she was supposed to be, removed from all social relationships. *How* that condition would be conceived by Hobbes, moreover, was probably not uninfluenced by his own relationship to the independents, from whose fanaticism for equality he had developed his idea. For he utterly detested the outlook of that party, both because of his principles, which attached him to the monarchical party, and his position as the teacher of Charles II as well as his own character, which was naturally timid and gentle. The equality of the state of nature became for him all the more easily merely a general destruction. From the unrestrained human desires an equal right of all to everything would arise under that condition and from that necessarily a war of all against all. Such a condition would destroy humanity unless it was brought to an end. It could only come to an end by means of a *compact*, by which all the individual wills submitted to an external, coercive higher power, as an expression of the common will that desired security. That submission must again of necessity be *unrestricted*, for if that highest power were to be restricted, that could either be done by an *equal* – in which case you would again have the former conflict – or by a *higher* one – but then the highest power would not be the highest. From that Hobbes concluded with irresistible logic that such a power could not be bound to any laws by the subjects – for what power would guarantee that it would uphold them? – On the contrary, as only it brought a condition of complete lawlessness to an end, it must itself be at once the source of all power and all law and in *every respect* unlimited.[153] Thus Hobbes arrived from an opposite direction in the theory of the state at an even harsher despotism than what Filmer had derived from the divine right and paternal authority of the kings, harsher, I say, because paternal authority naturally also involves mildness, while here, on the other hand, a government found itself in the relationship to the subjects of an absolute external coercive power. One sees that this state, which nullifies the state of nature in order to establish itself, also nullifies itself; for the insecurity in the face of violence, which was after all supposed to be the rationale for establishing the state, is the only thing that is certain in that state.

By two principles Hobbes did, however, become the father of the subsequently dominant political theories and have the greatest influence, namely that the state is an external institution of coercion and security – and that this institution has arisen through a compact. Both belong among the half-true propositions that precisely through their half-ness are especially suitable to be widely disseminated and to flourish in the half-light that constitutes the enlightenment of the masses. It is therefore interesting and very necessary to trace such opinions to their source. *There* you can be sure to find them in their most distinct, strongest form; for without an original force and distinctiveness no opinion will initially make headway. If one now goes to Hobbes' theory one finds not only the two abovementioned principles very clearly set out but also elaborated with such a self-defeating consistency that their actual outcome may be regarded as their refutation. But that consistency in the originator was abandoned by his successors. They nevertheless retained the principles, which is already evidence that they were no longer clearly and distinctively understood; otherwise Hobbes, who merely sought a desperate way out of civil troubles, would have been both the first and the last adherent of his own theory. If one considers the reason, it can only be found in the increasing influence gained by the abstract-empirical outlook that we have described above. It viewed society as it did the individual, attempting to define the inner nature of both by superficialities and *could* not do otherwise; it was therefore blind to the consequences of its own system. That the state is a security apparatus can by no means be denied; that is undoubtedly everywhere its external, evident aspect. He who would only explain it in that way, however, would be subject to exactly the same illusion as he who would only see in the human being the external, physical being, without the living connection in which the latter stands to the immortal inner one. The mechanical view of the state is merely a materialism applied to a larger object, which in society, if it is consistent, denies God, the soul and freedom. A blind, external necessity remains and, as that cannot explain itself, freedom is invoked only in the need to establish it and will then itself perish, which is to say that the irresistible coercive power arises from a compact. That such a compact, so conceived, is an absurdity is easily demonstrated. For each and every compact has to contain something binding, some guarantee, and as this doctrine recognises no other guarantee than that given by an external power, then the social compact itself already presupposes that same highest power which was first to be established by the compact? The state power, as a coercive power, must always have coerced, or else the state would not have emerged, and each and every compact for that purpose would have been powerless and ineffective. Thus we see how those who, by allowing society to emerge by nullifying a so-called state of nature, have actually deprived it of all natural reality and have attributed it as an external, temporary institution to a free agreement cannot themselves understand that as anything but a blind necessity, freedom merely as arbitrariness and the law as despotism. – In that way every extreme suffers not only its own torments but also necessarily those of its antithesis, just as cold shivers also represent fever. – Thus one antithesis, taken separately, constantly moves towards the other. – Reconciliation, unity, peace, where others see only an external struggle and destruction, exist only for those who grasp matters in their living core. As that is entirely lacking in the abstract-empirical outlook, one can already expect in advance that the improvement made to Hobbes' theory by the renowned Locke would not be able to eliminate its fundamental flaw, which is to perceive all relationships merely as *external* ones. In order simultaneously to avoid the despotic outcome produced by Hobbes' social compact, in which the people gave away everything and retained nothing, which again necessarily followed from its principle that the highest power was *indivisible* and could only be entrusted undivided to a government – in order, I say, to simultaneously avoid that extreme and the other democratic one, revealed in the doctrine of the independents, according to which the highest power *could* not be transferred but remained undivided with the people – Locke took a middle way, leading to the doctrine of the *separation of state powers*, whose real author he is. The highest power, he remarked, divided itself into *legislative* and *executive* power. The former belonged to the people or those to whom the people wished to entrust it, the latter to the government, and a law-based, free constitution could only exist where those two powers had been *separated*. One can see that, instead of the absolute *predominance* that Hobbes reserved for the highest power, he wished by means of separation to introduce an *equilibrium*, and it was from that time that the balance between the powers in the state played such an important role in the theories and became the highest purpose of politics and their essential arcanum. Whether that equilibrium will possess any real significance or not, however, depends entirely on the way in which it is perceived and expresses itself. It can have quite a healthy significance. But if by that one means only two or more external powers in that state that counterbalance each other, or a balance of power in general, then the balance itself is only a disguised and temporarily dormant hostility and Hobbes could with reason object that this simply served to locate within the highest power the *conflict* that, precisely by the establishment of a highest power, ought to have ceased and without the cessation of which the state of nature (which always expresses itself in *conflict between equals*) has not ceased either. The objection is irrefutable as soon as one, like Locke, occupies the same ground as Hobbes. It must be possible to present a *third* aspect, in which the separate powers are *one* and can be combined. But if that third aspect is perceived merely in an external, mechanical way, nothing is gained by that either. Out of fear of despotism Locke would still always need to posit alongside that third highest power a fourth one as a counterweight, Hobbes, for fear of anarchy, above those two a fifth one as the highest one again and so on for ever. Such are the insoluble difficulties of the mechanical theory of the state. That Locke does occupy that ground is clear from the whole of his philosophical character, which would necessarily lead him (although his noble practical life was not at all ordered according to those principles) to overlook and deny in the state as in the human being the internal and original, for which reason it is for him also merely an external institution, created especially for the security of property, having emerged by a compact from an abstract state of nature, which he assumes to have been like that of Hobbes, though he describes it differently. That is made even clearer by the consequences of his doctrine. – What was the main political error that after the convening of the States General, instead of the transformation of the arbitrary power into a lawful one and the introduction of a free constitution, precipitated France into the vortex of revolution and with each successive constitution drove it ever further along the same course, until the revolutionary cycle was completed? Was it not above all the purely literal, mechanical notion of the necessary separation between the *legislative* and *executive* power that led to the belief that one could not strictly enough establish the boundaries of both in order to make each of them *pure*, so that the paragraphs in the constitution really represent sentries between two hostile powers? Those two abstract powers, detached from their unity, did indeed relate to each other as to enemies and the legislative power destroyed the executive one (which was the republic) only to be suppressed and engulfed in turn by the latter (which was the empire). And can it be denied that those principles were consistently derived from the theory of Locke, just as French materialism in general was merely a development of the Lockean philosophy? – One now hears the best writers in France assert that they never wanted anything there other than the English constitution. – That assertion contains an ambiguity that is worth the trouble to elucidate. It was not the English constitution they wanted but rather a more perfect development and application of the theory on which that constitution was *believed* to be based, although imperfectly based. They regarded themselves as having taken a step beyond it, so great that it could be compared to the move from political barbarism to enlightenment, and from the earlier writings of Madame Staël one could also adduce sufficient evidence of that notion. That this theory, which formed the basis of the revolutionary constitutions, was *not* the one on which

276

that of England rested, was best demonstrated by the effects of those constitutions. They were from the beginning, however, consistently developed from the Lockean theory; and did that naturally also contain the principles of the English constitution? That we allow ourselves to doubt; we would rather admit that Locke's political writings contain the effects of the English constitution.

And the latter, which is at least partly so, also explains why his political theory gained a classic reputation precisely in England. Locke's *Treatises of Government*, which appeared in 1689, were namely intended to justify the revolution that stabilised the happy constitution of England. In that the author had the great advantage that the effects he had in mind was already present in reality; he simply subordinated it to his principles. It is in the connection between the two that his weak side lies; for that connection is vague, inadequate and often exists only by a great ambiguity, as a result of which he presupposes that which was to be demonstrated. – On the whole his work is a partisan tract, of great intelligence, composed in the spirit of *Whig* principles, though also containing much that follows consistently neither from his own nor his party's principles but was a collective effect, shared by all parties, of the active political life of the English state. And that common good, which in practice mitigates any extremes of a one-sided theory, we regard as the best aspect of that work. That circumstance is remarkable in view of the whole of English philosophy after Locke. For who does not know that all the audacious or even dangerous philosophical ideas that emerged from the abstract-empirical mode of thought and undeniably had a very detrimental influence in France derived their origin from England and there first appeared in their clearest and boldest forms? Nevertheless, they can there be seen not to have produced anything like the same destructive results but, as if by a secret power of their own, to have been neutralised and made innocuous for the state. Nothing provides better evidence that the essence of the English constitution lay deeper than all those theories and could not be touched or adversely affected by them. But it was *its* strength that made all their aberrations harmless; its wide practical application was what pricked all the bubbles of abstraction as soon as they came near it. Whereas in France, on the contrary, they wished to make that foundational which in England was merely external and superficial.

For our real aim in going through the theories referred to has been to enable us to distinguish the superficial from the essential. People's opinions not only change things but also, once a change has taken place, attach themselves to that which has occurred and give it its external appearance, its colour. And yet one has to distinguish between that preceding and subsequent effect of the opinions. For no change in reality is merely the result of the influence of an opinion or a certain mode of thought but of a conflict between the effect of various opinions. Even the victor is modified by his adversary, having been obliged to recognise and indeed associate his enemy with himself, albeit in a mitigated form. That is how things everywhere really are. On the other hand it is in the quality and appearance of what has occurred that the prevailing opinion shows its unlimited dominance. For it takes the credit for *everything*, from it emanates the light in which the change appears, and the superficial observer mistakes the colouring for the real thing. These observations are particularly instructive when applied to our present subject. The English revolution was altogether a national affair, not a party affair. The defenders of royal rule and of the rights of the people, Tories and Whigs, were in complete agreement on the main question; the influence of the different opinions revealed itself in regard to form and manner. The former, or the Tories, who had been obliged to admit an exception from their political doctrine for the sake of the general good, naturally attempted in every possible way to maintain their consistency and to associate the new situation with the old opinions as best they could. The latter, or the Whigs, were on the contrary on their own ground with regard to what had happened and from *their* doctrine the entire revolution would of necessity take on its colour, all the more so as that doctrine was theoretically presented by such a superior genius as Locke. Thus Locke's theory came to be regarded as the theory of the English constitution, although the distinguishing feature of that constitution was that, along with a republican element in the state, it assimilated the feudal-monarchical one in a form of organic action and counter-action, which, consistently realised, can have no place in Locke's theory.

We substantiate these statements with historical evidence. – In the convention or interim parliament in which in the year 1688, on account of the flight of James II and the necessary exclusion of the House of Stuart from the throne, the highest political questions were debated with such instructive thoroughness, we find both doctrines (that of those who derive all power from the people by a compact as well as of those who see in the highest power an originally divine order preceding all compacts) argued between Whigs and Tories with reference to the current extraordinary situation. It followed from the feudalist nature of the latter's principle that one should find most of them in the upper house, or in that element of the constitution that was distinguished by personal representation and hereditary rights of precedence. – That was indeed the case. – The main content of the bill sent up by the lower house –1) that state power existed through a compact; 2) that king James II, by breaking that compact and fleeing the country had abdicated – became the subject of lively debates in the upper house, not because they desired the change but because they wished to be formally consistent; for which reason the proposal for a regency, in particular, was voted down, though in vain. With a majority of only 53 votes to 46 the first question was answered in the affirmative; the second one faced even greater difficulties in and of itself as the upper house instead of *'abdicated'* wished to use the expression that James had *'deserted'* the throne as being more appropriate. That was not accepted, and with regard to everything concerning colouring and significance the revolution was of course the triumph of Whig principles. But just as the Tory ones had modified the issue itself, that is to say had an important influence on the constitution that was now adopted, they were also preserved in a constitutional sense, as much as the others. Both, having evolved in practice through protracted struggles in society, would increasingly manifest themselves as living, active political forces and it was that which placed the feudal element in such a unique relationship to the republican one in England. The English constitution recognises both. For that reason the revolution of 1688 was also, if not in its form nevertheless in essence a compact between those two principles or their representatives in society. The sequel to this essay will show whether *such* a one is not the only *real* social compact that can be concluded.

Two world events in particular have determined the internal and external conditions of the European states until the most recent upheavals. 1) The Reformation. 2) The discovery of the Indies. – We have considered the first of those great changes in its effect on the political concepts. It remains to consider the latter from the same point of view, or what *commerce* and the objects connected with it have brought about in the same regard. That will be our subject next, when we hope to be able to present in an even clearer light much that it has not hitherto been possible to express with sufficient certainty. Until that has been done, however, I request that no one will over-hastily draw conclusions from what has already been said and find myself so much more justified in issuing that warning, as nothing is so much the object of antagonistic partisan comments as *impartiality* and as I have at least endeavoured to observe that great historical duty.

Notes

The footnotes in this English translation have been shortened and simplified. Footnotes 89 and 90 have changed places since this seems to have been an error in the translated text-version. Some few new additions have been made to explain some of the terms in the essay.

1　The author expresses his detestation of the hypocrisy in the French revolution: "Statecraft ought to know the need to be honest of necessity; for it is more difficult than ever to deceive the nations."

2　Lycurgus is said to have asked a supporter of democracy: would you introduce that form of rule in your house?

3　The freed slaves formed a separate class: "Freedmen rank little higher than slaves" (Tacitus, *Germania,* ch. 25). That the conditions of the domestic slaves were not harsh is shown by Snorri Sturluson, *Heimskringla* (Peringskiöld ed.), I, 396.

4　"Kings they choose for their birth" (Tacitus, ch. 7).

5　"Distinction of birth or great deeds done by their fathers confer on mere lads the rank of chief" (Tacitus, ch. 13). For the Norse "kings of hosts" see Snorri, 'Olaf Haraldsson's saga' and 'Saint Olaf's saga', ch. 4 (both in Heimskringla).

6　Some of the terms for deities and priests were related (*god/gydja, diar*). See also Ste Croix, *Recherches sur les mystères du paganisme* (Paris, 1784).

7　"But no one is allowed to punish or bind or even flog the soldiers except the priests" (Tacitus, ch. 7). Kings had also been priests in early times among the Romans and Greeks.

8　Free status was forfeited by heinous crimes. The right of freemen to be judged by their peers was transferred to the nobility and the priesthood ('benefit of clergy').

9　For popular agreement to foreign wars in the case of the Swedish king Olof Skotkonung, see *Heimskringla,* I, 484.

10 "Where one of the chieftains announces in the assemblies that he intends to conduct a campaign, so that whoever would follow him could volunteer, all those stand up who approve of the cause and the man" (Caesar, *Gallic war*, VI. 22).

11 "And they do not blush to be seen among their retainers" (Tacitus, ch. 13).

12 "It is shameful for a leader to be surpassed in valour, shameful for his retinue to lag behind. In addition, infamy and lifelong scandal await the man who outlives his leader by retreating from the battle-line" (Tacitus, ch. 14).

13 The oldest Nordic law concerning the royal retinue is that of Canute the Great, called the 'Vitherlag law', from 'vitherlag', association (societas).

14 'Allshärjar-thing' meant the assembly of the entire army. "Nothing of a public or private nature is dealt with except under arms" (Tacitus, ch. 13).

15 "If their native state grows sluggish from prolonged peace and leisure, many well-born youths actively seek tribes that are then involved in a war ... while a large retinue is hard to maintain except by violence and war" (Tacitus, ch. 14).

16 "This among them is both status and strength: always to be surrounded by a large throng of picked young men, a distinction in peace and protection in war. That is a man's renown and that is his glory, not only among his own people but in neighbouring states as well, if his retinue excels in number and valour; for then they are sought by embassies and honoured with gifts, and

often by reputation alone all but bring wars to an end" (Tacitus, ch. 13). Most warfare consisted of private expeditions of the kings with their retinues.

17 "Indeed, there are even degrees in the retinue itself, determined by the man they attend. There is keen rivalry both among retainers, as to who will rank first with their leader, and among the leaders, as to whose retinues are most numerous and brave" (Tacitus, ch. 13). Compare the 'Vitherlag law' of Canute the Great (Langebek, *Scriptores rerum danicarum medii aevi*, III, 139). The head of the retinue was among us the *jarl* (earl).

18 According to the Vitherlag law that should be done eight days after Yule (Christmas).

19 "The means for this munificence comes from robbery and war" (Tacitus, ch. 14).

20 "It is customary for states to confer on the leaders a share of cattle or crops, voluntarily and man by man; this they receive as an honour, but it also supplies their needs" (Tacitus, ch. 15).

21 "Banquets and a lavish if unpolished pomp serve the men as pay" (Tacitus, ch. 14).

22 Cf. Nyerup, *Historisk statistisk Skildring af Tilstaandet i Danmark of Norge i ældre og nyere Tider* (Copenhagen, 1803), I, 180.

23 According to *Heimskringla* (II, 29) the only fief of a jarl was the *veitsla*.

24 Veitsla and fiefs are also found separately in the Nordic countries) (*Heimskringla*, I, 579).

25 That was eventually banned in Sweden: "A king may not give away or grant Upsala öd," according to the provincial law of Västergötland.

26 "Wer wissen will, woher wir sein,/ Von Schwedenland
   sind wir heran" it says in an old Swiss folk song
   (Neikter, *Dissertatio academica de colonia Suecorum in
   Helvetiam egressa*, Upsala, 1787).

27 The Salic law among the Franks, dating from the
   time of Clovis, knew no other nobles than those in
   the king's retinue (*antrustiones, leudes*) (C.F. Eichhorn,
   Deutsche Staats- und Rechts-Geschichte, Göttingen, 1808,
   I, 107) but refers in its prologue to an older royal
   nobility, consisting of "*proceres* (nobles) of that
   people, who – when the people of the Franks were still
   barbarians – were the *rectores* (tribal chieftains, kings)
   among them."

28 On the Carolingian constitution and its degeneration,
   see Möser, *Osnabrückische Geschichte*, I, 229-264, 375 ff.

29 Their oldest name in Scandinavia was 'house-carls'.
   (Cf. Vitherlag law, the Norwegian 'King's Mirror'
   and Sturluson.) 'Hirdmän' (from *hird*, 'family') and
   'hofmän' (from *hof*, 'house, farm') meant the same
   thing. Among the Franks the leader of the 'followers'
   (as they are called in the Norwegian *Hirdskrá*) was
   the *major domus*, the followers being members of the
   domus regia (royal household) and thus also known as
   familiares.

30 The common title of 'senior' for a feudal lord recalls
   the duties owed to paternal age within a family. *Señor,
   signore* and *seigneur* are all derived from it.

31 Thus *miles* ('warrior') became synonymous with
   'vassal'. The Vitherlag law, the first Nordic curial law,
   was therefore also the first *articles of war* (lex castrensis).

"Military men who are called *ministeriales* (officials)"
are mentioned in a document of the emperor Henry IV
of 1073 (Eichhorn, II, 479).

32 The reason why the nobleman is always regarded as
owing personal loyalty to his king is that the nobility
arose from the royal household (*maison du roi*). A non-
noble courtier thus remains a contradiction in terms.

33 Nothing has confused the concept of the medieval
constitution more than the fact that *ministeriales* (royal
officials) occur both as *unfree* (Remer, *Handbuch der
mittleren Geschichte,* 236) and as 'nobles' and 'free men'
(liberi) (Möser, II. 119). The solution appears to be that
when the first feudal nobility became hereditary these
were not accepted as equals, but due to royal favour
they achieved the same status, so that ministeriales
later became feudal nobles (Eichhorn, II, 902). Tacitus
already noted that unfree men rose by royal favour in
Germanic *kingdoms* above both free men and nobles. In
the Lombard laws the king's slave was valued as highly
as a free man, his liberated slave equalling a nobleman.
Among the nations with a developed kingship Tacitus
includes the *Suiones* (ch. 46). The reason for a more
extended kingship among the ancient Swedes than
other Germanic peoples is that the kings there retained
the priestly authority the longest, while they were
transformed into leaders of the warrior estate among
the others.

34 "No others are allowed the duty of fealty except to
us and their respective *lord* (senior), to our advantage
and that of the lord" (*Caroli Magni Capit.* 2, of 805,
in Baluz). "Vassals shall have the power to take
men in trust and to strengthen their *king* and be

286

given the title *huskarl*" (Norwegian *Hirdskrá* of king
Magnus Lagaböter, around 1273, edited by Dolmer,
Copenhagen, 1666, 119).

35 Knighthood corresponded to the grade of master;
the apprentices were in Scandinavia called servants
(svenner, knapar) or men-at-arms (väpnare). The old
royal warrior retinue also had grades.

36 Cf. Heeren, *Utvecklingen af korstågens följder för Europa*
(Strengnäs, 1816), 162. No nobility except the royal
one can trace its ancestry beyond the crusading period.

37 The Nordic sworn brotherhood could only be
expressed by *symbolic* acts, as among most peoples.
So also in marriage or old Norse friendship pacts,
where both parties laid a piece of turf on their heads,
as a sign of loyalty until death, and shared a drink
containing drops of blood from each. The symbolic act
on entering domestic service was a handshake from
the master. All agreements in the feudal system were
symbolic, from their very nature.

38 The warrior relationship between feudal lord and
vassal was one of equality. A remarkable example
of that occurs in Sveno Aggonis' 'Historia legum
castrensium regis Canuti Magni' (Langebek, III, 150).
King Canute broke the law when he killed one of his
house-carls while drunk. The retinue considered how
that should be atoned for, including death, but finally
accepted a heavy fine in compensation.

39 What was done beyond the legal requirements was
said to occur "out of *noble* duty," which shows the close
relationship between *honour* and *nobility*.

40 With regard to personal insults a Swedish nobleman is therefore bound not only by the general law but by the regulations on duelling.

41 In the case of serfdom it should be remembered that it was customary and represented the lowest level of *personal* dependence, in which a nobleman also stood to the king, though it was unlimited and lacked the equalising comradeship within the military class. The worst form of oppression came with civil order and laws, if they were applied in the service of a tyrant, as when a republican administration was subordinated to tyrants such as the Roman emperors or Napoleon, when the entire constitution becomes a living lie.

42 States can only arise on a religious foundation. What distinguishes them from a state of nature is "a positive religion."

43 The name given to the collection of estates which was the property of the Swedish Crown in medieval Sweden. *Nationalencyklopedin*, (1996).

44 Sturluson, 'Ynglinga saga', ch. 2, 20. See the word 'drott' in Björn Halldorson's Icelandic dictionary and Loccenius' *Lexicon juris sveo-gothici.*

45 "There God is the ruler of all, the rest being subject and obedient" (Tacitus, ch. 39).

46 Tacitus refers to the special office of a "priest of the state."

47 Sturluson, ch. 20.

48 The word 'hun(d)' or 'chun' meant 100, from which both 'king' and 'hundred-man' (centurio, centenaries) derive. Tacitus mentions the military division into hundreds and that a title arose from it: "What was

at first a *number* is now a *title* and an *honour*" (ch. 6).
Cf. Ihre, *Glossarium sviogothicum* under 'konung' and
'hundrade'.

49 "Then the realm and the kingship was divided between
kindreds, as they branched out" says Sturluson (ch. 40)
in describing the origin of the many subordinate kings
in Sweden.

50 All physical and death penalties come from the "court
of the overlord" (Möser, I, 22) and were originally
alien to the law of the *free*. The principles of the
Germanic constitution are excellently described by
Möser.

51 "A wedge is formed not by accident or random
conglomeration but through family connections and
kinship" (Tacitus, ch. 7).

52 "They pay out part of the fine to the king or the state,
part to the plaintiff himself or his kin" (Tacitus, ch.
12). The king's share accrued to him as defender
of the general peace but is probably later than that
of the hundred (Burman, 'Kritisk afhandling om
provinslagarna' in *Vitterhets Academiens Handlingar*,
6, 255). The king was party to the breaches of what
were later called the *royal* forms of peace, at assemblies
(ting), in homes towards women and in churches, for
which the perpetrator was made an outlaw throughout
the realm.

53 Östergötland laws (Homicide section), pt 3. Cf.
Västergötland laws (Assemblies section), pt 12.

54 "The son of a farmer shall the lawman be, for all the
farmers shall rule by the mercy of God" (Västergötland
laws, Assemblies section, pt 1).

55 The oldest titles of officials in Sweden are *lawman* and *hundred chieftain*, down to twelfthman, sixthman and fourthman, of which the last two referred to the varying subdivisions of the hundreds themselves. All are ancient and of a purely republican origin.

56 When the king 'rode Eriksgata' around the kingdom after his election, such hostages were given and taken at the boundary of each province. When one of them, Ragvald Knaphövde, arrived at the Västergötland provincial assembly without them he was slain by the local inhabitants, "because of the offence he gave to all the people of Västergötland" (regnal list in the Västergötland law code).

57 For that reason a foreigner could in the 11th century still judge the Nordic constitution, apart from in war, to be purely democratic: "At home they enjoy the status of *equals*; going to war they give all their obedience to the king" (Adam of Bremen, *De situ Daniae*). It had always been the custom of Swedish kings, said king Olof Skotkonung himself at an assembly, "that they have let the farmers rule with them" (Sturluson, I. 485).

58 The oath of homage of the old estates of Aragon was: "We, who are as good as you, recognise you as our lord and king on condition that you respect our freedom and rights; otherwise not."

59 The Visigothic, Salic, Burgundian, Ripuarian, Alemannic, Bavarian, Longobard, Frisian, Saxon and Thuringian laws (A. Georgisch, *Corpus juris germanici antiqui*, Halle, 1783).

60 As in Westphalia (Möser, *Osnabrückische Geschichte*, I, 243).

61 Cf. von Savigny, *Ueber germanische Gerichts-Verfassung*, ch. 4, and Eichhorn, I, 203.

62 As conciliation presupposes injury, all Germanic law was mostly criminal law, which was also the only public law, developed in continual practice to a successively more elaborated state among the members of society.

63 *Plegium* actually signified a guarantee, whether from a hundred or a lordly protector, but both were prescribed in the old English laws (Wilkins, *Leges anglo-saxonicae*, London, 1721, 241).

64 While all feudal law arose from curial law, which (primarily applying to the *ministeriales*) was later separated from the laws governing fiefs and the various forms of feudal relationships.

65 Cf. Ihre, Glossarium sviogothicum, under the word 'tukka'.

66 The Västergötland laws also deny royal officials the competence to give evidence in cases concerning boundary disputes between them and local farmers (section on land laws, pt 9).

67 Regarding the relationship of judge and jury to each other, compare C.J. Schlyter, 'Anmärkningar i anledning af den nyligen förda striden angående det fordna förhållandet mellan domare och nämnd' in the journal *Svea*, no. 1 (Upsala, 1824), 250. [Editorial note, 1850.]

68 The Vitherlag law, by which offenders were expelled from court, was strictly upheld until the time of Nils, (who became king of Denmark in 1104) who allowed a criminal (nobleman) with a powerful family to pay a fine instead, which subsequently became the norm

(Langebek, III, 152, 162). Compare the Swedish king Magnus Eriksson's curial law of 1319, edited by Hadorph.

69 Cf. W.G. Lagus, *Dissertatio de remediis juris contra sententias in genere et de submissione sententiae speciatim* (Åbo, 1823), 55.

70 "They cannot even stand dwellings joined together" (Tacitus, ch. 16).

71 During the reign of the emperor Otto I in the 10th century, according to Simonde de Sismondi, *Histoire des républiques italiennes du moyen age* (Zurich, 1807), I.

72 "In the ordering of the cities and the preservation of the state the ingenuity of the ancients was imitated. They finally desired freedom so much that, to avoid the pressures of power, they were governed by the decrees of the consuls rather than of the emperors" says a contemporary witness, bishop Otto of Freising (d. 1185), of the Lombard republics (*De gestis Friderici* I, II, ch. 13).

73 The continued existence of the Roman municipal constitution during the middle ages, a link between antiquity and the modern world, is importantlydemonstrated in von Savigny's classic work *Geschichte des römischen Rechts im Mittelalter*.

74 See the evidence for that in von Savigny, I, 90, 354, 257, 283, 342 ff.

75 "We decree that the conduct of cases between Romans be determined by Roman laws," according to a law of Chlothar around 560 (Baluz, I, 7). The same principle is recognised in the Langobard laws of Liutprand (VI, 37). The Ostrogothic king Theodoric produced a legal code for his Goths, the *'Edictum Theodorici'* (c.

500). The Visigothic king Alaric (484-507) provided a summary of Roman law for his Roman subjects, the so-called *'Breviarium Alaricianum'*, of which there is also a Burgundian example: *'Lex romana Burgundionum vulgo Papianus'*.

76 For the restrictions to be applied in that regard, see von Savigny, I. 92.

77 For the-evidence, see von Savigny, I, ch. 5.

78 Heeren, *Korstågens följder*, 183 ff.

79 Sismondi, *Histoire des républiques italiennes du moyen age* (Zurich, 1807), II, 116, 197.

80 J. von Müller, *Allgemeine Geschichte*, II, 223.

81 Eichhorn, II, 483 note a.

82 In Germany municipal laws and their domain were both called *Weichbild*, the etymology of which is disputed. 'Weichbilds-Recht' was the same as the Nordic *'birke-rätt'*, laws governing market places or "burgher right".

83 Rühs, *Handbuch der Geschichte des Mittelalters* (Berlin, 1816), 584.

84 Robertson, *The history of the reign of the emperor Charles V*, II, 236.

85 Eichhorn, II, 560.

86 The landowner in places even exercised such a right of confiscation (as with shipwrecks) when a waggon carrying goods broke down while crossing his property (Remer, 279).

87 Robertson, *The history of the reign of the emperor Charles V*, I, 224; II, 243.

88 Guibert, abbot of Nogent: "Those cursed communities into which, contrary to law and custom, serfs escape the justice of the lords in an unruly manner" (Du Cange, s.v. 'communia').

89 Heeren, 206; Eichhorn, II, 605; Robertson, II, 204. That almost universal right of cities was taken long before it was granted.

90 Sismondi, II, 245.

91 Tournaments were the favourite entertainments of the nobility. Nuremberg banned any of its burghers from jousting within or outside the city.

92 Cf. J. von Müller, *Schweizer Geschichte* (vol. 4, ch. 2) on the revolution in Zurich, which gave the guilds there a majority in the administration.

93 Hume, *History of England, ch, XII.*

94 Mezeray, *Abrégé chronologique de l'histoire de France*, II, 119.

95 Cf. Robertson, introduction and book 3.

96 The old Swedish nobility was not, as in the rest of Europe, largely of feudal origin but was mostly a royal nobility, closely related to the ruling dynasties. That gave it the great power and renown that it had, even before all privileges.

97 Thus the so-called "ecclesiastical men" or "serfs of the house of God" (Gotteshausleute) had a higher weregild and could answer for themselves in court (Potgiesser, *De statu servorum*, Lemgo, 1736, 177). Such rights were then transferred to the *royal* serfs, while the kings followed the example of the church in encouraging manumission. That the hereditary royal court servants *(ministeriales)* were originally in a condition analogous to serfdom is shown by the fact that it could only be

terminated by *emancipation* (Eichhorn, II, 904). Yet from those ministerial posts there emerged the highest offices in the state, such as that of the chief minister (*drots, Truchsess* – originally the one who brought dishes to the king's table, the *dapifer*), the *marshal*, originally the master of the stable) etc. – In Alemannic law the steward (seneschallus) and marshal, those in charge of swine and sheep, the cook and goldsmith were of equal status, their positions also being military.

98 Among the Romans a slave was called *mancipium* (*manu captus* – a prisoner of war). Among the Germanic nations the word 'slave' was derived from the ethnic name of the Slavic peoples, arising during the protracted wars against them in eastern and northern Germany. "Träl" as used for slaves in Scandinavia is probably similar to "troll".

99 Thus the Livonian serfdom was far harsher than that in Russia itself, as the former was based on conquest by Germans, who enslaved the natives.

100 This is the moral aspect of finance, which has not yet found its Adam Smith. The only known preparatory work on that higher national economy is found in the writings of the brilliant Adam Müller. – What is the abovementioned public spirit but the most perfect reciprocal trust? It reveals itself in *credit* and, for society as a whole, as *national credit*, as bills of exchange based on the national character, order, industriousness and patriotism. Without those guarantees, that of the metals would not prevent the monetary system from becoming a social cancer.

101 In conversation with an Austrian envoy on 10 March
     1813, after his return to Paris from Russia, Napoleon
     said: "In the eyes of their sovereigns people are mere
     abstractions, which they use to solve important political
     problems," explaining the metaphysical expression by
     an image: "They are often in his eyes nothing but frogs
     (des grenouilles)."

102 Due to this principle the increased activity of the *royal*
     courts of justice, by providing a more certain and
     quicker justice, became a very important means of
     extending royal authority, especially in France.

103 "You told me that there are no *hofmän* in Sweden," said
     king Christian II to Thure Jönsson during the invasion
     of Sweden in 1532 as he saw the Swedish cavalry
     approaching, "What then are these, whom I see; are
     they perhaps women?" (Tegel, I, 301).

104 One recalls the so-called 'knight service' in Sweden.

105 Hüllmann, *Historische und staatswissenschaftliche
     Untersuchungen über die Natural-Dienste der
     Gutsunterthanen nach fränkisch-deutscher Verfassung,
     und die Verwandlung derselben in Geld-Dienste* (Berlin,
     1803). *Tallia*, taille, generally denoted all extraordinary
     imposts, apart from the personal ones. The word
     comes from 'cut' *(tailler)* and refers to the tally (talea)
     on which the account was incised, after which the tally
     was split and each party kept one half of it. Du Cange
     (s.v. 'tallia') mentions four instancs, but there were
     others, either obligatory or voluntary. Related words in
     English are *toll* (customs duties) and *stocks* (interest on
     public loans).

106 "Louis VIII regarded all cities in which there were
     communes as his" (Du Cange, s.v. 'communia').

107 It is remarkable that the decay not only of the
republican spirit but also earlier of the feudal system
had nonetheless begun to show itself in *hired fighters*.
Since commerce had from the beginning of the 12th
century made money more common, higher-ranking
knights, counts and princes had been willing to go to
war in return for payment in place of others – kings
or their own equals (Hüllmann, *Geschichte des Urprungs
der Stände in Deutschland*, II, 240). The fief here was
a standing loan, the interest paid by the borrower
through war service.

108 In Augsburg the art of casting and using firearms was
a secret within a particular guild and three cannon
with an immense calibre are said to have been cast
there as early as 1378. In 1377 firearms began to be
used in Lubeck. Soon almost every city had its own
gun-founders, producing cannon from which initially
balls of stone were fired. The invention of smaller
guns, pistols and muskets came at the end of the
14th century. Handguns were militarily significant in
the Franco-Italian wars at the beginning of the 16th
century. Stockholm already had canon and gunpowder
and a salaried master of ordnance and gun-founder in
1431 (Muhrberg, *Vitterhets Academiens handlingar*, pt 4).

109 Sismondi, IV, 335. Compare Gibbon for that period.

110 Cf. Henault, *Abrégé*, I, 129.

111 "A gathering of mercenaries from almost every nation
under heaven," says an old chronicler (Schiphower,
Oldenburg chronicle, in Menken, *Scriptores rerum
germanicarum*, II, 189). "Ravagers, the impious hands
of men, for nothing was held sacred" (Alb. Krantius,
Saxon laws, 13, ch. 23; Vandal laws, 14, ch. 27).

297

112 Cf. Krause, *Geschichte des heutigen Europa*, I, 153, 372;
Dalin, *Svea rikes historia*, II, 832.

113 Müller, *Schweizer Geschichte*, IV. 53.

114 See Müller, *op. cit., 124.*

115 Charles VII's companies of orderlies numbered 9,000
mounted men, the free aerchers 16,000 foot. Louis
increased the standing cavalry to 15,000, the infantry
to 25,000 (Remer, note on Robertson), but Duclos
states that Louis left an army of 60,000 men (*Histoire
de Louis XI*, II, 423). The expenditure rose from
1,800,000 to 3,700,000 livres.

116 See the content of the first subsidy treaty between
France and Switzerland in 1474 in Duclos (*op. cit.,* 124).
The Swiss, apart from the annual subsidies, stipulated
a certain sum for each soldier (four and a half Rhenish
florins a month).

117 Hüllmann, *Deutsche Finanz-Geschichte des Mittelalters*
(Berlin, 1805), 40.

118 When Charles VII borrowed 100,000 ducats from
the Genoese for his Italian campaign in 1495, he had
to pay them 14,000 ducats for 4 months in interest
(Remer, *Handbuch der mittleren Geschichte,* 529). During
the same period, however, the Venetians could borrow
any sums whatever at 5 per cent – proof that the credit
of the kings was not the best.

119 When the political society is in its *essence* corrupted,
the revived religion has a generally *destructive* influence
on the whole of that corrupted social order, which
will only thereby make room for a healthier one. Thus
Christianity was undoubtedly a principal cause of
the destruction of the Roman empire and the ancient
world rather than the barbarians. That explains the

hostile view of Christianity among historians, both ancient and modern (Gibbon), who cling to the name of Rome, as if its mere name could make amends for the misery extended to such a large proportion of humanity. For what was even the epoch of the Antonines but an unsecured truce of tyranny?

120 "*L'état c'est moi*" (Louis XIV, Napoleon); the Spanish "*Yo el rey*" (I, the king). – The thought expressed is simply the old monarchical one, for as long as monarchs have existed. Everything depends on the sense.

121 Even Charles V therefore did his utmost, using all possible means, in order to settle the religious conflict by some middle way and conciliation.

122 The sincere confession before Christendom of the honest Hadrian VI regarding the corruption and failings of the Roman curia undoubtedly damaged papal authority as much as, if not more than, the vices of the preceding and subsequent popes, which is even admitted by papal historians (Pallavicini, *Historia Concilii Tridentini*, II, 7).

123 Hugo Grotius, born 10 April 1583 in Delft. Practising lawyer before the age of 17. Maurice of Orange used the strictly Calvinist or Gomerist party against the Arminians, who were protected by Barneveld, to bring his old benefactor to the scaffold on 13 May 1619. Grotius became involved in his fall and was condemned on 18 May that year to life imprisonment, fled to France, returned after several years to the Netherlands, had to flee again, entered Swedish service in 1634 and was for almost 11 years the Swedish envoy in Paris, was recalled due to a court intrigue in

Stockholm and died on the journey from there on 28 August 1645 at Rostock. His book *De jure belli ac pacis* was published in Paris in 1625.

124 Seven editions within 20 years. The most renowned translator, Barbeyrac, notes in his preface that 50 years after the author's death his work was published *"cum notis variorum'* (by Becman, 1691), an honour usually accorded only to ancient classical authors.

125 Barbeyrac, *op. cit.* However, at first Grotius' work was banned in Rome in 1627 (Bayle). Gustavus Adolphus constantly carried it with him (Archenholtz, Mémoires de Christine, I, 6).

126 Cf. *De jure belli ac pacis,* Prolegomena.

127 "I saw across the Christian world or among barbarian peoples the repugnant arbitrariness of war, the resort to arms for frivolous or no reasons, and having once taken them up, no reverence either for divine or human law, plainly as if seized with a madness caused by the issuing of a single edict for every crime" *(ibid.).*

128 To that party the great French jurists generally belonged during this period. Jurisprudence is a republican science.

129 Jansenius, bishop of Ypres (1585-1681). His book *Augustinus,* in which he defended the concept of grace of that church father and drew closer to protestant doctrine, was only published after his death.

130 The whole of Rousseau' political theory, which gained such an exceptional influence in France, is not only that of the thinker but of the citizen of Geneva.

131 The cruellest war fought in modern times, because unscrupulous court intrigues and the interests of political factions mingled with the fury of the militant

religious zeal, here more than anywhere else in the world. The reigns of Francis II, Charles XI, Henry III – or in place of all of them that of Catherine de Medicis – what regimes!

132 F. Schlegel, *Ueber die neuere Geschichte.*

133 What first separated conformists and non-conformists, the supporters of the episcopal church and the puritans, was not even the episcopal hierarchy; it was the episcopal vestments. Furthermore, all symbolic practices in the service, such as making the sign of the cross or kneeling, were a target for the most profound abhorrence of the puritans. Some puritan members of the parliament of 1571 complained that such gross abuses were questions that touched on salvation, against which crowns, kingdoms or even universal rule were mere trifles (Hume, *History of England*). To such things did a party difference initially attach itself, which would later have such important consequences for the state.

134 When such expressions caused too much offence, he also used to distinguish between a king in *abstracto* and a king in *concreto*, the former absolute, the latter bound by the laws of the land. ('King James's works', cited by Hume, *op. cit.*).

135 "Gentlemen," he said to the nobles, "in London you are like ships on the open sea, which look like nothing. In the country on your estates you are like ships on a river, which look like great things" (Hume, *op. cit.*).

136 "Samuel," said Knox to Mary," feared not to slay Agag, the fat king of the Amaleklites, whom Saul had saved; nor did Elias spare the false prophets and Baal priests of Jezebel," which is what Knox used to call Mary

herself, "although king Ahab was present ... And thus Your Grace may see that others than high officials may lawfully impose punishments for such crimes as are forbidden in the law of God" (Hume, *op. cit.*, under 1561). How different was the doctrine of Luther: "you shall not accomplish it with violence and force." – "Power shall be broken by none but the one who has established it." The least known aspect of Luther's character was his deep abhorrence of all *violence* as such.

137 Jacob Arminius or Herrman, born 1560. Professor of theology in Leiden, d. 1609. His milder doctrine on grace was condemned at the synod of Dordrecht in 1618-19. From that time the Arminians in the reformed church were separatists. They distinguished themselves by their tolerance.

138 All these are propositions presented by the lawyer Prynne in his book *Histrio-mastix*, in which he bitterly attacked the high church. He was held in high regard by the puritans but was condemned to the stocks and to have his ears cut off in 1633 (Hume).

139 Bishop of London, then archbishop of Canterbury, decapitated in 1645.

140 Hume, *op. cit.* Parliament then banned all entertainments on Sundays and had the king's decree regarding them burned by the executioner. Christmas was turned from a festival of joy into one of penance and fasting. A strict ordinance appeared against may-poles.

141 Hume, referring to 1629.

142 House preachers were appointed to spy on the master
and mistress. Servants were used for the same purpose
by the clergy. In Scotland Hume describes an event in
1651 when a synod of churchmen in Perth summoned
the population, which had expressed dissatisfaction
with their spiritual rule. The men being absent, 120
women turned up armed with cudgels, half of whom
entered the church, beat up the clergymen and put
them to flight. A dozen of the refugees gathered some
miles away and voted that the town should be cursed
and no women in future be counted among *the godly*.

143 A single English artilleryman stayed on board the ships
that arrived at Dieppe when it became known that
they would be used against La Rochelle. All of England
then rejoiced at the news that the man had been shot
during the siege.

144 Charles II demanded 200,000 pounds sterling as the
price for officially changing his religion. Louis would
only pay 150,000, but a treaty was signed on 1 January
1678 which included provisions for partitioneing
the Netherland and Louis' promise to assist Charles
against parliament (Flassan, *Histoire générale et raisonée
de la diplomatie française,* with summaries in German
by Benzel-Sternau, I, 421). Louis also promised him a
pension of 100,000 pounds in a secret treaty of 1673.
His ministry (the cabal) was also in receipt of French
bribes. One of history's most infamous princes.

145 The Spanish envoy Ronquillo warned the king not to
listen too much to the advice of his catholic priests.
James nonetheless appointed his confessor, a Jesuit, as
privy counsellor.

146 Mary, married to William III, Anne to prince George
of Denmark, both brought up as protestants. His
brother-in-law George secretly went to the camp of the
prince of Orange and Anne likewise left London before
the crisis.

147 The court party accused their opponents of an affinity
with the religious fanatics in Scotland known as *Whigs*.
The country party saw a resemblance between the
hierarchical court party and the catholic outlaws in
Ireland who were called *Tories*. Both were originally
terms of abuse.

148 The doctrines of passive obedience (non-resistance)
and resistance with regard to the limits of royal
authority were from the 1670's onward often the
subject of the most lively debates in parliament.
Even the *coffee houses* became so important due to the
political disputes that Charles banned them in 1675.

149 'Patriarcha, or the natural power of kings' forms part
of the *Political discourses* (London, 1682) of Robert
Filmer. The summary of his and Sidney's principles is
based on Heeren, *Ueber die Entstehung, die Ausbildung
und den praktischen Einfluss der politischen Theorien in
dem neuesten Europa* (Kleine historische Schriften,
Göttingen, 1805).

150 Algernon Sidney, son of the earl of Leicester, was born
in 1622, from his youth an enthusiastic worshipper
of freedom, took part in the civil war against Charles
I, fearlessly opposed the usurpation of Cromwell,
emigrated at the restoration, returned in 1677, was
accused of planning an insurrection and participating
in the so-called Rye House plot in 1683. Nothing could
be proved, but his *Discourses on government* were found

among his papers and he was condemned to death
for high treason and was executed. During the reign
of William III the judgement was overturned and
Sidney's writings appeared in print.

151 Thomas Hobbes, born in 1588, Charles II's teacher
when the prince was in exile in France. His book *De
cive* was written in Paris and published in 1642. His
Leviathan, sive de materia, forma et potestate civitatis
(1651) expands on the same subject. – John Locke, so
renowned in the history of philosophy, was born in
1632, studied medicine, spent part of his life outside
England, especially in the Netherlands, where he
wrote his famous work on human reason; returned ti
England with William III in 1688, published his *Two
treatises on government* the following year and drew
his countrymen's attention to the national economy
by his *Considerations of the consequences of lowering the
interest and raising the value of money*; was one of the
Commissioners of Trade from 1695 to 1700, when he
retired due to ill health; died 28 October 1704 ('Life of
John Locke', prefaced to his collected works, London,
1777).

152 Empiricism in this form is simply inverted abstraction.
A false philosophy is always the one that has lost the
idea of the living unity that connects *concept* and *thing*,
the inner with the external. That can reveal itself in
two ways, either dogmatically, when one wishes to
derive the thing from the empty formal concept, or
empirically, when one allows the multiplicity of things
to create the concept. The correct theory is the same

as the correct empirical procedure and they are both in accord in seeing and following the living idea in reality itself.

153 Hobbes combined in the highest power not only the legislative and judicial power but also the power to determine what shall generally be regarded as right and wrong by the subjects, thus also an absolute power over opinions (ch. VI, § 16). – At least Hobbes does not separate *ethics* and *politics* but, on the contrary, asserts *the unity of the two*, although that unity in his system cannot be achieved without the destruction of the former, or ethics.

3. Reflections on the Establishment of the European Colonial Dominions

1819

To what power, to what immense influence over the peoples of the earth has not this little Europe, by no means richly endowed by nature, ascended! To *such* a global dominion history has nothing even remotely comparable to offer. Europe closed in upon itself, still largely unknown to itself; Europe embracing the earth and the oceans by force of arms, colonies, trade and civilisation: see there the contrasting spectacles presented by the 15th and 18th centuries! – And it was *the discovery of the Indies* that initiated that great course of events. What a transformation within three centuries! And yet, however great and significant that *past* era may appear, what is it compared to the *future* one, which is already emerging from it, partly in reality and partly in the imagination! How significant is not *the freedom of America*! A youthful future may never have presented itself to the view of mankind with a more extensive prospect. At the expense of Europe, it will be said. We doubt that. But one has to admit that this freedom – even if its fruits may ripen slowly – is the greatest triumph that European civilisation has yet achieved. For all civilisation is that of freedom – and whoever would dominate the world by force should begin by banishing all sciences, all arts; for every one of them contains the divine spark of freedom.

We have called that power of Europe a global dominion, and the remark just made already suffices to define its true nature. It would be able to justify the name even if one looks only at the extent of European conquests and possessions on other continents. Rome ascribed to itself dominion over the world for something infinitely smaller. But the distinguishing aspect is that this dominion – not established exclusively by a single state but by several competing ones – owes its origin as much to the arts of *peace* as of *war*; indeed, its chief means has been a steadily expanding active intercourse between all the peoples of the world, engendered by *trade*. The role of Europe as a go-between in this great world context, gained and sustained by its cultural superiority, is what we really mean by the dominion or, if preferable, the European *hegemony* to which we just referred. Whatever means may have been or are still used to maintain that superiority, in so far as it is itself based on the power of a higher civilisation and endures thanks to that, it must eventually in that regard introduce the relationship of *mutuality* in which freedom alone exists. Europe will by the very nature of its dominion eventually put its own superiority at stake but at the same time also awaken within itself and others the incalculable abundance of energies which an unrestricted *free competition* among the nations of the earth will release. – And that is the future on the threshold of which we already stand. The chance of seeing at least a ray of that dawning world morning illuminate our subject is the reason why we have at once gazed up towards it. In its time success will seem more pleasing and even the misfortunes more bearable, as they are sacrifices for such a great purpose.

One cannot return often enough to the amazing era that forms the beginning of modern history. Discoveries have been made subsequently, in themselves no less important than those that then introduced a new order of things, but they have occurred along already beaten tracks and in a context of endeavours in which one feels plausibly able to infer the later developments from the earlier ones, the greater from the lesser. The inventions of the 15th century, on the other hand, in their immense consequences, relate so little to the obscure, relatively insignificant circumstances out of which they evolved, at once removing the veil from so much that was astonishing and unknown until then, that their novelty never wears off for the observer and in particular reminds us of the intuitive presentiment of the secrets of nature that is the singular attribute of the genius. That is what constitutes their eternal youthfulness, however old the world becomes, their imperishably fresh appeal to the imagination. That applies above all to the discovery of America. Whose mind has not been stirred by the account of the voyage of Columbus, after which the ocean was no longer a barrier for mankind! – even by the very enterprise of sailing across an open, previously unknown sea, the most audacious voyage that had been undertaken within the memory of man. For if the Portuguese finally found the way around the tip of Africa to the East Indies, it was only because they extended further than all others that coasting trade to which all navigation had previously been restricted, and once they had arrived on the eastern coast of Africa they only needed to follow an already existing commercial route across a sea easily navigated by means of the trade winds to a specific and at least in general terms already known goal. Columbus was the first to sail across the ocean, and what was *his* goal? Where was the new Indian world that he sought? That had remained in his imagination for eighteen years before he set eyes on it: eighteen years, devoted with an incomparable perseverance to vain attempts, first in one state, then in another, simply to find someone willing to venture the very modest expense of the attempt, until the good humour of a Spanish queen in the moment after a victory grants the three small ships with which Columbus discovered a new world for Spain. Later, too, indifference, unresponsiveness and at times persecution replaced the initial enthusiasm, although the entire life of the discoverer from that day onward was a sequence of great achievements and incredible hardships. – What an unhappy fate so often awaits those who by the power within themselves are called upon to effect one of those great changes on which the future of millions will depend for better or worse! Their place is too elevated for the tranquillity of an ordinary fate. – Columbus died[1] with a heart broken by ingratitude and sorrow and wished to have placed in his tomb the chains in which he was once removed to Spain from the new world that he had discovered for its monarchs. For a long time the ever-expanding discoveries in America then continued to be treated with some indifference by the government. It was always individual men, warlike adventurers, with almost superhuman courage and renowned for exploits that one cannot help but admire while deploring the cruelties that so often accompanied them, who subjugated to Spain the richest countries in the world. Cortez and Pizarro conquered two empires for Charles V with a handful of people, while Charles exhausted the strength of the greatest European monarchy in the unremarkable wars with Francis I. With less power, the Portuguese, not diverted by involvement in the affairs of the rest of Europe, showed greater consistency and calculation in the discoveries that eventually led them around the coasts of Africa to India and there established their dominion. But what would even excellent kings such as Emanuel (1495-1521) have achieved without the national spirit, animated by the splendid new prospects, that now created Portugal's brief but so illustrious heroic age – without men such as Vasco da Gama, an Almeida and the great Albuquerque, to whom such unlimited power had to be entrusted in the distant regions that were the scene of their exploits that it often enough became the object of the suspicions and apprehension of the government. "Down into the grave, unhappy old man!" said Alfonzo Albuquerque when he was informed on his deathbed of his dismissal and the disfavour of king Emanuel. He wrote to his monarch without complaining and commended his son to him. "Of India I say nothing," he concluded, "it will speak both for itself and for me." – He was the real founder of the Portuguese empire. Under his successors and during the subsequent era of a soon corrupted power one often saw the unfortunate Hindustanis making sacrifices on his grave and imploring the shade of the great Albuquerque for protection against the violence to which they were subjected.[2] In short, if one considers the way in which the initial possessions in the two Indies were acquired, they were less the outcome of any deliberate plan than of an elevated and audacious spirit of adventure which, when it had begun to disappear in the rest of Europe following the decline of chivalry and the emergence of civic order, was still active among the nations of the Pyrenean peninsula, acquired a new sphere of activity through the great discoveries and played its final role on the oceans and in the Indies. For that reason one finds in those distant exploits the same noble-mindedness and cruelty, the same unselfishness and rapacity, above all the same splendid, invincible courage that alternately arouses our admiration and abhorrence in considering the heroes, feats of arms and customs of the age of chivalry. For that reason they were also so congenial to poetry, and they have been celebrated in verse, as the power of imagination was already an original element in them and found new nourishment among wonderful scenes in distant climes. Ercilla wrote his heroic poem *La Auracana*[3] in the wilderness at the foot of the Cordilleras, during wars with savage tribes or on voyages on distant seas. The greatest among Portugal's poets and one of the noblest that European literature has to show, Camoens, went to the East Indies as a soldier (1550) and celebrated in verse his great compatriot Vasco da Gama, the discovery of India and the glory of his fatherland on the very same shores that had witnessed the exploits that he glorified. And if the poetry of Spain and Portugal in general has a certain alien charm, which distinguishes it from that of its sisters, it is also partly because it carries the reflection of the sun, the colours and the marvels of the Indies. – Portuguese and Spaniards have performed the heroic poetry of the European colonial system. The prose began with the Dutchman and the Englishman. – To the former trade itself was not yet the only or the chief purpose. They

312

fought for the church, now in distant parts of the world, as formerly within their own country against the Moors. On the conversion of the heathen both of them based that right to the newly discovered lands that they requested and obtained from the pope.

The famous papal dividing line (1,000 kilometres west of the islands of the Azores) separated them[4] from each other. – The ignorance that here by the stroke of a pen partitioned the world did not conceive of the further possibility of a *westerly* route to the East Indies; but with the newly opened navigation the discoveries and the claims made such enormous strides that disputes concerning faraway Indian islands – the Moluccas – could soon become the subject of a special treaty[5] between Portugal and Spain (1529), having already brought about the first circumnavigation of the globe by Magellan (1519-1522). – Within barely more than half a century after the first great discoveries the trade and influence of the Portuguese extended by way of Hormuz and Muscat over Arabia (where several petty princes were obliged to pay tribute to them) – over Persia, Egypt and Abyssinia (with whose Christian ruler they were in contact) – from Malacca (which, like Hormuz and Muscat, was conquered by the great Albuquerque) by way of a chain of trading posts and possessions over the islands of Sunda and the Moluccas, over a large part of the eastern Indian peninsula to China, where they subsequently acquired Macao, and even to the distant Japan, where their power became significant enough to imprudently provoke a great internal revolution in the next century, which simultaneously expelled both themselves and the Christian faith that they had introduced.[6] From the seat of the Portuguese viceroy in Goa Portugal's influence extended across the whole of western India, where the Malabar coast together with part of Coromandel and Ceylon were subject to them. On the eastern coast of Africa they controlled Mozambique, the gold-rich Sofala and Malindi, on the western one (apart from the possessions in Guinea) Congo and Angola (from 1578), in America Brazil. And at the same time as that great empire was rapidly brought to its peak the Spaniards had already laid the extensive foundations of their immense power in the new world, which matured more slowly but all the more solidly, by the conquest of Mexico, Peru and Chile, by the occupation of Terra Firma, New Granada and the West Indian islands; and by taking possession of the Philippines, which was the outcome of the first circumnavigation of the world, they had already become neighbours of the Portuguese in the East Indian seas. The founding of the European colonial system by the Portuguese and the Spaniards at the same time already established the main difference within it, a difference that has been constantly maintained since then.

Colonies, according to their nature, are either *agricultural* and *mining* colonies, necessarily associated with taking possession of the land itself by colonisers from the mother country, who engage in actual production, or else *trading colonies*, the purpose of which is the exchange and acquisition of products of nature or craftsmanship that have already been produced, which necessarily implies an already existing culture in the foreign country, for which reason those colonies, though generally based on conquest, provide less scope for settlers. – A third kind of colonies, the so-called *plantation colonies*, which, though their purpose is to cultivate natural crops, are in their whole nature an *artificial product* of trade and thus in a peculiar manner combine in themselves the characteristics of the two preceding ones, constitute a class of their own. They do not belong to the beginnings of the colonial system but constitute the luxury end of it. – The difference referred to was naturally determined by the varying nature of the countries discovered to the east and the west. In the East Indies the Portuguese found an already ancient culture, the institutions of which have with a marvellous firmness withstood the storms of numerous foreign conquests until our era. They had to content themselves with bringing certain important localities under their control, in order to hold the natives in check from there by their superiority in courage, shrewdness and weaponry and under the protection of that power in an all the more advantageous manner to acquire the treasures of India, so abundant in crafts and products. Even where no significant older culture opposed their progress, as on some of the islands and in Africa, they nevertheless confronted aggressive nations experienced in warfare, which by their great natural strength and ability, in which the peoples of the old world seemed to surpass the natives of America, associated any more extensive occupation of the land itself with almost insuperable difficulties. They everywhere remained *visitors*, and even if as such they might be overlords, they had no firmly established dominion. – The situation in America was quite different. Despite the dazzling accounts that the first conquerors disseminated about the culture and power of Mexico and Peru, the conquests themselves and their consequences are sufficient to modify those panegyrics to a considerable extent. Powerful civilised states are not overthrown by a handful of military adventurers, even if they included such a great man as Cortez. Nations that have drunk from the vital source of civilisation do not virtually disappear from the earth as a result of external violence. Let us concede that Mexico and Peru – the former a military, the latter a hieratic state, both founded by strangers, of unknown origin but possibly of an originally Asiatic derivation – let us concede that those countries far surpassed in culture the other natives of America, who were either savage hunting peoples, having not even raised themselves by *cattle herding* – which in the old world everywhere accompanies the nomadic life – to the first level above the lowest and most uncertain of all human conditions, or else, if they were not entirely ignorant of agriculture, as in the tropical regions of America, where the incredible lushness of the vegetation so superabundantly rewards even the humblest worker, in many other regards nonetheless approached utter savagery; if in making such a comparison we concede that Mexico's *pyramids*, Peru's *royal highways*, the greatest monuments of the new world, provide reasonable evidence of an ancient culture, constituting a remarkable exception to the otherwise general backwardness, yet we find lacking even among the foremost nations of America the most distinctive tokens and means of civilisation, which are extremely ancient on the old continent. – They knew no true form of *writing*. The Mexican hieroglyphs are merely a crude pictorial script, used to assist memory, and that practice was not here, as among the Egyptians, followed by knowledge of phonetic writing. The only annals of the Peruvians were knots on leather straps (quipos). – They did not know, or at least only in a very limited sense, the use of a *currency*,[7] which is otherwise everywhere the surest sign of a civic society. –

316

They were, finally, ignorant of *iron*, although that most powerful of metals in the hands of humanity existed in sufficient quantities in the same mountains, perhaps the richest in ore on earth, which gave them, without the need for technology, that gold and silver of which the abundance became so damaging both to themselves and to their first conquerors. The childhood tales of the false power of *the prince of this world*, which especially through the magical lustre and strange allure of the precious metals entices people to perdition and deprives them of life and salvation, can never appear more vividly to our imagination than in the narrative of the earliest fortunes of the Europeans in the new world. The thirst for gold took possession of their minds with a kind of delirium and debased even to inhumanity the lofty spirit that otherwise revealed itself as active in so many remarkable exploits. – "Gold," wrote the great Columbus himself in his last letter to king Ferdinand[8] – "gold, Your Majesty, is the noblest of all metals. He who possesses it can achieve whatever he wishes in this world, indeed convey souls to Paradise." – Those utterances by a profoundly unhappy man, who tried to emphasise the importance of his long unappreciated discovery by appealing to one of the most terrible human passions, have a peculiar resonance; and if one bears in mind his own grim predicament when he wrote them down,[9] shipwrecked among savages on an unfamiliar island, where the most inhuman envy left him to languish for over a year combatting revolts among his own men, attacks by barbarians and every conceivable distress, then that tableau of misery may be regarded as an omen of the misfortunes that afflicted those whom the thirst for gold subsequently drove to follow in his footsteps and made

317

the masters of the new world. Cortez died unrewarded and neglected, Almagro and Pizarro, the vanquishers of Peru, fell in mutual conflict. Nor did the fate that thus befell the leading men spare the mass of the so-called *conquistadores* (conquerors), whose descendants right down to this latest era in Spanish America formed a particular kind of nobility, though more hated than respected, for the memories that it evokes, the collective condemnation of which attached itself to all, even to those who, in those times of a peculiar mixture of rapacity and enthusiasm, had not defiled themselves with any crimes. The majority sought after gold with a kind of frenzy that had no less damaging effects on them than on the unfortunate Indians. The treasures amassed in the initial plundering were soon exhausted. The mountains contained immense riches, but ignorance was not always fortunate enough to find them. By futile mining operations many destroyed all their wealth and condemned themselves to want and misery, as impoverished slaves of the barren metal, amidst the blessings of a luxuriant nature. If one considers in a general way the difficulties with which each and every settler must necessarily begin to strive, how all his efforts had to be directed towards providing for his primary needs in still uncertain circumstances, what would the consequences then not be of an exclusive focus on the precious metals, while neglecting agriculture? But that was initially the case with all the Spanish colonies in the new world. They were mining colonies before they also became agricultural colonies. The greatest burden of that naturally fell upon the natives, who *at the same time* had to work the soil and the mountains for their new masters. If one adds that they were neither generally numerous nor accustomed to labouring or naturally robust, one sees in outline an insupportably destructive situation, which explains the tremendous demographic losses that accompanied the initial colonisation by the Spaniards in the new world.

On the West Indian islands there were within a short time hardly any traces left of the original population. Mexico and Peru, more civilised, resisted more effectively, but even there the decline was so rapid that a few years after the conquest what had been narrated of the former prosperity of those countries seemed incredible. Nor did the victors themselves fail to become aware of those effects. The emigration from the mother country, at first so extensive, diminished so quickly that 60 years after their discovery a contemporary writer reckons that there were no more than 15,000 Spaniards in the new world.[10] But the government had now begun to show more active concern and the nature of the colonies was enough to ensure their permanence.

Thus the Spanish colonies survived that initial transformation which in other regions, no less well endowed by nature, caused the downfall of the Portuguese ones, I mean the inclination towards corruption that is so often brought about by the rapid acquisition of great wealth. Portuguese power in India was not one born of the soil which, like the giant in the fable, could derive new strength from it after a defeat. Its stage was set amidst civilised, wealthy nations, in countries that, due to the precious stones, pearls, spices and silk, in a word almost everything that the human desire for splendour and pleasure most strongly craves, had from time immemorial attracted conquerors and corrupted them by luxurious living. The heroic age of Portugal, as glorious as it was brief, soon came to an end, in which

319

the arrogance bred by the treasures of the East was not the least contributory factor. In India the name of the Portuguese, formerly so feared, became an object of detestation for the peoples as a result of oppression and excesses of every kind. Soon India cost more than it yielded, and when the mother country fell under the sceptre of Spain (1580) that hastened the downfall of a power in the colonies that was already in itself tottering. Only Brazil, as it was not a mere trading colony, would in the future become a possession of great importance.

If the Spanish monarchs contributed little to the first great discoveries and conquests, no government has on the other hand devoted to its colonies, once they had been acquired, a greater concern, if not always in its effects a happy one, than the Spanish. One will find no laws in which greater solicitude appears for the preservation, security and prosperity of the peoples than in the Spanish laws on the administration of the Indies.[11] That was already organised by the ordinances of Charles V (from the year 1542), which forbade the enslavement of the natives. Of all the new conquests the king was regarded as the autocratic ruler and sole proprietor, so that all power emanated from him alone, not only in secular but, under a special papal bull (of Julius II), also in spiritual matters. As a result, all the institutions of the catholic church were transferred to the colonies. That hierarchy may have subsequently had many deleterious effects; what is certain is that we have generally most unjustly blamed the zeal of the Spanish clergy for the violence inflicted on the Indians. – According to the most reliable information, the case is the very opposite.[12] The clergy were those who first took up the case of that unhappy oppressed people, refuted the

degrading notions that covetousness sought to dissemi-
nate about them, procured for them rights under the law
and became the guardians of those rights. The Indians in
Spanish America still regard the clergy as their natural
protectors, and the law itself has recognised them in that
honourable capacity, as one of the ordinances of Charles
V already specifically enjoins on every priest to take care
that the native is not enslaved or oppressed. The highest
secular authority lay with the Spanish viceroys. The power of those officials naturally had to be rather extensive.
It was counterbalanced on the one hand by the rights of
the clergy and on the other hand by the wise care with
which the administration of the law and the higher courts
(audiencias) were made independent of the viceroys. The
centre-point of the entire system was the great *Council
of the Indies* in Madrid, already established by Ferdinand
and elaborated by Charles V, an institution by which the
Spanish colonial policy acquired the homogeneity and stability that distinguished it. What other nation has for two
and a half centuries maintained such a distant rule over
the richest colonies in the world? We by no means approve
of all the measures by which that has been achieved. However – what a spectacle did Spanish America not provide
for the most famous traveller of recent times! In the interior of the country and by the large cities on the coasts,
brought into existence by profitable mines, commerce and
centres of government – public works and structures that
rivalled the greatest European ones – a regular postal service across the vast expanse of all the colonies – flourishing fields, sometimes reminiscent of the most advanced
cultivation in Germany and France – in Lima, in the imperial city of Mexico, which Humboldt found to exceed in

beauty and splendour the most famous capitals of Europe, scientific institutions of every kind and of great excellence – often capable and enlightened officials – everywhere a good-hearted people, the Indian protected, the Negro treated more humanely than anywhere else in the world – all the *degrees* of culture, the missions, its outposts in the interior of the forests of the undeveloped lands, then following them across the fertile savannahs, the agriculture and cattle farming of the ever-advancing settlers, finally the intensive cultivation in the coastal regions engendered by towns and trade[13] – all the climate zones combined under the brilliance of a tropical sky along the rising peaks of the Cordilleras – prodigious vegetation, a majestic nature, the greatest abundance of precious metals and a general superfluity of the most valuable products of nature! – And should one then generally and always with a Raynal wish to see only the traces of the blood and oppression of the initial conquest in these wonderful lands and not acknowledge the great handiwork of mankind that has quietly but mightily expanded and flourished there for centuries!

But in what then lies the cause of the defection of these same countries? – In that very same handiwork, we reply – in the nature of all colonies associated with genuine settlement and cultivation to mature at some point towards freedom. That the defection has been accompanied by bitterness towards the motherland is presumably a consequence of the nature of every *such* conflict but also has specific causes in the very distrustful and harsh overseas policy that Spain has always pursued in regard to its American dominions, in order to ensure their complete dependence on the motherland, a policy that can never succeed beyond a certain point. Hardly any state has kept its colonies in a stricter tutelage and with greater distrust deprived them of everything that could involve or give the impression of *political* rights, which are the ultimate and the highest goal that the nations seek. As a result, not only was *all foreign* influence excluded, whether it consisted of immigration (even that from the motherland was placed under strict supervision) or of trade, which was restricted to the motherland (and even that was controlled and subject to tight regulations), but in addition only European Spaniards could be appointed to government posts in Spanish America, and the caution went so far that the latter could not become domiciled in the colonies. The whole numerous class of Spaniards born in America, or the *Creoles*, was thereby entirely condemned to political impotence, and they would eventually, despite their natural insouciance, feel that exclusion all the more keenly, as they must continually experience the restrictions of Spain's excessively strict regulatory decrees in the only spheres of activity that remained to them, namely industry and trade.[14] – It is primarily that class which has carried out the revolution in Spanish America, encouraged to do so by its own strength and the condition of the motherland, and the outcome is no longer in doubt, although it is already apparent how wrong we have been to expect the same results here as those that are evolving from the liberty of the former English America. The differences are in every respect great, and a *single* difference, which we wish to point out (without referring to the many important ones relating to climate, origins, customs, belief and mind-set), is sufficient to have exerted an immense influence on the future destiny of Spanish America. The English colonies in North America, established among

323

savage hunting nations, did not wish to or could not incorporate the latter into their civilisation or, even if that
was attempted, it has had no effect. The wandering natives
were *forced out* and the greater part of the population of
the colonies came to be European, at least in the *northern*
states; for the *southern* ones have along with Negro slavery, which predominates there and is becoming ever more
oppressive, imposed on themselves all the hazards of a
black future. The Spaniards, on the other hand, establishing their empire in the wealthier, already previously more
civilised countries, have, ever since the time when Spanish America became the object of the government's concern, always *included* the natives in their colonial system,
the consequence of which have been that, alongside the
Indian, the Negro and the American Europeans, numerous *intermediate classes* have come into existence from their
mingling, which, given that these were also distinguished
by specific forms of civil status and professions, have created a real *division into castes*. Among these the dominant
one, that of the Creoles, who put themselves at the head
of the revolution, constitute a kind of aristocracy, elevated in their own and in general opinion above the others.
The common struggle against the Europeans may have
appeared to unite them, but whoever is aware of the deeply rooted difference that the mind-set and customs of the
new world establish between *white* people and the *coloured*
ones of every degree and of however distant ancestry,
whoever recollects that in republics (and all the states of
the new world become particular kinds of republics, due
not to an excess of republican virtues but to necessity, as
they lack heroic memories and history) the freedom of *one*
dominant group is for the others generally associated with

324

a far stricter subservience than is ever the case in monarchies, can scarcely doubt that those circumstances will in the future also become politically significant here, just as they have already shown themselves to be on the islands. The liberty of English America was achieved by a *single* revolution; that of Spanish America embraces *many*, the course and outcome of which no human mind can predict.

The reason for the long duration of the Spanish colonial empire lay in its nature and in the spirit of the initial legislation; the growing prosperity of the colonies, which gave them the courage to reach for the forbidden fruit of liberty, was chiefly derived from the more liberal principles for the relations both between themselves and with the mother country, by which the influence of the 18th century manifested itself even in Spain during the energetic regime of Charles III (1759-1788), distinguished by many wise ordinances, which had a beneficial effect on America. From as early as the elevation of the Bourbon dynasty to the throne, after the loss of the dependent territories in Europe, the American possessions acquired a greater importance for the mother country. The expanding activity of world trade exerted an ever-increasing influence on them, irrespective of the wishes of the government. But between that epoch and the founding of the Spanish colonial empire there extends a long interval of time that saw the growing powerlessness and decay of a formerly great name, at home and in America, from the reign of Philip II, despite the fact that by the conquest of Portugal he became the lord of *both* Indies, until the end of the house of Habsburg in Spain, fading away in debility, and that intermediate era is also the period during which

the other nations that are prominent in the history of the
European colonial system set out along the track that the
Portuguese and Spaniards had first opened up.

That remarkable change outside Europe again reminds
us of the reformation, which by the power and vitality that
it conveyed even shifted the weights on the great scales of
commerce in favour of those nations that developed new
powers in the era of the new liberty. The connections with
the rest of the world were already so close that an internal
change in the heart of Europe could be felt by its effects
in the most distant parts of the world. One could with
reason call the colonial system that now arose in the hands
of others a *protestant* one. Not merely because the struggle
in which it was acquired by the *Dutch* and the *English* was
simultaneously a struggle against catholicism and Spain,
being one in consequence of the other, and was conducted by the forces awakened by the reformation, but also
because the struggle began with an actual *protest* against
the claims by which Philip II intended to bind the lands
and the seas, as he would consciences by the bonds of the
church. That protest against the *exclusive* dominion over
the two Indies and their seas, so strictly maintained by
Spain, was pursued by the Dutch and the English with
the sword, as by the great Grotius with the pen.[15] And it
is with a peculiar feeling that one sees the same England
that now treats the ocean as a conquered province begin
its career as a naval power under Elizabeth with a protest
for the freedom of the seas. Thus fortune transforms nations as it does the individual, and to arouse loathing of
all arbitrary dominion even the observation would suffice
that whoever *possesses* power is already quite *different* from
the one who *acquired* it. – We remarked with reference to

the initial establishment of the European colonial system that it happened much less according to any plan of the governments than to the spirit of the nations that made the first great discoveries. Exactly the same applies to what we have now called the protestant colonial system. It was the same spirit that made the Dutchman free and that despite a thousand hazards brought him to India, the same spirit that in England resisted Philip's invincible armada and brought Walter Raleigh to North America, Francis Drake around the globe,[16] and that at a time when Dutch merchant ships fought their way through Spanish fleets – heroes created from merchants.[17] Thus we also find in this context an already familiar truth, namely that it is only by the energy of higher interests that inspire the peoples, that great events occur. Policy has *created* nothing. It is wise if it can bring order to things and sustain them. Of all the states that have played a more active part in the European colonial enterprise, *France* is the only really significant European state in which the government itself has desired to create colonies and trade without being supported in that endeavour by a real national trend. And what were the results? – reckoning from Law's system until the participation of France in the American war.

The new colonial system arose, we said, through a protest against Spain's exclusive claims; and why not compare that to protestantism in another respect as well, as the comparison offers itself spontaneously and is instructive? Among the Spaniards and Portuguese, who based their rights to the countries of which they had taken possession on a papal deed of gift to the monarchs for the propagation of Christianity, the entire colonial system subsequently remained in the truest sense *royal*. We have noted that with regard to Spanish America. The same applies to the Portuguese in the East Indies. All communication with India was conducted by royal fleets, and although the East Indian possessions, as trading colonies, really ought to be important, what profitable trade could a nation without industries of its own maintain in the long run? The result was an ever-expanding system of conquest and plunder in India, which enriched individuals but contained within itself the seeds of its own destruction and, as it diverted attention ever more from the exploitation of one's own resources through personal labour, impoverished the mother country instead of enriching it. The strict royal direction of colonial affairs had no less damaging effects on Spain. Industriousness cannot be prescribed. Philip II's literally lethal policy drove it out of Spain and made himself poor, in spite of all the silver and gold of America, which, as if by an inherent curse, continually disappeared without leaving any traces of themselves in a land without a productive economy, although even in the days of Charles V it had been among the richest in crafts and industriousness in Europe. The strictly monarchical maxims of the colonial system are reminiscent of the old church, on the basis of which they had developed. Among the protestants the demand for freedom in that regard became a consequence of the general freedom of thought that the reformation introduced, and that powerful sense of liberty survived and achieved great things as long as it *needed* to protest, as long as it was involved in a life-and-death struggle with the old coercion. Once it had succeeded in securing its position the circumstances changed, and we see in the secular sphere of trade a repetition of those phenomena that characterised the spiritual protestantism, which, when resistance to the old could not alone remain its guiding principle, and as no human affairs are compatible with an entirely unrestricted liberty, soon surrounded itself with a bulwark of dogmas and declined internally into *sects*. But the sects in the free realm of commerce are the *monopolising corporations*, and it is they, or the great privileged trading companies in the Netherlands and England – following the initial protest of the national spirit in those countries for the freedom of the seas and of trade – that chiefly denote the new form that the European colonial system now adopted. What it has become in that form is evidenced by the hundreds of millions of people who are now subject to English merchants in the East Indies. One could call that a monopoly that has outgrown itself and which will no doubt be transformed into *the freedom of world trade* – if Europe can maintain freedom within itself.

Notes

1   20 May 1506. The death of his protectress Isabella in 1504 made a deep impression on him. Ferdinand had never been favourably disposed towards him.

2   Albuquerque died in Goa on 16 Dec. 1515.

3   An epic poem in which he celebrates a war in which he himself took part against the Araucanians, a brave people in Chile, around 1556.

4   1493. The line of demarcation was moved by an agreement the following year to 3,700 kilometres west of those islands, which was confirmed by a new papal bull in 1506. Whatever lay to the east of that line was to belong to Portugal, the rest to Spain.

5 Charles V, though to the disapproval of the Spanish
nation, sold his claims to the Moluccan islands to
Portugal for 550,000 ducats.

6 The eradication of Christianity in Japan and the
expulsion of the Portuguese, 1639.

7 The Mexicans made use of cocoa beans as small
change.

8 Cf. Humboldt, *Voyage au nouveau continent*, vol. 2, p.
618.

9 This letter of Columbus, first published in 1810 in
Italy, was written during his fourth and last voyage
and is dated from Jamaica 7 July 1503. Having reached
the American mainland for the second time during
that voyage and discovered the isthmus of Panama, he
suffered shipwreck at the beginning of the year 1503
at Jamaica. Although he managed to send information
about his situation from there to the Spanish governor
Oviedo on San Domingo, the latter nevertheless failed
to help him until August 1504 and even mocked his
misfortune. On the quite incredible difficulties that
Columbus had to struggle with here, see Robertson,
History of America, pt I, p. 216 (Swedish translation).

10 Benzoni, cited by Robertson, pt IV, p. 206.

11 Robertson, *History of America*, pt IV, p. 127.

12 See Robertson.

13 Cf. Humboldt's description of Caracas, *Voyage au
nouveau continent*, ch. XIII.

14 Even those were only opened to them as a result of the
more liberal principles on the reciprocal trade between
the colonies as well as with the mother country that

have applied in Spain since the reign of Charles III and
had the most fortunate consequences for the prosperity
of the whole of Spanish America.

15 Hugo Grotius, *Mare liberum, sive de jure, quod Batavis
competit ad indicana commercia*. Leyden, 1618.

16 The discovery of Virginia in 1584. – The first English
circumnavigation of the world 1577-80.

17 In 1601 8 Dutch Indiamen fought their way through
a Spanish fleet of 30 ships sent out against them.
Geschichte der ostindischen Handlungs-Gesellschaften, in the
Allgemeine Weltgeschichte, vol. XXVI, p. 298.

4. On Slavery

Published in Post- och Inrikes
Tidningar 1845, nos. 16, 17.

I F INJUSTICE COULD be vindicated by tradition, slavery would have the oldest one on its side, for it has existed from time immemorial.

In the entire ancient pagan world there was not even a doubt as to its legitimacy, and slavery still finds its only excuse in *paganism*. For the really distinctive feature of paganism is that it knows only the worship of *power* in heaven and on earth. It is therefore quite appropriate to it that *might goes before right*, as in *nature*, which is the God of the pagans, multiple like the powers of the latter.

The God of the *moral* world has become known to mankind later than the divine power in nature. Only in that more elevated world is God the only God – superior to nature – himself the lord of nature. Human beings approach him and at the same time one another more closely.

The relationship of human beings to one another is essentially determined by their shared one to God. But the fact that God is the God of *all* human beings and not only the God of certain human beings; that all human beings are in that respect *equal* before him; that all justice between them is therefore *reciprocal* and is grounded in the *human personality* itself – that great truth was first revealed to mankind through *Christianity*. That only certain human beings possess rights but that the human being as such is without rights: that notion underlies the origin and long history of slavery – and it defines the still on-going conflict between paganism and Christianity.

That a *person can be owned by another person*, with a complete right of property, like a thing – that first principle of slavery originally arose from the old pagan household, in which the master of the house regarded himself as the owner of his wife, children and domestic servants. Property rights have generally been attached by the laws of the different nations to the family. But the family itself constituted the first property, and the right of the head of the household over it was absolute. When the first laws arose by agreement between the individually absolute heads of households, that at once gave rise to a separate class of masters, who acknowledged each other's rights. But the chief prerogative of the *free man* lay in his being acknowledged as the head of a family. The distinctive mark of the *unfree man* was that he could not legally own anyone. Even when laws had developed one therefore sees enough traces of the old absolute power of the head of the household. The Gauls boasted before Caesar that they were masters over the lives of their wives and children. In ancient Rome the father reserved the right to determine the life and death of his son throughout his lifetime. Among pagan peoples it depended, and still depends today, on the arbitrary will of the father whether he recognises his new-born child or allows it to be exposed to die, and only Christianity abolished that cruel iniquitous custom even among our ancestors. But generally speaking many children constituted a man's wealth. He therefore had several wives or, if only one, also concubines, brought into the household by abduction or purchase, like other property. That is the rea-

334

son why marriage still retains the form of *purchase* among so many nations. Even among the ancient Hebrews, the bride was purchased. In one case Moses determines the price (V Moses, ch. 22:29). It is equivalent to the highest one for a male slave (in fact a temple slave: III Moses, ch. 27:3). The Mosaic legislation is incidentally the most equitable with regard to slavery of all the ancient ones. It could not abolish it as long as it permitted *polygamy*, and as a consequence of that permission *domestic* slavery has likewise remained irremovable among the Muhammedans. Thus even the purer religions were encumbered with the heritage of paganism.

In some respects one may regard domestic slavery as the mildest form, and for that reason one still hears the most recent defenders of slavery exalt that inherently most violent of all conditions as a *patriarchal* institution. But domestic slavery proper did not remain the only form among the ancients. The number of slaves was increased not only due to the original nature of the pagan household but even more through *warfare* and *trade*. And even if among the slaves acquired in that way the one who personally attended on his master occasionally rose to a position of influence and power, the fate of the slave captured in war or purchased from far away was still generally harsher than that of the home-born one. But soon the latter was also reared to be sold. As both captured and traded slaves were found to be insufficient for the increasing demand for slave labour that accompanied the growth of pagan civilisation, one already sees in the Roman Empire (as now in the North American slave states) how internal slave-breeding for sale became a profitable branch of commerce. In the ancient Roman Empire the entire labouring mass eventually consisted of slaves or serfs.

Such was the world in which Christianity made its appearance with its doctrine: that *all* human beings were God's children, but that he, the all-powerful ruler and creator of heaven and earth, did not *want*, like the earthly head of a household, to rule over slaves; that he had sent his own son, the brother of mankind, to incline their hearts to him by the greatest of all proofs of love and to purify them in the fire of divine love; that they were all called to be citizens in a heavenly and blissful society; and that their exclusion from its bliss was so far a matter of personal decision that the rejection of it must also be a self-condemnation. – That was a doctrine that could turn the world upside down. But being itself incompatible with violence – for had it not taught that even God's own supreme power did not desire to be worshipped purely *as* power? – it had from the beginning renounced all violent means. Its way was that of persuasion, its weapon that of suffering. Thus it wished to draw the attention of humanity to the inner voice, by which God speaks to all individuals in their conscience.

It finally became the state religion in the Roman empire, thereby itself acquiring power, and the temptation to make use of it as such became too great. It became political in its actions and no less in its pronouncements. For it had to overlook much, and the necessity to do so increased when it came into contact with the northern peoples who were conquering southern Europe, whose leaders soon became politically Christian and had their soldiers baptised en masse. One consequence of that was that the slavery that was indigenous to the old pagan world by and large persisted and only changed to the extent that, due to the varying relationships of the victors to the defeated and to their own peoples, several kinds of both freedom and unfreedom arose. Slavery proper generally gave way to *serfdom*, which nonetheless, by custom or law, entailed certain rights, in particular for the agricultural serf, whereas the serf in the master's household was for better or worse more subject to the mere whims of the master and thereby in all of the old sense a slave.

The *church*, it is true, was a refuge for the slave, and it endeavoured to alleviate his fate. But he only became *free*, without the satisfaction of a free choice, by actually entering it as a priest or monk. In this and many other respects the church obtained freedom for *itself* and first made itself independent of secular society, which it ended up controlling during the Middle Ages. But in the struggle between spiritual and secular power civic freedom emerged between the two and encroached on the sphere of the church itself, when the reformation assailed and, in so far as it was victorious, abolished the previously accepted essential distinction between *priest* and *layman*.

It was a great step towards freedom in both a spiritual and secular sense, and the new Christian congregations (the protestant ones) thereby differed collectively from the old churches, founded more on tradition than on the word of God, which in that main regard are all in reality, if not in name, papist.

At the same time, however, slavery received new and extensive support. We have seen that it is essentially a part of paganism. The excuse of the latter was that it lacked the concept of the human personality. It was aware of the family, the kindred and the tribe and accepted those natural social bonds as valid. It neither perceived nor recognised any *human* relationships and provided no doctrine concerning them through the religions. For all the pagan mythologies, derived from the influence, or rather infantile compulsion, of the imagination, are in accord in regarding one's own people, if not solely then at least pre-eminently, as *human beings*. The others appear in them as monsters, giants, dwarves and trolls, in a word as enemies, and even with advancing culture *stranger* long meant the same as enemy. Christianity broke down that barrier but raised another between *the world* and *itself*. The church alone became the sacred society, while the world remained the unholy one, which could be tolerated in so far as it, at least outwardly, submitted to the commandments of the church. Its tolerance extended no further than that, and the *heretic* became *the enemy without rights*. But just as the hierarchy, not least through the brutal wars against the heretics, had itself begun to transform its power, the misanthropic differences were brought to bear elsewhere. The *different human races* had by the circumnavigation of Africa and the discovery of the new world become better known to Europe than previously, and those different races, which one hesitated to accept as equals, were also heretics, they were pagans. The church approved of their conversion by force. Then the thirst for the gold of the new world was freely quenched under the cloak of religion, and slavery, which Christianity had expelled from paganism, gained immense new realms once Christianity had reimposed it on the pagans.

War and trade, which had already shown themselves in the old world to be the causes of slavery in its worst form, became far more extensive and effective means of propagating it after the discovery of the new one. One now sees the *Christian slave trade* arise (the mere name sufficiently expressing the horror of the matter), based on war and violent abduction.

It was not introduced without remonstrations, and the compassion for the initial woeful fate of the American Indians also played its part in the rise of the *Negro trade*. Due to the violence of the Spanish conquest and even more due to the harsh slave labour inflicted on the natives, almost the entire original population of the West Indian islands died out within a short space of time.[1] A pious Spanish bishop, Las Casas, then suggested, out of consideration for that remnant, that in place of the Indians Negroes should be used, with whom the Portuguese had already begun to conduct a trade in slaves. Formal permission for such a trade was granted in 1517 by Charles V. The emperor later regretted his decision and rescinded the permission he had given before he abdicated. His son Philip II renewed it, and the slave trade was already in full operation.

It remained in the hands of Spaniards and Portuguese until, towards the end of the sixteenth century and at the beginning of the following one, other nations of Europe, the English, the Dutch and the French, began to take part in it.[2] From the peace of Utrecht in 1713, when England acquired the right to supply Spanish America with slaves, the English, who would soon become the principal trading nation of the world, also occupied the leading position in that commerce.

339

It had not come to that without disapproving voices being heard. Several of the greatest theologians and philosophers of England condemned the slave trade in the most forceful language. In 1771 the high court judge Lord Mansfield declared, in the case of an appeal brought before him in the name of a Negro slave transported to England, that the law of England did not admit of any right to possess another as a slave. Not long after that (1776) the first motion against the slave trade was submitted in the House of Commons but gained little support. In 1787 the first private association for the abolition of the slave trade and slavery was formed in England, and we find among its members the names Wilberforce and Clarkson, so honourable for their steadfast perseverance in the most noble cause. After twenty years of tireless endeavours, during which that cause counted among its supporters the greatest statesmen of England, Pitt, Burke and Fox, the ban on slave trading was voted through in the English parliament and received royal confirmation on 25 March 1807. After twenty-six years of further struggle against the most powerful interests the growing number of friends of humanity was finally able to bring about the abolition of slavery in the British Empire within a certain number of years by an act of parliament that was granted royal assent on 28 Aug. 1833. The parliament voted 20 million pounds for compensation to the slave owners, and on 1 Aug. 1838 seven hundred and fifty thousand slaves were liberated in England's West Indian colonies, without the peace being disturbed or a drop of blood being shed.

That act of justice and magnanimity by a great nation is beyond praise. But the rightful recognition of that also includes the gratitude of the philanthropist for the brave, poor, humble preachers of the gospel whose voluntary zeal (for the wealthy Church of England did little in that regard and has only subsequently taken up the work of those men) had for so many previous years brought the slave from paganism to Christianity, before the law gave him freedom.

Nor had a more general opposition to slavery and the slave trade meanwhile been lacking in the rest of Europe, although the French Revolution harmed rather than promoted the good cause by the slave war that it conducted on San Domingo, where the coloured population nonetheless finally won for itself an independent state, which was recognised in 1804. The first ban on the slave trade is Danish. The royal ordinance of 16 March 1792 enacted that it would not be allowed to be undertaken by any Danish citizen as from 1803. The united American states banned the African slave trade in 1794 and more comprehensively in 1807, although Negro slavery continued to prevail and still prevails in the Southern states of the union. At the Congress of Vienna in 1814 the slave trade was declared to be irreconcilable with the demands of humanity and morality. France reserved it for itself for several more years, although Napoleon banned it on his return from Elba. The Netherlands abolished it in 1814. Spain and Portugal undertook, in return for £1,830,000, which England paid, not to engage in slave trading north of the equator, and under the treaties between Spain and England of 5 July and 28 Aug. 1814 the Spanish slave trade was to cease entirely in 1820. Sweden committed itself by the treaties with England of 6 Nov. 1824 and with France of 21 May 1836 to combined efforts to suppress the slave trade, a commerce for which by the royal decree of 7 Jan. 1830, with the amendment of 1 March the same year, a life sentence was imposed.

There is now no Christian society into which slaves may *legally* be introduced, and the only Christian peoples who still conduct the trade in *contravention* of law and treaties are Spaniards to the Spanish West Indian islands of Cuba and Porto Rico and Portuguese to the Portuguese African islands and to Brazil. But the secret slave trade continues and the cruelty inflicted on its victims has increased along with the bans and the measures of surveillance. National distrust between France and England and between America and England, with regard to the right to search slave ships, has complicated the issue, and the desire for profit has interposed itself between the laws and their implementation. The profit from this infamous traffic is so great that it is reckoned at 180 per cent for every African slave whom it succeeds in importing. What a temptation for avarice, when it is otherwise known from the experience of the greatest trading nation in the world that any illicit trade whatsoever that yields a 30 per cent profit defies every form of surveillance!

The united detestation of all nations is therefore required to abolish the brutal trade in human beings. As late as 1839 the annual importation of slaves, the majority of them to Cuba and Brazil, was reckoned at 150,000, of which commonly a quarter, most often a third or more, perish from the hardships during the crossing.[3]

The history of the slave trade confirms the truth that every institution based on the neglect or denial of human rights necessarily *becomes worse*, unless it is completely abolished. That applies equally to the slave trade and to

slavery itself, which of necessity becomes more tyrannical the more and the longer it has to harden itself against
divine and human justice. The slave trade and slavery
go hand in hand, although the latter can also exist independently of foreign slave imports. It then makes up for
its losses by *internal* slave breeding and slave trading. That
is now the main basis of slavery within one part of the
North American union, and several of the most terrible
features of slavery, the cruelty with which spouses, parents and children are torn from each other, the barbarity
with which the slave is debarred from all education, even
by harsh punishments, appear most detestable precisely in
the treatment of the home-born slave. The leading Southern free states in North America, originally founded on
slave labour as English colonies, have indeed had that imposed on them as a hereditary misfortune. But they have
themselves subsequently fostered, acclaimed and extended
that evil in the name and under the pretext of freedom.[4]
And on that soil the final battle of slavery and freedom
within the Christian world is also likely to be fought. The
most ardent *abolitionists* (as the supporters of the banning
of slavery call themselves) are now to be found in large
and constantly growing numbers in the Northern states
of the union, which are not slave states. Their population,
free from the outset, their well-being, enlightenment and
wealth have increased incredibly and far more than the
growth in population and prosperity of the Southern
states, where the number of the slaves has nevertheless
already grown to two and a half million[5] but the wealth
has mostly been concentrated within the class of the great
slave-owners. And yet it is the latter, incidentally with
loudly proclaimed democratic opinions, who have hith-

erto exercised the greatest political influence within the union. During 56 years, from the establishment of the central government of the united North American free states to the present day, the presidency has been held by slave-owners for 44 years; the recently elected president is one as well, as is his predecessor.

The attempts by Sweden during its era of conquests to acquire possessions and colonies, which could have made it complicit in the shame of the slave trade and slavery, were soon, one may say fortunately, reduced to nothing. On the little island of St Barthelemy acquired from France during the reign of king Gustav III, slavery has existed since the French period and still exists, though not in its worst form and to a modest extent. May the representatives of the Swedish people, may the delegates of the nation that itself earlier than any other abolished the pagan heritage of serfdom also annihilate this last remnant of it on Swedish territory and thereby meet the wishes of a noble-minded monarch!

Notes

1 In 1492 Columbus discovered San Domingo or, as the island is now called again, Haiti. Fifteen years later, according to the Spaniards' own account, nineteen twentieths of the natives had perished.

2 In 1588 the first English slave-trading company was granted a charter by queen Elizabeth. From 1631, when king Charles I gave an even larger company a charter for the same purpose, the English slave trade

continually increased. The Dutch and the French
had already followed that example, in step with the
expansion of their American possessions.

3 Fowell Buxton, *The African slave trade*, London, 1839.

4 For that reason the incorporation of *Texas*, a new slave
state, into the American union is now one of the chief
means of strengthening the slavery interest, favoured
by the outgoing president John Tyler from Virginia
and, it is said, by the incoming James Polk from
Tennessee.

5 2,487,113 according to the *American Almanac* for 1842.

5. On the Internal Social Conditions of Our Time, with Particular Reference to the Fatherland

Three lectures from the history course given in the autumn of 1844 in Upsala

Preface to the first edition

VARIOUS ACCOUNTS OF the content of these lectures have persuaded me to publish them, in a more elaborate form than they could have in their original brief, oral delivery. In view of the importance of the questions that they deal with, they may be regarded as too brief even in their present form, and that is doubtless not their only shortcoming.

They should, however, serve to some extent to analyse the conditions that were their object. They may also function as a conclusion to the articles begun in the supplement to *Literaturbladet*.

First lecture (17 October)

It is twenty-five years since I had the honour to address a gathering of listeners and students in this room, among whom the present king of Sweden and Norway, then the crown prince of the united kingdoms of Sweden and Norway, had graciously deigned to take a seat. That was twenty-five years ago – and the prospect that again meets my eye here today and links old memories to new, solemn hopes is in every respect designed to move me to the innermost part of my being. I must crave your indulgence, Sirs, should I be unable to satisfy the demands that the importance both of the occasion and of the subject impose on me.

How often during the past years has not the circle of students around me been transformed! The old university teacher has spent his life among always young, but constantly changing generations. His profession has its great rewards but also its great losses and regrets, and the academic garrison life that he leads can hardly avoid finally imbuing him with a deep sense of *loneliness*. He needs, in order to sustain himself, to be personally refreshed with a draught from the spring of youth, from that inner, eternal spring of youth, which is as invigorating for all ages, but is relished most in old age. Fortunately it should not be too far away from him. For if the life of the scholar possesses any advantage, it is to be found in the fact that he is obliged, by his vocation, to the life-giving reflection on the imperishable, the eternally youthful, which no vicissitudes will remove but which should emerge ever more clearly from the experience of life.

My audience is no longer the same as in former days. I myself am no longer the same – a quarter of a century passes no-one by and leaves him unchanged. The times are no longer the same. I do not say that with reference to the changing opinions of the day. I say it with reference to the great shifts in the epoch itself, which have more than ever touched, as they do now, the interests of *all* and which have laid the highest problems of humanity as it were on everyone's doorstep. – He who still remembers the end of the eighteenth century and has lived with the nineteenth until this day; he who in the dim perceptions of his childhood still sensed, like a distant roll of thunder, the outbreak of the French Revolution; he whose youth was confronted by its effects, which shook Europe; he who in the rise and fall of Napoleon has been a witness to the greatest changes that human fates seem able to offer; he who has then, after the great wars, experienced and personally felt the nature of the peace that followed them – a peace that, with an increasingly deep inner disquiet, has feared external arms less, as it appears to face the danger of civil war – he who has seen and considered all that, what has he not experienced, what ought he not to have learned? – even if he lived in an out-of-the-way corner of the world, as I have lived, and even if his own life were obscure and insignificant, as mine has been.

It is the *past* that will engage us. In order to be instructive, however, this discourse must not ignore the *present*. We shall therefore begin by taking a look at the latter. In doing so, we cannot confine ourselves to the fatherland. It is concerns that are common to us, to Europe, to the world, that will initially demand our attention.

Our age has more than any other been distinguished by great external upheavals. Yet it is not that which has most distinguished it, but even more that those enormous external changes more clearly than ever before can be derived from inner causes. It is the inner world that is shifting in its foundations, in its faith, its convictions, its knowledge. Our age is an age that suffers from its own ideas. If, on the other hand, one wishes to give a name to the fundamental and productive idea, that desires to emerge here and is finding a way, and during the birth pangs of which the world trembles, it is none other than *the principle of personality*, the irruption of which into *the general political sphere* we have experienced.

It was the night before the 4 August 1789 when, during the discussion begun on *the rights of man*, enthusiasm rapidly seized every mind in the French national assembly. The nobility rose and gave up its rights of precedence, the clergy and the deputies from towns and provinces, their privileges. Within a few hours there had been decided: the abolition of every form of personal serfdom in France, with all the territorial revenues and rights into which it had over time been converted, together with the patrimonial jurisdiction of the nobility over its tenants; the redemption of tithes, the equality of imposts, open access for all citizens to the offices of the state, the cessation of all purchasing of commissions, the repeal of all exclusive privileges for corporations and guilds. Shortly after that *the declaration of the rights of man* was placed at the head of the constitution of France.

That remarkable night has subsequently been called *la nuit des dupes*, and many probably soon regretted what they had surrendered in their initial rapture. Even the declaration of the rights of man, the original notion of which was borrowed from the free America, how vague, ambiguous, confusing did it not appear on closer reflection! I have before me a later confession relating to that by a man who, together with Mirabeau, had taken part in writing one of the drafts for it.[1] He calls it "a *childish fiction*" (une fiction puérile). – What was it then in that childishness that touched every heart and moved every mind? What was the cause of that general involvement, which elicits from the author the following confession: "one could say that everything in Europe that was not aristocracy had trembled for the fate of the third estate in France and had felt its liberation as that of the whole of mankind. It was the action of the human race against the ruling and encroaching classes. The unhappy events that have impressed on the revolution the stamp of an unhappy fate now also cast a grim shadow over its cradle; one is ashamed of having initially admired what one subsequently had to hate; but the impartial chronicler should recall that there was at that time a general ferment, a sort of delirium of hopes, and that the enthusiasm aroused by the magnitude of the cause deadened the sense of disorders, which were regarded as unfortunate accidentals in a national triumph" (p. 135). – Be it far from us to wish to close our eyes and hearts to the horrors of the revolution! But nor can we close them to the great step that humanity had taken with it. We turn away with revulsion from the crimes, but we do not only have curses for those who in that great cause acted and suffered on behalf of many generations. It was the hour of birth of the modern era. Ever since then the interests of estates and corporations have had to yield to higher and more general ones.

351

It is a new departure in human society that we have experienced. *Human* society has only recently begun to exist.
It was not present at the beginning of the individual societies, nor for a long time during their evolution. *Society* appears to be older than *the state*, which cannot be conceived
of without a *governmental power*. But in its *simplest* sense
such a power is inseparable even from the earliest society,
and not even the *family* can exist without it. That power
was in the ancient pagan household vested absolutely in
its head, who *owned* wives, children, servants, his original
property as well as his wealth. From agreements between
such heads of households arose the first laws, and all ancient laws bear traces of the initially absolute power of the
head. One difference between the power and authority of
the father and *the right of property* (as over a *thing*) seems to
have originated with the appearance of the actual slave in
the ancient household, to which he would seem originally
not to have belonged other than in the form of *the son*. But
the slave entered the household by the right of *war*, and
only *his* complete lack of rights first raised the status of
the son.

On that nature of the ancient pagan household *the
structure of kinship* has been founded throughout the world.
One sees kindred relating to kindred as subsequently state
to state. Domestic law is also state law, and breaches of
domestic peace, such as the abduction of kings' daughters,
are the great causes of war in antiquity. There are no *penalties* except by the will of the head of the household or as
a propitiatory sacrifice to the gods ordained by the priest.
Affronts are otherwise avenged by *war* or resolved by a
peace agreement, and the tariff of fines eventually agreed
upon between the heads of households by which such

affronts could, without dishonour, be compensated for – that is to say a conditional peace agreement, arranged in advance – is the original germ of both *criminal* and *civil law* as well as the first *public law*. The *collectivity* of the heads of households evinced in such agreements is the first beginning of *political society*, in which those heads of households also appear as the only ones with entitlement. Everything else is *unfree* in relation to them.[2]

Thus *political rights* – which are defined by participation in legislation and government – have been not only the *first*, but for a long time the *only* ones, and they have also been completely *abstracted from human rights*. How should *the law* have regard for the latter, when such a large proportion of mankind, the majority of it, was excluded from them and therefore without legal rights? How should *religion* speak of it, when God was the God not of *all* but only of *some* human beings, of the family, the tribe, the nation; when in the mythologies one's *own* people alone or at least preferentially were *human beings* and when *stranger* for so long meant the same as *enemy*?

The relationship of human beings to one another is essentially determined by their common one to God.[3] *Religion*, it is said, is the knowledge of God. But no knowledge can simply exist or be communicated from outside. The noblest gifts are those that cannot be received as mere presents but which one must also assimilate independently. Truth is above all a gift of that divine kind. It *cannot* be given away. From that follows that the being to whom God has communicated the high privilege of knowledge of himself must also be equipped by him with the independent capability that is required for that purpose and that the manner of understanding God also depends on

353

the development of that capability. If that capability has received the law of its development from God Himself, then he has also made the nature of the knowledge of himself dependent on that development. He has done so because he *desires* only to be worshipped with a discerning, voluntary submissiveness. That is his glory, that is the goal of his creation.

The first religion was that of *fear*, in which the human being only knew how to conceive of God as *power* and worshipped him in the forces of nature. That is paganism. In that religion might naturally goes before right. Serfdom has its origin in it, and everywhere that it [serfdom] reappears it is a new paganism.

To paganism one commonly opposes *revelation*, to which, however, regarded in a wider sense, paganism also belonged in a certain way. Revelation merges with the concept of *miracles*. Miracles are what we call that which cannot be explained by anything preceding it. That inexplicability may be illusory, has often enough been so, and with increased knowledge the miracles disappear. But will *all* of them? Does not science also have its miracles, the more wonderful the more they are contemplated, the more closely they are examined? There are such ineradicable miracles, and even natural science has had to admit it. That there are no leaps in nature but that one thing there evolves from another has been the first general principle of modern natural science. It has found itself compelled to progressively limit that principle. The latter applies *within* the separate domains of nature, each regarded by itself. It does not apply *between* the domains. Between each of them there is a leap, a new beginning, which can only be explained on its own terms. It is thus an impossibility to derive *organic* nature from the *inorganic*. The laws of life can be ever more clearly manifested and explored in their overall connection. It cannot in itself be derived from any external cause. It is and remains a miracle – and, like everything that is only explicable in terms of itself, a reflection of the divine. The pagan has therefore worshipped God in *life*, as the revelation of God in nature.

But just as impossible as it is to explain *life* from the *lifeless*, it is equally impossible to derive *the self-aware* from the *unconscious*, even if alive, or to explain reason as a product of nature. The dawning realisation that *reason* is *above* nature is also the realisation that *God* is *above* nature, as such being unique in himself, and creator of heaven and earth. That is God's *second* revelation. It first occurred to pagan minds. Thus the wondrous diffraction of that light in its first rising above a horizon obscured by mists: God, the only God, moreover the God of a single nation; his law an external one that equates the moral with the ceremonial; the obedience blind, the hopes earthly. This second form of worship is the religion of mere *obedience*. That is how the ancient Hebrews worshipped him. And even after Christianity that religion has evolved in the doctrine of Muhammad into *religious fatalism*. Freedom is unknown to that religion. For that reason it has preserved domestic slavery, in association with polygamy.

A *communicated independence*, we said, is the precondition for a knowledge of God. Even as *communicated*, that independence elevates human beings above nature and is inexplicable by it. They must seek that explanation simultaneously within themselves and *above* themselves. But everything higher is incomprehensible to the lower unless it communicates itself. That is what happened with the absolute miracle, the *real* revelation, in which God, who is also *above* reason, has descended to mankind. That God so deeply loves the *free* being created by him, who has therefore also had the ability to desert him, that he sent his son, the brother of mankind, to the human beings thus immersed in temporality, in order to move their hearts by the greatest of all proofs of love to turn towards *him*; that is God's mercy, which exceeds all reason. Love is above reason. One cannot arrive at it by a conclusion or construal. It must come towards one, it must be *experienced*. That field of experience is opened up in the *third* religion, which is the religion of love. That God, the almighty, did not wish merely to be worshipped in his *power*, that he is not satisfied with a blind *obedience*, that he desires to be loved, worshipped and obeyed in and for himself and with a willing, discerning mind: that is the humility of God, in relation to which all human pride as well as humility is reduced to nothing and can only dissolve in adoration.

The *true human being* and the *true God* were revealed simultaneously. That late concept of the human being appeared in history with Christianity. It appeared with a human being emanating from God, returning to God, and who suffered the punishment of a slave, in order that nothing human should be beneath him, just as nothing is above him, as he taught that the human being is of divine origin and has eternal hope – in other respects, in what he did and suffered, still more a person and a fact than an image and a doctrine, and the latter only by means of the former. But he also came to be born and arise in every breast.

With *Christianity* the *concept of human personality* first arose. Thousands of years had been required for that. Eighteen hundred years were still needed before it moved from *the church* and *the congregation* to within the bounds of the state. It had by then lost its connection with the religion of that era and turned against it in a hostile manner. Its connection with religion will be restored, more deeply, more generally. For Christianity is also the religion of the future. It already reveals itself, as such, in the increasingly acknowledged, although in themselves far too powerless, general demands of morality. But the ever more revealed *moral ideal* in the human mind is not a merely intellectual image; it is a *divine presence* and a *divine help*, where such help is correctly sought. It is in itself the presence of a judge and of a redeemer.

It is our intention, as an introduction to these lectures, to provide a brief overview of the history of rights in European society. In that regard we have proceeded from the ancient pagan family and the kinship structure determined by it, the essential features of which are also found among the peoples that established the first European states after the fall of Rome. The Middle Ages are quite rightly regarded as the epoch of the actual *formation of estates*. But the entire social development of the Middle Ages is also a dissolution and transformation of the original nature of the pagan household. That has been a slow process. The *son* first achieved independence through *war*, the *wife* her rights through the *church*, the *servant* finally his portion of freedom and rights through *the emergence of the third estate*. The son achieved independence and property through war. The wife obtained the right to monogamy and a share in authority over the household and inheritance through the church, or, as the sainted king Erik decreed for Swedish wives, the right to a status of "honour and matron-hood, to locks and keys, to half a bed and a

357

legal third of the domestic property." When the *free cities* emerged, the unfree servant finally found a refuge in them, and what the burgher previously lacked and only won when he gained his freedom is best demonstrated by the letters of freedom, in which he is granted the right to marry off his children, to dispose over his property and to personally inherit. From the mass of the people even those rights were still long withheld. The rights of the Christian family were not even through the church generally extended to the serf. He did not live in a formal marriage, and the epoch that was made brilliant by chivalry and its gallantry trampled without hesitation on the rights of the inferior woman.

War had first become a major occupation among the Germanic peoples through the great so-called *migration of peoples*. One tends to think too often in that regard of migrations by entire nations. The European region has, under successive regimes and designations, ever since the development of agriculture – and even the Germans were familiar with it – seen far less change than is generally thought in the basic composition of its population. That era of historical science has now passed, when in the obscurity of ancient history nations were moved hither and thither. The migration of peoples – with the odd exception of onrushing nomadic horsemen – forms a progressive military occupation of the provinces of the West Roman Empire by the sons in the ancient Germanic household who had the leisure for war, often mingled together from several nations mixed together, but appearing under national names according to the ancestry of their leader or the native region of the majority of them. It is the Germanic military kings with their warlike followings who assault the Roman Empire and who destroy it, once Rome in its civilised decay increasingly incorporates the Germanic armies into its own system. They finally needed only to establish their arms on Roman territory and say 'it is mine', and they did say that. The outcome of *the raids of the Norsemen* would later also be the same, and they likewise founded dynasties and kingdoms. It was a genuine conquest, barbarian military rule. The political rights adjusted themselves to that. The *free* man was the armed one, the *unfree* the unarmed. It had already been so in their homelands. War has everywhere among mankind first introduced commanders and obedience on an extended scale. To bear arms for one's nation or one's country was a sign that one had a voice in public affairs. Thus the *army* was among our ancestors the national assembly, and the Swedish people was referred to as *the army of the Swedes*. The previous condition of things was already a state of war in relation to the rest of the world. The conquests led to a new modification of the martial society.

That modification manifests itself at two levels: from above by the superior power of the conquerors, who are initially a garrison army among the subjugated peoples; from below by the influence of the civilisation of the subjugated, which soon makes the warlike barbarians addicted to it. In that way a mixture of freedom and unfreedom of several kinds arises, all of them, however, ultimately determined by armed force. In general terms, one sees the martial society expand into ever wider circles of greater or lesser forms of subservience, all the way down to the serf, to the subservience of the slave without any legal protection; and on the model of the family all of these develop towards heritable status. *Feudalism* is in effect merely an attempted extension of the martial households of the military kings, a transformation of the state on the pattern of the old military *maison du roi*, often with adopted Roman designations and, in so as far as they understood them and were able to, with the introduction of Roman conditions of service. But *one* limit remained the decisive one in all these circumstances – the use and honour of arms – and *one* freedom, the sign of which was comradeship in arms, the preeminent one. That applied in every part of the feudal, loosely integrated system of power, from the court of the king to the least among the feudal lords. It began as a *military*, it became an *aristocratic* society: first forming an estate of born warriors, who became equestrian to distinguish themselves from the common herd, finally represented by the most powerful landed proprietors and commanders.

Every social formation has had its day and its rationale. As long as military concerns predominated between societies and within them, power was with good reason entrusted to the warrior. But the interests of society are not only those of war, they are even more those of peace; and who was to take care of them, where war is the business of society? If peace and security were not to be sacrificed, they had to stand under the protection of higher powers, which in themselves, even without physical violence, are awe-inspiring. Such an awe-inspiring power presented itself to the warlike barbarians in the Christian Church.

With *Christianity* the concept of personality in a spiritual sense had first appeared among mankind. It had to make its way in a pagan world, disordered both in its civilisation and in its barbarity. It had to begin by setting itself against that world, as an inward society, directed only towards the eternal. – There was a time when St Peter called the entire congregation a *priesthood*.[4] Gradually the difference developed ever more between the *priest* and the *congregation*. On confronting the warlike barbarians, whose leaders, soon becoming politically Christian, had their soldiers baptised en masse, the church became increasingly an outward institution for atonement, in which the atonement (and the barbarian was familiar with atoning for his crimes by fines) was undertaken and performed by the clergy for offerings, penitences, then soon redeemed penitences and thus new gifts. In its very concept, however, the spiritual power was superior to the temporal one. The hierarchy also arose above the latter and separated the church entirely from secular society, in order all the more securely to control it. The church now sanctified everything for its purposes, including war, which it unleashed on the East in the crusades and at home turned against heretics. In the new departure that arose from that, both the military and peaceful concerns of society were released from the bonds of the church. It had originally achieved dominance in particular by all the means of peaceful social power. In a violent age all peaceful professions and livelihoods had at first taken refuge in its shade. Trade was conducted under its protection. The word 'mässa' denoted both a religious service and a market.[5] Improvements in agriculture, mining and horticulture emanated in Northern countries from bishops and monasteries. Bishops entered the royal courts as chancellors. Chanceries, administration and finances were only transferred from the hands of the clergy to secular society during the Middle Ages. The first basic tax was the tithe that they introduced. The concept of *general* law in place of tribal and provincial laws came first from the church, and on legislation it has had the most profound influence. It was the *learned* estate; for a long time it also represented *civil* society. The founding of *universities* is its achievement. But it would thereby initiate the separation of the learned estate from the priestly one. Such a separation expressed itself first in the emergence of a particular *civil estate*, especially through the *jurists*, although the latter themselves had originally come from schools of theology. They were to strengthen the temporal power, which expanded both from above and below. The *cities*, originally mainly gathering-places for an unfree population engaged in peaceful pursuits, threw off the yoke of feudalism, became free communities, combined for common defence and soon also gave war a new appearance by the renewed importance of infantry, by the use of firearms and by means of mercenary troops. The military profession began to detach itself from the aristocratic knighthood, while the civilians detached themselves from the priests and the scholars turned against the church. The new secular power, strengthened in every respect, fell into the hands of the *kings*, at the same time as the *reformation* shattered the edifice of the hierarchy.

It is only from a political point of view that the reformation can here become an object of our attention. Alongside the aristocratic-martial, the spiritual and soon especially priestly concept of personality had entered society. It had, like the former, expressed itself in the form of a separate estate. It became all the more powerful as it based its rights on divine authority and thereby drew a sharp dividing line between priests and laymen. The two were separated by *the mystical concept of priesthood*, according to which it is a vocation established and perpetuated by the founder of each congregation through his blessing and laying on of hands, already thereby provided with its own divine gifts of grace. It is what in the language of the church is called the *successio apostolica*, to which particular significance is again beginning to be attached here and there, even within the bosom of protestantism. It implies a specific, indelible sacred character of the priestly office, perpetuated in that manner, impressed on it in the *ordination*, as by a *sacrament*, for which reason ordination is also a sacrament in the old churches. In that regard they are all *papistical*, even if a papal power only arose in the West, as it was here from the beginning freer from the imperial power, which in the Eastern-Greek Church also combined with itself the supreme spiritual authority. The return of the reformation to the practice of the earliest Christianity, in which the office of teacher was by no means restricted to the apostles and their successors (what Paul records about the relationship of the bishops to the congregation is clear evidence of that), abolished that old distinction between priest and layman. With that, the spiritual principle of personality had escaped from the *church* and into the *congregation*. Priesthood became a function, a commission within the latter, the priest a teacher, preacher of the word, administrator of the means of grace, no longer a performer of offerings and a mediator, through the sacrifice of the mass, between God and human beings. Salvation had become a common concern. With that, the real basis of the hierarchy was destroyed.

To the same degree as these new circumstances developed, royal power had gained a new position. Let us take a look at that new position! The kings have accomplished a great task in the history of Europe. That task may be briefly expressed as follows: just as the formation of social estates in the Middle Ages broke both the ancient freedom and serfdom that derived from the pagan family, so in more recent history *the power of the estates* has been curbed by the *royal power*. The kings have performed that task as the first representatives of *the unity of the state*. The latter had not been able to assert itself without protesting against the ostensibly divine privilege by which the church, itself the first estate as well as the antithesis of secular society, had desired to dominate and curb the latter. It is the declaration of independence of secular society, and it was first proclaimed by the kings. All the new means of power therefore evolved in response to them. The new bodies of soldiery, the new learning, the new civil status, the administrative and municipal finance system that had first originated in the church and then been developed in the cities, all offered them their services. In the administration of justice they intervened between and above the individual corporations. The ever-expanding wars increasingly gave them control over expenditure. After the wars of the reformation their power was consolidated, no less in the catholic than in the protestant world. It is the position of the kings as representatives of *the unity of the state*, both externally and internally, that brought them to predominance, even to autocracy. That principle was higher than the principle of the estate and corporation. It is the kings who *broke* the latter. How could they any longer *support* themselves on it? For three hundred years they had unceasingly undermined and finally destroyed the old independence of the estates. The revolution that our epoch has witnessed as a consequence of that is in fact their own work. They did not recognise it, all the less so as they had positioned themselves not at the centre of society, where they belong, but on the edge of society, namely on the side where those higher estates were, at first subdued and then supported and privileged by them, which would later claim rights of precedence of their own as those of the throne. But in reality the royal power is most elevated and irresistible in the fact that it is the guardian of the rights of *all*. It has paid the price for having broken the power of the estates, only in so far as it was inconvenient for the throne, but left the field open for the oppression by the estates and the privileged abuses with regard to the people. What therefore happened was that the unity of the state, the essential expression of which will always be equality before the law, turned around and flared up, with the demand for general rights, in opposition to the throne and despite the throne, among *the people*. That reversal was the *revolution*. In France it became a contest between the two extremes of democracy and autocracy, or at least the consequences of the latter, until the autocracy was reborn from the democracy in the form of a new martial authority figure, killed its mother and scattered the bones of its children across the battlefields of Europe.

We have returned to the point where we began, the political turning-point that we have experienced, which raised the question of the rights of *the human being* within *the state*. – *That* the turning point exists cannot be denied; it has rocked the civilised world to its foundations. *How*, on the other hand, human rights relate to the state is the second question, with the solution to which the world is occupied, and if one considers the long time it has required to arrive at the first question, the time needed for resolving the second one is not likely to be short either.

That period has begun with the conflict between the old political forces and the new society. The latter resorted to the desperate measure of an initially *demagogic* and then *military dictatorship*, in order to create space for itself, and it did thereby create space enough for itself in Europe, which it almost vanquished. In so doing it had itself in practice abandoned the question and had to pay for that in turn by being vanquished by the old powers. But even that victory could only become an accommodation between the old and the new interests, so powerful were the latter already. During the truce initiated in that way the question itself has increasingly changed from an external to an internal one, which must ultimately be resolved in the minds of people themselves. To be able to make a contribution to that is what we would wish. What is required for that is a closer determination both of the question itself and of its present status.

That all human beings are born and remain equal in rights was the principle that the revolution placed at the head of the Declaration of Human Rights. It is so far from being an axiom that it can at most merely be regarded as a postulate, which presupposes an investigation concerning in *what* regard human beings are and remain *equal*. For if one looks at the reality, what strikes one most is, on the contrary, the natural inequality. One also finds from history that *all* rights are in fact *acquired*; even the so-called *innate* rights – such as the right to life, property, freedom of conscience – are the ones most dearly and slowly acquired and have by no means been granted to the majority of people but were, among the minority that for a long time alone or especially possessed rights, an attribute of *power*, not of *justice*. For justice exists only if it is *reciprocal*.

But that inherent *reciprocity* of justice is also its only form of *equality*. That the human personality is the subject of rights in general is thereby admitted, but the objective extent of the rights is not at the same time determined. One sees the laws determine that in different ways. Only after the appearance of the principle of personality in the world have they been obliged to conclude that no human being is without rights. That was news eighteen hundred years ago. Another conclusion derived from the same principle has appeared in the world in our time, namely that there are no other barriers in the state to the *acquisition* of rights than those that apply to *all* and are based on the equal right of all in that regard. It is the equality before the law demanded today. It has turned against all the old traditional limitations on that general right. What it is most clearly conscious of is having opened up the competition for merit in every area.

The conviction that is imposing itself on everyone is that a man no longer is or should be dependent on his social status, but his status on himself as judged by civic merit. The principle of estates feels itself subordinated to the civic one. That is the new, undeniable fact in the social universe, which we merely need to mention.

If one considers its real basis, that is none other than *the legally free competition that has entered society and is asserting itself with all its consequences*. All so-called *liberal ideas* are comprised in that single concept, and against the correctness and justice of the principle it appears that there is nothing to be said. The opposition it has faced and still has to combat is well known. – One can classify that opposition as being of three kinds. The first is the *opposition of the estates*, which fights, as for its vital principle, against the new subordination of the interests of the estates to the civic ones. The second is the *monarchical* opposition, which had itself first defeated the estates by creating the competition based on merit, but the more it has succeeded in developing the *military* and *civilian service state* and to rule by means of it, the less does it wish to hear of the new application of the principle to the *whole* of society and in the interest of freedom, not only of power. The third is the *religious* opposition, which virtually regards the appearance of the principle of personality in the state as a new fall of mankind, considering it to be the bad egoistic principle. There is much that could be said of those three kinds of opposition, which reinforce each other. One could object against the first that the old estates possess their own highest significance precisely in the fact that Providence has entrusted a property to them, which was actually intended for common use and has also finally come to that. No one can deny, for instance, that *ancestry* is a natural distinction. An irreproachable, good or honourable descent are merits that are willingly acknowledged by the simplest intellect and are not contested by the most enlightened one. To preserve and maintain within the families that irreproachability, that honour, is one of the most attractive and purest human motives, which could not be eradicated from society without the most pernicious consequences. Such is the principle of a natural *nobility* in all estates, which – as I once said[6] – can only appear in its full power and vitality when it has broken through the shell of the aristocracy embedded in privileges and, so to speak, unfolded its wings. If we turn to the spiritual estate, it has most of all the distinguishing feature of having fostered within itself what we might call the *aristocracy of abilities*.

That neither ancestry nor wealth should entitle one to the offices of the church is something for which it has always striven, and none of its epochs has lacked examples of it having awarded its highest positions of honour to merit, even if that has emerged from the humblest abode. It has thus long preserved and respected a principle that the state would in turn come to adopt. The same circumstance applies with regard to *wealth* – in itself a fruit of *labour*, although privileged in many ways in the estates of the nobility, the clergy and the burghers. It is increasingly obliged to recall its origin, since with the accelerating development of social forces all privileged values must finally admit their dependence on *labour*. – With regard to the monarchical opposition one might remark that the royal power has been the principal cohesive one in the state, that the unity of the state has not only an *external* but also an *inward* significance, but that the latter is also necessarily moving on and making itself felt in the external one, to the same extent that the multiplicity of social forces are able to develop freely, and that the *monarchical principle* can for that reason undoubtedly also be strengthened instead of being weakened. – One could remind the religious opposition that the egoistic interpretation of the principle of personality is neither the only nor the correct one, that the human personality on the contrary must in its development increasingly admit that every single *I* implies and presupposes a *you*,[7] that the *necessary* reciprocity of justice lies therein, but that only *the religion of love* can transform that necessity into mutual happiness. – One could say all this and would not thereby have said little. But the *kind* of reaction against liberalism that our time has most recently seen emerging and which is still in full stride is not entirely explained by those three, already old oppositions. A new, a fourth one has been added to them, and it makes an all the greater impression as it emanates from the camp of the liberals themselves.

They have begun to despair of their own principle – of *free competition*. It has already produced results that are becoming ever more disquieting and which appear to counsel us, if possible, to at least stop half way. That most recent phenomenon, more or less general but everywhere observable, indicates difficulties, without a resolution of which the great social question would also appear to be insoluble.

That reaction is also based on a fact that begins to assume the character of a *fait accompli*. The new class that has assumed its place in society after the revolution and is increasingly consolidating itself in the long calm of peace after its storms is the so-called *middle class*. We saw it at first form itself as a result of the progressive dissolution of the old estates and originally comprise all those who did *not* belong to any of them, yet both by their wealth and education had justifiable claims to set against the exclusive rights of the latter. We see it finally, passing from that negative significance to a more positive one, consolidate itself as a new estate with a character of its own, as it is far more extensive than any of the old estates and is therefore moving toward a steadily increasing power. That character consists in the fact that its boundary *upwards* is indefinite, so that the middle class can absorb into itself and in reality does ever more combine in itself the genuine interests also of the higher classes, whereas, on the other hand, it defines itself ever more sharply *downwards* and becomes exclusive with regard to the mass of the people. That boundary has become the one of *wealth*, with *a certain amount of wealth being the precondition for all exercise of political rights.*

That *material wealth* should achieve such dominance would be inexplicable if it had not long before then become as it were permeated by the power of *intelligence*, become itself at once a result of education and a means to education. Only to that extent could wealth also appear suitable as a political measure of worth.

That association of wealth and intelligence had been formed a long time previously. The development of industry itself is nothing but the development of the community of human labour. That developing communal aspect is precisely the share of *intelligence* in the work, which incessantly *increases*, just as the individual labour is represented by human physical strength, the share of which in work, on the contrary, *decreases*. That in turn means that intelligence increasingly permeates *all* of human labour. From which it follows that the *mental* labour, on the one hand, the *physical* form on the other (originally separated by such a great divide that the workers in each respective area were not regarded as belonging to the same, equally entitled society, but that the superior and learned work merely utilised the inferior and unlearned labour as a *means*) are gradually – and yet in the end unexpectedly enough – to be found on the same level as each other, the latter no less than the former with claims to be an intelligent activity. – The *machine system*, for example, by which human strength is at once generalised and multiplied, is merely *one* aspect of that development. The first machine was the human being as such, utilised by human beings as a machine, namely *the slave*. The first barbarous machinery

371

was the enslaved human bodily strength. The immensely high level to which that was developed in ancient times is evidenced by such monuments as the pyramids of Egypt or the temple caves of India. The invention and perfection of machinery as of *all* the industrial aids provided by science, from the first crude attempts in that regard until science has finally in our time become the *greatest* power of industry, are in reality – or *ought* to be – a progressive *emancipation of labour*.

But *work is mobile*; so *how could property be made permanent*? The work is necessarily *always* being performed. That applies in *all* spheres of human labour – to the higher, mental labour as well as to the lower, physical form – to the static religious dogma versus progressive science – to the nobility of birth versus the nobility of service – to the bourgeois guild regulations versus the ever more liberated labour produced by the advances of industry itself. Everywhere the protest of the superseded labour against the fresh new form eventually becomes futile, although the capital of the past, augmented by new enterprise, will always be a great advantage in the competitive race.

That is the effect of *enlightenment* in society, which is itself merely a growing common possession and mutuality of knowledge. Its effects are by no means only gratifying. Complaints have long been made that, with the growth of enlightenment, destitution and degradation have also increased. If one restricted oneself to asserting that they thereby became more visible, there would be nothing to object to in that. The silence and darkness of former times were responsible for much. But there is also another side to the question. One formerly heard much less, it is said, about disunity, much less of conflicts about rights – Naturally! – For there to be a conflict about something, it must first exist. But even if rights as such are conceptually inseparable from the human being, they are despite that far from *recognised* in reality. The recognition is the first step to their realisation, and that recognition is *enlightenment*, a *common* and *mutual* knowledge. In the absence of such knowledge, the right as such does not exist either. It slumbers, it has not yet opened its eyes. It then exists only as *power*, or emanates from power as *favour* and *privilege*, but it does not yet exist as a *right*. However, both knowledge in general and the knowledge of rights in particular emerge out of a given external authority, as out of their natural carapace, until that which was initially accepted in good faith, or allowed by some authority, becomes transformed and purified into insight and right. The issues of contention thus necessarily increase in society with the advances in enlightenment. If one adds that with this rising enlightenment, which is everywhere the growing portion of intelligence in work, human beings *become ever more dependent on each other* for the satisfaction of their needs and that this rising mutual dependence is the inevitable outcome of *civilisation*, one is confronted with a *necessity* of a truly *alarming* nature. And yet that necessity is none other than the inherent *law* of intelligence itself. And yet that necessarily increasing dependence of human beings on one another is a condition that *justice* can more and more order, that *fairness* can more and more mitigate, that *love* can turn into reciprocal gain! – *can*, I say – namely *depending on how human beings respond to that law*. For they may as a consequence of their freedom of choice deny and deride it; they can transform its effects into auspicious or inauspicious ones. But they are unable to alter its validity in the slightest degree. That law progresses, bringing human beings ever closer to each other, it progresses incessantly, in dissension if not in concord, in hatred if not in love, for the worse if not for the better – a source of misery or felicity, the blessing or curse of civilisation – depending on how each of us responds to it. – But if a lively sense of that sublime necessity, interconnecting everything that is human, should instantaneously pervade the human mind in all its profundity – human beings would turn around and recognise each other as brethren.

What the law has to achieve in society we would call the work of *justice*, what customs add to it that of *fairness*, what religion finally perfects that of *love*. The *static* mode of thought, in contrast to the *revolutionary* one, has always laid particular emphasis on the last two. Morality and religion are above all *its* motto, apart from being the *permanent element* in laws and institutions, as morality and religion should serve to enable one to be content with that permanency, even if it cannot endure before the demands of justice. Evidently a false position! – For *the work of justice is the primary one in society* and *becomes* so increasingly through the acknowledged reciprocity of justice; it occupies that place in the view of morality and religion themselves, for which reason the public morality and devoutness that are unwilling to acknowledge it cannot be of the right kind either. The revolutionaries are well aware of that, for which reason they attack such a morality and piety with scorn and derision, comparing it to an opiate, which is given to the masses as an anaesthetic. For *them*, on the other hand, the purely *juridical* aspect of society is not only the *primary* one, which is quite correct nowadays, but virtually the *only* one, which is false. But the danger of a revolution is no less on the one side than on the other. Religion and morality, prescribed as numbing substances against injustice, really are that opiate, which can lead to slumber but also, how often, to an awakening accompanied by blasphemous curses! Where are the limits of *justice*, where are those of *fairness* in *such* an awakening? – What ought to become the effect of *love* becomes that of *hatred* – and prides itself on that![8]

Thus I spoke several years ago, and one cannot reproach me with having omitted the shadier side of the picture. The darkest feature in it was absent, however. That the old society rested all too much on *the right of the stronger* is what we criticise it for. But what would *free competition* be if it merely became one additional means of oppressing the weak and of reintroducing into society the right of the stronger? – What would the celebrated *emancipation of labour* be if one of its consequences were the *unfreedom of the labourer*? – What would *enlightenment* be if it were merely to teach the constantly growing mass of the defenceless and propertyless wandering on the outskirts of present-day society about everything that they appear doomed to lack? – Such are the questions, by the answers to which even the most liberal person, with his eye on the signs of the times, tends to be taken aback and hesitate.

What we have experienced is a more unrestricted rule of wealth or property than the world has hitherto seen, and that rule is also decidedly the rule of *movable* property over its *fixed* form. It is the first time that property positions itself at the forefront of society, namely as merely private property, for it has previously been linked to wider personal relationships. Fixed property was *family property* and *property of an estate* before it became purely *private*

375

property. That was the case with the *nobility*, which was legitimated in the maintenance of a larger amount of property within the families by the fact that it bore arms on behalf of society and ought to become a defence even for the defenceless. That was the case with the *church*, whose property was regarded as entailed and held in trust for the spiritual estate as a whole; it was expected, apart from the liturgy, to engage in care for the propertyless, for which reason the church had also liked to call its property the property of the poor. The power of purely private property began with *the third estate* and found its theoretical justification in the ancient Roman law revived by the jurists. The very origin of bourgeois property explains its varying character.

Even with the fullest property right, according to feudal notions, there were limitations that we no longer attach to it. In the feudal system an absolute right to private property, if not unknown, was by no means the predominant one. The property was hedged in on every side by a network of personal relationships, which transformed every *property right* into a *personal right* and thereby made the bond between owner and property into a reciprocal, in fact a moral bond. An hereditary, inalienable property, attached by personal relationships to the state possessed a nobler value than mere private property. And precisely because *things* were also owned in the feudal system in a more personal way, *persons* could also be owned in it under property law, without that immediately leading to the human degradation that is quite inseparable from the modern mercantile concepts of property, where they are applied to persons. – All feudal property was in particular connected with the land. But the first and simplest agri-

cultural production is distinguished by the fact that it preserves human beings *whole*, dividing neither their powers
nor their needs, requires capable men and preserves them
as men, without the occupation itself ever transforming
them into mere tools. For that reason all agriculture so
easily associates itself with personal hardships and duties,
as the occupation itself demands an undivided personality. It is different with secondary production, which involves the refinement of the primary products. An endless
variety of activities here replace the original simplicity,
each of which requires a capable man, and he who chooses
one of those activities for the exercise of his skill must be
able to expect to acquire from the primary production not
only what is necessary for his basic needs but also of other
artificial products what is required for the satisfaction of
the new needs generated by the technologies themselves.
In a word: *the division of labour* arises. When work of that
kind either first gives value to the material through technology, or at least enhances it, then that secondary production, or the refinement, is necessarily associated with a
more unrestricted right of disposition over property. For
that reason, whereas in the feudalistic sector of society
we see that property rights are curtailed and subjected to
various restrictions, all property in the bourgeois sector
naturally assumes the character of absolute private property. But what property rights have thus gained in force
they have lost in scope. Everyone most immediately owns
his own production, but when that has been distributed
among a number of persons by the division of labour, the
production of each individual needs to be complemented
by that of the others, if the individual is to be able to exist, and precisely because he unrestrictedly owns the thing

that he knows how to produce, he has become dependent on all other things that he needs and cannot produce. An exchange thus becomes necessary and for the sake of that exchange, something *par excellence* that represents all other things, for which they can be acquired and by means of which the unavoidable complementation just referred to can take place. Such a thing is *money*, may it otherwise be anything you like. For even precious metal, which is most often used for that purpose, first acquires its value as money by the necessary exchange of products that it mediates, that is to say, without its circulation it is not money. The bourgeois sector of society becomes above all the sphere of money; not as if the primary production could entirely do without it, yet the latter is conceivable without money – the bourgeois, on the contrary, is not.

Since we have now seen how within the actual field of the division of labour things complement each other according to need, the same issue nonetheless remains at a higher level: how are *human beings* themselves complemented under those conditions? – how are the powers of the complete human being, split asunder by the division of labour and distributed among various individuals, reunited again? – One will easily realise that the question is not superfluous. For the same disparity that exists between the individual artificial product and the totality of human needs, the same disparity applies to the specially developed skill in relation to the totality of human abilities, and yet everyone wishes to be regarded as a whole, complete human being, wishes to know himself in the full power of his humanity and personality and therefore desires completion in that regard, if he has been obliged to develop only a certain part of his ability. The answer is

that every individual power can only achieve such fulfilment in so far as it *feels itself to be part of the whole*. But that
feeling, which, in permeating every individual, makes him
a participant in the power of the whole, is *public spirit*.[9]

Such was the principle of life in the great corporations
of the Middle Ages. The third estate emerged from the
conflicts of that time equipped with the organisation of
the guild. That was the armour it had donned against feudalism. What it had to protect in the past was not only the
unappreciated and suppressed freedom of labour, it was
human, Christian and civic justice. Such are also the traditions of the *guilds*, which are ancient enough. Those guilds
and societies had in past times not only an *industrial* but
a *religious* and *political* significance. Nowadays they have
even lost the remembrance of their former possession of
that higher significance, and yet it was precisely *that* which
made them into what they once were, great industrial institutions and at the same time a support for civic freedom
and justice. Whoever would restore to them their former
significance must also reawaken their former spirit! – But
precisely *that* is now active at higher levels for the same
goals by other means. – Such is also generally the history of the *commune*. Its initial life was *political*, and what is
left of its life remains so even today. The commune was
originally civic society on a small scale. Now civic society
exists on a large scale and has taken over the major social
guarantees, but even the lesser local ones that are left to
the care of the communes wither away without the vitality that is only provided by the connection with the great
interests of society. The commune began by being a centre
of political life. Nowadays it presupposes, for its own existence, a national social life, in which the commune is in-

deed a subordinate but nonetheless a necessarily interactive part. Everywhere, even in despotic states, where there are traces of a *communal constitution* one sees in it the remnants of a better, freer time. Everywhere that one wishes to reintroduce such a constitution, though only as a kind of private-household and police arrangement, without the commune also becoming one of the simple forms of a nation's political life, one creates lifeless regulations.

With the waves of *crusades, feudalism* was transformed; with the *wars of the reformation* the church *hierarchy* was transformed. From the *revolutionary wars* of our time the strength of the *third estate* finally emerged, at first favoured but then restrained by the royal power, and that estate appears already to be embarrassed by the victory it has won. It is the *burgher* who has finally defeated the *nobleman* and the *priest*. But *below* the burgher in society there is also a people – namely the so-called *common people* – a people whose labour prepares the harvest and moistens the workshops with its sweat – a people in which the first and simplest needs of humanity are reflected, and those simplest human needs also include to have *something to respect, to venerate*. Being well acquainted with *unavoidable* sacrifices, the people finds the objects for such respect and veneration primarily in *the ability of the volunteers*, and that was the original secret of the power of the higher estates. For both the profession of the warrior and of the priest is a *life-and-death* one and thereby elevated above both. The *judge*, in the conscientious exercise of his profession, stands no less high. The masses know and understand such matters and follow and even allow themselves for a time to be ruled by the semblance, even if the reality ever more disappears. They naturally respect the *social status* of the priest, the judge, the warrior; they do not respect the status as such in the burgher intent only on acquisition, although they can respect the human being behind the status. – What are the means, then, that remain for an essentially *bourgeois* society to gain from the people the respect that it previously gave to the *higher classes*, but which it seems far less inclined to grant to advantages that lie closer to its own sphere? What remains is only to allow the worth of the *human being* to permeate that of the social status. In reality, everyone is progressively descending to the level of the third estate. The latter estate is thereby more than ever subjected to the necessity of replacing and absorbing into itself the other estates. Not without reason arms are now borne not only by the *soldier* but by the *citizen*; not without reason the church is no longer exclusively the concern of the *clergy* but of the *Christian congregation*. – The comfortable repose of the capitalist after well performed mundane business is not the goal of humanity. Against a class that would dare to regard it as such, the masses throw their lives away in desperate uprisings – if only in order to demonstrate their contempt for them. Should *such* a kind of new bourgeois nobility – an aristocracy of bumblebees and drones – wish to consolidate itself, it will fail owing to its very origins. A *nobility* arose in the world because it was originally based on *duties that cannot be paid for*, and for that reason *honour* was its soul, and it cannot exist in any other way. But in the last resort life's account cannot be balanced for anyone unless one *pays with one's own person*, and even the burgher must learn – at the risk of otherwise being cast out with ignominy from the position in which the evolution of society has placed him – that it is *that* payment that will ultimately be demanded – that he does not exist to have defence as well as pastoral care and justice comfortably provided to him, for a fee, but that the advantages of society must be purchased with genuine civic activity. In reality, if a *middle class* has ever more encroached on the areas of the former estates, it can only maintain its position by fulfilling *all* the duties of the citizen and human being.[10]

Part of that is also the recognition of *all* human rights, and given that, as we have seen, the entry of *human rights* into secular society in reality reveals itself in *free competition*, the recognition of that principle also embraces *all its consequences*. It is from that recognition that the liberalism of the middle class recoils. – We shall explain.

It is the *nature* of those consequences, we said, that have given rise to the hesitation. What, then, is so terrible about those consequences, not only for the class that is now rising to predominance but for *all*? We have already defined it. We seem to find that the most immediate effect of free, unchecked competition has been to *reintroduce into society the right of the stronger*. It reinforces the strength of the powerful, it diminishes the ability of the weak, it increases the burden. In the gigantically expanding realm of modern industry an ever greater chasm opens up and consolidates itself between wealth and poverty. To the same degree destitution and crime increase and produce, in a growth as rapid as it is horrifying, a mass of *proletarians* that, ever more deprived of all the advantages of society, sustain themselves only by their hostility towards the society. It is the distinction of the ancient world between the *free* and the *unfree* that is again, in the very name of freedom, manifesting itself.

Work is mobile – we have said – so how could wealth remain fixed? – It is free competition that has set work free and thereby given rise to the new mobility of property. Why has that development turned out so much to the detriment of the weaker that he whose only capital is his labour power so often, even with the assiduous use of it, is exposed to the danger of sinking into ever deeper dependence? What is it that lowers the value of the personal capital when the opportunities for work have opened up in all directions? There must be an advantage *apart from* labour that produces a decisive superiority on the competitive track. There is such an *additional factor* that could assure victory in advance to those who possess it. That factor in labour is the *finished* labour and the right of disposal over it. But *capital*, in itself and in an impersonal sense, is in reality merely *finished labour* – and *the money that represents finished labour is, for that very reason, a means of exchange for new labour*.[11] The *dominance of capital* represented by money could thus have an oppressive effect on the labour that lacks capital. That corresponds to the general opinion that what in our own time has succeeded aristocratic dominance, priestly authority and royal power is *plutocracy* – the dominance of wealth, of money.

But *how* can the impersonal capital, the power of money have such a deleterious effect on the personal capital, on the individual labour power? That lies in the natural predominance of *collective* labour over *isolated* labour. *Capital* is the means whereby the *collective unity* of labour evolves to precisely the same degree as the *division of labour*. It draws to itself the isolated labourers, it combines them into great masses, it produces all the advantages of *large-scale* industry over the *small-scale*: simultaneously a

383

greater and *superior* production with *lower* costs of production. The progress along the track that makes the labourer ever more dependent on his master and his own fate nonetheless thereby ever more uncertain is as rapid as it is inescapable. It is in fact the *growing share* of *intelligence* in the work that irresistibly progresses.

Could its nature actually be one of necessarily increasing to *the ruin of the masses*? – Impossible. – Something must have been overlooked here, something mistaken. Could that error not actually be that, while we have left the growing share of intelligence in the work free scope in *one* direction, we continue to *obstruct it in another* – that, while we claim to support free competition, we have in reality *not* recognised the principle in *all* its consequences, or at least overlooked and misunderstood the only but necessary precondition by which those consequences can freely develop and perhaps become generally beneficial?

The evil is recognised everywhere, by the people and by the governments, and both have wished to intervene, each in their own way. Among the people it has merely expressed itself in a sense of a malaise, for which the specific cure is unknown. The *proletarians*, the mass of whom constantly grows in modern society,[12] protest against *property*: they do so in action and they have now begun to do so in theory and conviction. The crime statistics provide the evidence for the former; *communism*, whose only article of faith is the demand for the community or equality of property, provides evidence for the latter. Socialism stands a step higher and at least within the bounds of reason. It works with what is called *the organisation of labour*, according to the intrinsically correct premise that the *small capitals, combined and properly administered*, ought to function like the *large* ones, and to the profit of *all* participants. And it is true: *the principle of association* is a means of salvation in our time, but surely not only in the *industrial* context. That requires the principle of association itself gaining a higher, nobler life, that it be animated by that same *social spirit* of which we have spoken, but which nowadays in the commune, the corporation, the estate has lost its former political meaning. How narrowly the socialists have conceived of their principle is already shown by the fact that they increasingly leave both *religion* and *state* out of consideration. They have, however, referred to one important demand addressed to the legislators. It has already long been admitted that neither the *criminal* nor the *civil* legislation can be allowed to be the outcome of arbitrariness or circumstance. The time has come when the same demand is increasingly extended to the *economic* legislation of society, when it is ever more clearly realised that in this latter case, no less than in the former, the issue is *everyone's right*, from which it specifically follows – as money itself is subject to the laws of labour – that the legislation that, instead of adapting itself to that, attempts to create or regulate money *arbitrarily*, in so doing inevitably *disorganises labour*. And what very important consequences are not already implied by that realisation! – The governments, on their part, have paid ever greater attention to the economic and administrative legislation, the principal issues of which are also, with the evolution of society, increasingly transformed into *issues of rights*. They have treated that legislation more than ever in a preventative and corrective sense with regard to the needs of the lower classes. They have made provision for a more general poor-relief system, a more general system of education; they have ameliorated the criminal law; they have transformed the prisons into correctional institutions; they have in various ways sought to intervene in the relationship between master and labourer and also allowed themselves to set dubious restrictions on the former's right of disposal over his wealth; all apparently in vain. Several of the means employed would even appear to have aggravated the evil.

What follows from all that? Clearly that the power of the moral, personal capital must be *strengthened*, if it is not to be increasingly suffocated by the rule of the impersonal, material capital. We have drawn attention to *the principle of association*. That is actually the *public spirit* itself, which in our time has broken the fetters of the corporations and led to free enterprise. One would perhaps not really be able – I once said – to describe the character of the social revolution that we daily observe more accurately than with these words: that the state is engaged in the winding up of the bankruptcy of the corporations. It has certainly thereby incurred an excessive load of work, and if it is not assisted in time by a newly revived spirit of association, it will probably not be equal to the task. We could add that the breaking up of the corporations, obdurate in their exclusive rights, liberates precisely the natural spirit of association, which also manifests itself, within the ever more legally determined area of the *permissible*, in far more numerous forms than before. In industrial and financial, literary and scientific, moral and religious respects that new spirit of association is manifesting itself. All these companies, societies and associations for private and for public purposes are among the signs of the times. It is also the *corporation*, which has likewise become *mobile* along with the mobility of labour, in which the approaching relief forces of the new state begin to become visible.[13] But the essential expression of the public spirit is *the state*. It has had its time with *the estates*, each of which in its own way once sought to dominate the whole of society. They are, regarded in themselves, only expressions of the immature principle of association. The real life of the latter is *political*. It has thus once expressed itself in a dominant nobility, in a dominant clergy, in the rising free commune, until, following mutual conflicts, that aggregate of corporations that was medieval society fell under the dominion of the state unit and royal power. That outward unity of the state has finally changed course and emerged as the need for an inward unity of the state among the people. That need has given rise to the awareness that no class among the members of society can now or ought to be excluded from also sharing in the *political rights*. It is the political life that has penetrated right down to the people. To admit that is simply to admit *what exists*.

Such an extension of the political rights was what *the revolution* attempted to bring about in a violent way. It is what *reform* has to accomplish in a lawful way – a way that can again only be kept open by giving full validity to the following principle: *obedience to current law*, *but an open right to demand a better one, and free discussion of the means to achieve that aim*.[14] Where that road to improvement is cut off, there *compulsion* eventually becomes the only guarantee of obedience, which in the long term is not effective and is merely the revolution in its germinal state. In order to deflect the danger, people have indeed resorted in several countries, as a form of alleviation, to promoting as far as possible the *material* prosperity of society, while the higher preconditions for that prosperity remain inhibited.

Such an emollient – which could be called the revolutionary palliative – is comparable to the hot compresses that cause a swelling to come to a head. It hastens the outbreak of the evil. An apparent material prosperity generated in that way has often enough preceded and brought to maturity internal revolutions. That is due to the fact that man does not live from bread alone and that whoever debars him from freedom and light harms his vital spirits. Those times are also gone when the prosperity of society could with any semblance of truth be promoted by some artificial means. That the *higher* conditions for that prosperity are precisely the most important ones for the *material* prosperity as well has, on the contrary, become ever clearer.

It was under the influence of such thoughts that I, as a member of parliament in 1840 expressed my conviction that the *issue of representation* now rested on the *principle of personality*. I excluded both those who were under age and those whose most immediate obligation is to educate the future citizen within the *family*, the *congregation* and the *secondary school* – I excluded from political representation the *woman* and the *priest* and was inclined to extend that exclusion to the *secular teacher*, not as if they lacked rights in that regard, but because they ought to find themselves called upon by *higher* obligations not to descend to the battlefield of the political passions and would work best even for the welfare of the state by their influence on those general human concerns, the care of which has primarily been entrusted to them. Apart from that, I demanded a personal right to vote for every citizen who had come of age. The exercise of that right to vote should to my mind preferably be *indirect*, or occur through chosen electors.

Both for *those* and for the representatives I posed a requirement for a so-called *augmented personality* but could not find any other general criterion for that than a *substantial fortune*. I hesitated between the generally indirect suffrage and direct suffrage *within* the higher property level, while the indirect one should apply lower down. – My proposal remained incomplete.

The new *recommendation on representation* drawn up by the standing committee on the constitution that remained dormant in the parliament of 1840 referred to the *principle of personality* and was based on *general suffrage*, but had also made the exercise of the right to vote generally conditional on an *electoral register graded according to wealth*. The contradiction into which it thereby fell with the wide extent of the right to vote that already existed among us, particularly in the estate of the peasants, led to a depression of that register, so that it became illusory at its lower levels, nor could it at the higher levels ensure for the greater private fortunes the influence to which they laid claim. It generally turned out that every new proposal for representation in Sweden would find it fairly difficult not to *restrict* the political rights in the system of representation, bearing in mind the extensiveness of personal participation that was already present *within* our four old estates, rather than, in accord with the trend of the times, to *extend* them. Given the extensiveness that the new proposal nevertheless did provide for in that regard, the great majority of the estate of peasants and finally also a large part of the estate of the burghers and a part of the nobility also gave their support to that proposal, under an ever stronger resistance by those who held to the principle of *elections by estate* or – as they preferred to say – *by class*, due to which resistance the new proposal on representation has also succumbed in the present parliament.

Among us, too, a *reaction* has set in against the principles that have hitherto prevailed among the representatives, ever since the more liberal interpretation of our constitution of estates provided for in the constitution of 1809. That is connected with a general phenomenon in the European realm, to which we have already to some extent drawn attention. The *middle class* in those states that have moved furthest along the constitutional road has already come into possession of its new rights and is everywhere expanding in a way that will guarantee it a preponderant political influence. Wherever that influence has entrenched itself, the middle class has ceased to work for *the party of movement*. Based on the new power of wealth, it makes a certain level of wealth an ever more essential precondition for every kind of direct or indirect exercise of political rights and guards with all the greater suspiciousness the boundary, where it has once been set, the more so as the new mobility of wealth makes all possession insecure. In that sense the majority of representatives in all constitutional states have become decidedly *conservative*. It has become ever more doubtful regarding further change and at the same time ever more tolerant of the weakened remnants of the powers of the older society. But in fact the new conditions, introduced by the middle class, already differ so much, too, from the system of accommodation in the constitutional theories that it has adopted that it seems more than doubtful whether the pact between the *new* and the *old conservatism* will be effective in the long run.

The July Revolution in France has, for instance, condemned the *hereditary nature of the chamber of peers*. That the *chamber of peers itself* has therewith received its sentence is something that no one seems willing to admit. That is nevertheless the case, and the difficulty or even impossibility of constructing on some other basis a chamber of peers that will be more than a constitutional illusion is evident. With the collapse of the system of privilege, *two* or *more* chambers become merely a working arrangement – comparable to the activities of the *committees* within a *single* one. It should not for that reason be thought that the *mediating* element between monarchy and democracy that is looked for in a chamber of peers, following the example of England, has disappeared from the state. It has, on the contrary, entered it in a far more *powerful* and *general* way. That mediating element has become *the middle class itself* in its new conservative significance and power. One should look around in the representative states. Wherever the representative system has either possessed an old or gained a new stability, the political life of the representatives is ever more concentrated in its *lower* chamber, even in England in the *House of Commons*; and everywhere the majority of that representation has become *conservative*. It is generally no longer simply a question of *two parties*, ministry and opposition, in and through which the former aristocracy above all competed for the highest positions in government; there is a *third*, not merely a faction but a genuine social force, which has placed itself at the *centre*, between ultra-conservatism and radicalism, is an expression of the conservative majority of the middle class and has become the focal point on which every government can confidently support itself in maintaining peace, order and security. That conservative majority of the middle class expands daily. The whole relationship of *ministerial government* both to the crown and the representation has thereby been substantially altered. A ministry used to be a real intermediary power as long as the old aristocracy was one. It is so no longer, and for that reason *ministerial power* becomes increasingly an aristocratic fiction. The *royal power* itself develops a closer relationship to *the representation*, that is to say above all to the great predominant interests of the middle class, by which a government now feels empowered, and one cannot deny that such a position, even if it has its dangers, is in actual fact more *royal* than a throne, which merely emits the lustre of supreme power but with its substance transferred into other hands.

If one observes this *new social formation*, everything indicates that it is still far from completed and can therefore lay claim to a future. It is observable everywhere, even where it does not yet have any legal voice. Where a representative system is lacking, it is usually that element which demands it. Where it does exist, it seeks an assured influence within it and identifies the whole with itself. In France it rules since the July Revolution; in England it is an acknowledged power since the reform bill. It is *its* importance that maintains *peace* in Europe. For all its interests are peaceful. It regards war as its enemy, and in those states that are still based on war it has also made the least progress. Yet it generally finds itself in a difficult position. In war it fears its *external* enemy, in peace its *internal* one, for the ever more entrenched sovereignty of capital over the worker throws the latter increasingly back among the fearfully growing mass of proletarians. Whether that knot in the history of European civilisation will be *cut* by the sword and culture pass along other roads, or whether Europe will be able to *untie* it, is the most important question that it poses to the future. The latter appears to be possible in only *one* way – by a new and in both height and depth *more extensive* social formation. Such a one was once under way but has been repressed.

We have arrived at a point in our account where experience appears to directly contradict the assertion with which we began, namely that inner, spiritual causes have been and are principally at work in the upheavals of our time. We started out from an alleged ascendancy of *ideas* but have arrived at an actual one of *material interests*. Indeed, even the new *ideology* increasingly materialises itself. But it is not about that which I must speak here. On the other hand, we should be permitted to compare one experience with another and draw our conclusions from that.

It was with and through *Napoleon* that the effects of the French Revolution first took form and shape. *Two* immense means of power fell into his hands: one was a *centralisation* of it far beyond anything that the former monarchy could even have imagined; the other was *conscription*, but based on the legally recognised right of *every* citizen to bear arms for the fatherland. One was his *civil*, the other became his *military* strength. We must pay special attention to those factors, all the more so as they were connected and were in themselves merely manifestations of a *third* power that sustained both Napoleon and his regime.

The centralisation was a manifestation of the *unity of the state* that the old royal power had already given to society. But that unity became in its hands a kind of mystery, in the actual secrets of which only the higher estates that surrounded the throne and the main organs of the royal power itself in the military and civilian *service state* were knowing participants. The masses obeyed blindly. Their social spirit could only express itself directly within the remnants of the old corporations or within the tradition of the provincial or patrimonial jurisdictions. The storm of the revolution swept all that away. With the question of human rights free competition entered society. The liberated social spirit blazed up and found no other limits than *the state*. – That was when the unity of the state could no longer be represented only by the old royal power. It had to be represented by *the people*. – But *how?*

The more recent individual constitutions of France have sought to resolve that question in different ways, and one sees in all those attempts at once a certain consistency and a certain contradiction, according to whether they begin the resolution of the question with *personality* itself or with *property*. The first constituent national assembly, while paying particular attention to one, nevertheless did not wish to exclude the other. After placing the Declaration of *Human* Rights at the head of the constitution of 1791, it proceeds to the concept of *citizen* and determines who should be regarded as an *active* citizen. Excluded from that class are the servant and everyone who does not pay a direct tax (equivalent to at least three days' work), and it also prescribes the *indirect* form of election by electors appointed in the primary assemblies. The first republican constitution of 1793 rejected all those distinctions. It was a crude attempt to let the entire people directly exercise government power, for which reason that constitution was already suspended in its hour of birth and power was transferred to a demagogic dictatorship, with terrorism as a means of governing. The constitution of 1795, with its directorial government, not only returns to the distinctions suggested by the first but adds new ones. It determines the meaning of *citoyen actif*; it takes up again the indirect method of election by the introduction of dual electoral colleges; it decrees a new distinction, by demanding a certain higher level of wealth to qualify to be chosen as an elector. The constitution of 1799, with consular government, allows the reference to *wealth* to entirely lapse again, but adopts a threefold graded scale of personal and civic *trust*, according to which the electors of the *commune* determine those of the *departement* and they in turn those worthy of the trust of the *nation*. One sees a closer definition of the state powers, a conservative senate, appointed for life, a legislative body etc. and finally a government that possesses the entire executive power and alone proposes the laws. Into that government enters the man on whom the trust of the whole nation was to be focused and who therefore, although within and through the people, centralised all power in himself. That was the dominion of *Napoleon*.

In none of the changes that he subsequently made to the constitution of France has he touched or infringed that basis of his power, namely the *trust*, not in *wealth* but in *ability* as the vital principle of the new state. It was that which made him into a man of *the people*. He has remained that even after his downfall and will remain so.

And how could he have abandoned that foundation? How could he allow a line drawn through the nation according to a certain level of wealth become the limit for political rights? – He made quite different demands of every citizen. Every one was obliged to perform *military service*. It was the first and remained the only precondition for *active* citizenship. His greatness, his fame and his power had begun in arms. Even the initial republican spirit had necessarily become *martial* during the life-and-death struggle of France against the old powers. That spirit found its only sanctuary under the tyranny of the demagogic dictatorship in the armies; it long maintained itself there and was never completely extinguished, even during the imperial dictatorship. One cannot read the story of those military campaigns without recognising the spirit of the Roman legions, which survived long after the fall of the republic.

For his military violence against property, however, Napoleon finally fell. There followed the *restoration*, with its accommodation between the new and the old. The middle class, whose development had continued even during the great wars, now settled down after the peace, guarded its rights and became divorced from the people under the *charter*, due to the setting of a fairly high electoral qualification. That distinction between *middle class* and *people*, between the politically entitled and unentitled, has remained ever since but only after the July Revolution (although it lowered the electoral qualification) broken out into *opposition* between the two. During the restoration that was not yet very noticeable. The old royal power, when it marched in accompanied by all the claims of the old privileged estates, which it at first *could* not and then had no *desire* to restrain, ended by uniting against itself both middle class and people. It is only since the middle class turned the July revolution to its own advantage, only since the new dynasty openly bases its power on the support of the middle class, that an open division has also developed between the middle class and the people.[15]

Has the epoch of Napoleon then vanished without a trace for the internal development of the European community? Far from it. – Everything in that development that goes *beyond* the society based on the political power of the middle class, all the higher and more profound forces, which in all this point towards a more comprehensive social formation in the future, all of that is conscious of its connection with him and his time and has also evolved after him in recognisable forms. We wish particularly to draw attention to two of these: the new political weight and significance of the *nationalities* and of the *religious motivations*.

The first concrete form assumed by the initially abstract principle of personality as it entered the political arena is *nationality*. It is in that sense more than a mere feeling and habit, it is also an awareness of the connection opened up and liberated between the individual and the state, of the significance of *all* citizens with regard to the general good, of the entitlement and obligation of *all* to contribute to that and share in it. That awareness rests on the new extension of political rights. It represents the acceptance of the new unity of the state by *the people*. – France emerged from the first storms of the revolution with a heightened national consciousness. It initially depended in that regard on itself, after recovering from the propagandistic delirium of extending happiness to the whole of mankind with the new freedom and equality. It felt itself to be the *great nation*, which would soon come to mean the *dominant* one. Napoleon made the claim into a reality, in that he carried both the principle of equality under the law and the dependence of all civic distinction on merit as far as his dominion extended. That would confront its limit and soon its downfall due to the contradiction in which it had become involved. He extended political rights everywhere but also denied them all national significance of their own compared to the claims of the great nation. Thus *the national significance* was awakened to a new life, even in the subjugated or threatened nations. It was with the power of the *newly awakened nationalities* that the monarchs defeated Napoleon. A great political accommodation restored the outward calm in Europe. But the conflict between the old and new claims became instead an internal one, and the nations could not be content with having merely been used by the regimes as means for the latters' own purposes. Ever since then nationality has been a power in its own right and is making itself felt as such. Both the regimes that have *divided* the governance over a *single* nation between themselves and those that extend their great power across *several* distinct nations are experiencing that. The former feel the separate parts *striving to unite*; the latter feel the various combined entities ever more *separating themselves*. It is the newly awakened national consciousness that is active in both cases.

With the reformation the *ecclesiastical* consciousness had passed beyond the limits of the *clergy* and entered the *congregation*. The reformation also in effect established the sovereignty of the state over the church, and that sovereignty was exercised by the old royal power, as the representative of the unity of the state. The participation of the congregation itself in ecclesiastical affairs was increasingly suspended after the great wars of religion, in step with the consolidation of princely power. The church thus increasingly lost its connection with the people and soon became itself merely an external monarchical or aristocratic form, a *clerical* addition to the *military* and *civil service state*. That an autonomous power inhered in the church, both people and governments had had time to forget, when the political state-unit changed course and created a new basis for itself among the people with the doctrine of human rights. The claims of that new state-unit were greater and more extensive than those of the old regimes. The revolution abolished the concept of *state religion* – but has precisely thereby *emancipated* religion, and from that moment religion makes itself felt as a separate power. The outward signs of that are numerous and still chaotic but are undeniable. One sees them in the newly emergent life, not only ecclesiastical but popular, of the various confessions, in their new political significance and in the profound conflicts that they again provoke in society, in the sectarianism among the people and in the new relationships of both catholicism and protestantism, internally, to each other and to the state. In one respect, however, *all* confessions have become *protestant*. All of them protest against the sovereignty of the regimes in matters relating to faith. The regimes may declare themselves in the most religious and Christian terms; they are not believed as soon as they attempt to impose restraints on conviction, and *the present epoch has the most decided antipathy to every use of religion for political purposes. Holy alliances* become unholy from that point of view. *Unions*, politically imposed on closely related confessions, suddenly arouse the long-dormant awareness of old differences, at the very time when the secular power attempts to establish that relationship and consolidate it.

In several respects that new ecclesiastical tendency is *reactionary*. – It shares that fate with the new *national* tendency, which has for example also led to a revival of the old prohibitive system for industries and trade, which one is pleased to call *national*. With the new vitality of the confessions, their old intolerance is reviving. They quarrel among themselves, they quarrel with the state, they contend with it regarding both the spiritual and secular magisterium. Catholicism in particular advances the claims of the church in a manner reminiscent of that of the old hierarchy. But the hierarchy has itself lost its ancient basis, and the protest of the new religion turns equally, within catholicism, against that of the Pope himself. On the other hand, the reactionary element in that movement is counter-balanced by the transformation of the former religious indifference into an averred hostility to Christianity, or even to all religion, which has seized hold of many minds. And it will without doubt be from *the purgatory of that denial* that the new power of religion will emerge and the new relationship of the state to the church likewise thereby be defined. *The state* and its rights may in an abstract sense be elevated even to idolatry. It is of a truly divine kind in so far as it is connected with *all* the social forces of mankind and is therefore also subject to their influence. The state, the legitimate expression of human freedom, cannot detach itself from the highest and innermost law of that freedom, of being in itself *a communicated independence*, which has to seek its explanation not only below itself in things temporal, or within itself in the human element, but also above itself in the divine and in the connection of the human spirit with that. It is that connection which Christianity most purely represents. For that reason it is

400

immortal; for that reason it is not merely a doctrine but a *divine power*. "Christianity is a mighty essence, with which mankind has more than once restored itself," said Goethe, who was not regarded as orthodox and by many barely as a Christian. "The Gospel – as Napoleon remarked on St Helena – possesses a secret power, something indescribably forceful, a warmth that acts on reason and enchants the heart. One feels the same about it as when contemplating the heavens. It is not a book, it is a living essence with a power that overcomes everything that opposes its effect. It is a book of all books; I do not tire of reading it and read it every day with the same pleasure. Nowhere else does one find that succession of beautiful thoughts, of beautiful, moral principles, which march past like the battalions of the heavenly hosts and awaken in the soul the same emotion as that inspired by the sky gleaming in all its infinitude during a beautiful summer night. Reading it, one is not only captivated but overwhelmed, and the soul is never in danger of going astray with this book. If the faithful gospel has once taken possession of our soul, it loves us. God is our friend, our father, in truth our God. A mother takes no more tender care of the child that she nourishes at her breast."[16]

What we have presented here relates to the inner, the spiritual forces that set our era in motion and will soon dominate it. Their effect is and will be an ever more devoted expression of that *collective personality* which is ultimately the soul in every social combination and that evolves at precisely the same rate as the recognition of the rights of the *individual personality*. Such is *the real power of the personality principle*. Like the principle of estates formerly, it has had its *martial* phase of development, is entering its *religious* one and will likewise, having passed through those stages, fully develop its *political* character. He who anticipates that development is in no hurry. He can wait.

One more discourse remains. What is the relationship of our *fatherland* to the social evolution of the new era? – That relationship is a distinctive one.

The only form of unity of which the ancient constitution of estates was capable was an *aristocratic* one, namely in reality one such for each estate separately, thus a noble, a priestly and a bourgeois one, and therefore on the whole an internally contending aristocracy. That contention is the origin of the *privileges of the estates*. Everyone who is familiar with their history knows that they were initially mostly wrested from the royal power and also that they both were and were considered to be a separate transaction between the king and the estate, in which their congruity with the best interests of the state and universal rights was in no way considered. It was a relationship of power to power, which changed according to the varying distribution of power. However, even that need for a *royal privilege* involved a sense of dependency on the side of the estates, while the granting of the privilege was a *ius maiestaticum*. That royal right did often come into conflict with itself by assuring privileges to one estate that would be too disadvantageous for another, which was therefore remedied, if danger threatened, by compensatory privileges. But in all of that there was nevertheless a presentiment of and requirement for a *higher interconnectedness in the state* than that which existed in the estates. *That* is what has been represented by *the kings*: by right of *that* principle they have established their realm; every advance in their power has meant a weakening of the power of the estates, until finally, shortly before the great revolution that has in our time thrown the interconnectedness of the state inwards, the power of the estates had become an antiquity, which only remained in traditions and formalities. There are exceptions to that general European situation, but they are more apparent than real and also different from one another. – We would name *Germany – England – Sweden*. In Germany, where the illusion of the ancient imperial dominion impeded the development of royal power, the latter moved forward in a different way and under the cloak of the estates themselves. One has here come to see *sovereign estates*, though represented by the *imperial princes*, who have arrogated to themselves the former power of the estates, each of them having individually broken it within their territories, following which they have thrown off even in name the former dependence on the head of the empire. In England the aristocracy realised its *common* interests early enough to combine together. Both that of the nobility and of the clergy also jointly felt the need not only of approval from above but also of support from below. The English *House of Lords* can be said to have constructed a democratic basis for itself in the *House of Commons*; the last-named, as long as it remained under the control of the *aristocracy*, made the latter such a strong intermediate power between the crown and the people that, by means of some constitutional fictions, it became in reality the ruling power. How that situation has latterly changed is well known. – In Sweden the originally democratic basis of the constitution has not first been destroyed and then reconstituted by the aristocracy. It is and remains the indestructible foundation on which the constitution has evolved. Our estates all originate from the ancient Swedish *allodial freedom*, still unextinguished in the Swedish estate of peasants. To our constitution the words therefore apply in full measure that I once used about it: "A connection with the maternal soil is necessary for every plant, if it is not to fade away – without that connection neither the dew of heaven nor the rays of the sun will help it. The top should not imagine that it is a separate tree, even if it is situated so high that it does not see its root. If the nourishing sap does not rise to it from below, the next day will see it withered."[17] – Violent storms have tested, impeded and distorted the natural growth of the Swedish constitution. Among us, too, the aristocracy formerly felt the need to combine in order to rule. The Swedish one united with those of Denmark and Norway in order to maintain an association of the entire Scandinavian North in *the Union of Kalmar*, of which the people at that time experienced only the disadvantages. Sweden broke free from the trammels of the union with a reborn national sentiment, and on the compact between Swedish popular power and Swedish royal power, which was then consolidated, has never since then been dissolved and is indissoluble, the Swedish state was founded. The era of conquests and its consequences at first gave rise to the rule of the aristocracy in Sweden and then brought it down, when internal evils threatened the survival both of the kingdom and of freedom. The absolutism introduced by Charles XI with the assistance of the non-noble estates and the newer nobility was used by Charles XII with such martial recklessness that the power of both the king and of Sweden collapsed together. But for the fact that the *Swedish estates* could emerge from those ruins, themselves governing under a nominal king, the old and new aristocracy, whose victory that was, had not themselves to thank but the tradition that *the Swedish people* was fully represented in our estates by the presence of the estate of peasants, although it was excluded from all real influence on general affairs. In that new situation, however, the aristocracy itself sensed that its position had changed, as it thenceforward acted not as an *estate* but as a *party*. Party rule had to yield to a restored monarchical one, and that again, losing itself in the infatuation of autocracy, was followed by the constitution that is our present one, tempered by royal power, the power of the people, the growing influence of the middle class and the heightened national consciousness of the people. All the social elements of the new era are mingled in it with the old traditional ones in such a unique manner that their working against and with each other towards a *new* expression of the whole must be slower here than elsewhere. Royal absolutism has become impossible. The middle class, ever more incorporated into the system of government by the concessions made by the estates, cannot here generally apply its great political instrument of an electoral register based simply on wealth, as our ancient constitution stands *above* that, in that any electoral register would here curtail political rights that the majority of the people already possess. For a representation based on the principle of personality, which would here require a more consistent implementation than anywhere else, public opinion is not yet ready, while here, too, the divergence between the interests of the *propertied* and the *non-propertied* indicates the common social malady of our time. In our representation, divided by estates, we have thus also latterly seen the old *principle of estates* revived in connection with the new proposal on representation. But even that reaction – like all forms of reaction that have in Europe accompanied the consolidated power of *the middle class* or attached themselves to the resurgent *national* interests, the newly awakened *religious* needs – even *that* reaction, I say, suffers from having based itself on what is in reality a *forward-moving* social principle. For even the principle of estates is such a one. It is nowadays transformed. It has returned to the general sphere of civic life, and only from there can it again emerge in a freer, purer form. There is no defender of the old privileges of the estates who is not secretly aware of that and who can avoid an inner conflict while he fights for the latter.

Here I conclude this introductory discourse. I have freely expressed convictions that I hold profoundly. I leave a gentle judgment of them to the *faith*, the *love* and the *hope* that act in a reconciling fashion in all human affairs and by which I, too, live. – And what moment could more appropriately connect them than specifically the present one? – I have lived to see the sons of the prince to whom two nations now lovingly look up, on whose head rest the crowns of Sweden and Norway, united by his great father; I have lived to see them enter the same lecture room where I once saw him personally as a youth listening to the words of the teacher. I have lived to see the sons of king Oscar, surrounded by the youth that is moving towards its adult days, dedicate themselves in the temple of the sciences to the service of the fatherland and of mankind. – I welcome that as an auspicious sign for me, for this seat of learning, for the fatherland, for king and people. – An old man's blessing does no harm. So I wish to call down the blessing of heaven on these young princes, on the generation of youths that surrounds them, on the unknown future that resides in all these young breasts. May it be happy, may it be glorious! May it be full of the divine honour that is based on *justice* and *truth*! May it be worthy of the fatherland, whose fortunes we shall now proceed to contemplate!

Excerpt from the Third lecture
– 1844 (pages 408-426)

THE GOVERNMENT OF Gustaf III marks a strange transitional epoch in our history. It revealed internal contradictions both in the character of the king and in the constitution that he introduced. He had carried out the revolution of 19 August 1772 in a manner that was as audacious as it was light-handed and successful. It was a change on the political scene that was completed in a few hours, cost not a drop of blood, was greeted with delight by the people and was suited to display the mildness of the king in the most favourable light. He later boasted that he had for three days possessed the greatest sovereignty that any ruler had held and had voluntarily relinquished it.

The illusions of a government of estates and of parties had vanished, but others took their place. The king wished for autocracy in *substance* but not in *name*. That he shrank from the name was part of the general character of the enlightened-despotism school of rulers to which he belonged but also had other causes related to his own position. The word *sovereignty*, in the sense that was attached to it here, was a name that was with good reason feared in Sweden, where it recalled great misfortunes. Gustaf was not himself a great admirer of the epoch of Karl XI and Karl XII, whereas Gustaf Adolf was for him the object of unqualified admiration. One had seen the traditions of the era of Gustaf Adolf return even during the period of party conflict and be invoked by the nobility against the commoner estates, which on the contrary showed a preference for that of Karl XI. At a time when the 'Hats' still flattered Adolf Fredrik and Lovisa with the prospect of restoring royal power, that party had promised to base it again on the so-called 'form of government' of Gustaf Adolf – the nature and real originator of which we know. From 1748 onward the plan was approved of by France, the ally of the Hats, and the French cabinet compared that form of government to that of England.[18] Already after the death of king Fredrik in 1751 it became apparent that the ruling party did not intend to keep the promise that it had held out to the young royal couple, and the latter's unfortunate attempt at a revolution of its own in 1756, bloodily suppressed, completed the breach between the court and its former friends. It was the earliest, traumatic childhood memory of Gustaf III; it could never be effaced from his soul. He returns to it in his harsh address to the nobility in the parliament of 1789: "they had once dared to lay hands on his father's crown and perhaps meant to tussle with himself over his sceptre, but in his hand it would not waver." – On the other hand, after the fall of the Hat party during the parliament of 1766, the equal hostility to the throne of the Cap party, with even narrower views and greater cantankerousness, had filled him with a disgust and loathing that was intensified to contempt when the leaders of that party ever more openly placed themselves under Russian protection against their king.

That Gustaf III at the moment of the successful revolution of 1772 was aligned with the Swedish people,
which, being as tired of the autocracy as of party rule, had
been ready to rally round their king with a more extensive
representation than that of the old estates (which had already in part been demanded in 1719), that fact evaded his
otherwise sharp perception. It may perhaps have been less
dangerous then than during the subsequent crisis of 1789,
when the king considered changing the system of representation, though without carrying it out.[19] – But neither
he nor the time was ready for that. Gustaf III knew the
people only as a commoner estate, or as a party name, invoked by rival factions.

However, both council and estates had proved themselves all too dangerous next to the throne and had attached to themselves associations that were all too re-
pellent for them to be able to retain their rights. What
remained was to leave them the name of freedom but keep
dominion for oneself. That was what happened by means
of the form of government adopted in 1772, in which the
power of the king is even greater than it appears, as its
actual limits are left undefined. The king had forgotten to
make only one provision ambiguous, namely the requirement for the assent of the estates to a war of aggression,
and that is also the only one that he could not avoid openly infringing. Otherwise one sees the lustre of both the
throne and the aristocracy extending across everything.
The king loved both far too much not to want to combine
them. A predilection for the nobility was part of his nature, upbringing and habits. But he only wanted to have
the aristocracy as décor around the throne. For that purpose both the parliament act and the rules for the house of

the nobility from the time of Gustaf Adolf were searched out, and the method of governing during his glorious days was said to have been restored in Sweden.

Gustaf III's later revolution of 1789 – for that is what it was again, and such outbreaks of disease in the body politic now begin to recur periodically in Sweden – is in all respects the opposite to that of 1772. It is the illusion of 1772 that disappears. That the estates, so recently holding power, that the Swedish nobility in particular would be content with the delusion of a somewhat unequally distributed royal favour, while scarcely a shadow remained of its former political rights, was inconceivable. Fear of the former unrest, enjoyment of the subsequent tranquillity, the honeymoon of the new royal power, which lasted longer than usual, all of that contributed to suppress the discontent for a long time, and collisions could be avoided as long as the king did not need the estates. He had succeeded in making his first parliament (in 1778) almost entirely into a loyal ceremony. During the second one (in 1786) conditions had already changed so much that it had to be hurriedly dissolved. In the third one (1789) the conflict between him and all the traditions of the previous way of governing culminated. – The moment had come when he could neither do without the estates nor make use of them as they had existed until then. His position was already so difficult that he appears to have thrown himself into the Russian war in order to precipitate an internal breach. It did not fail to occur. The aristocratic opposition established itself in the actual camp between the king and the enemy. The king again positioned himself in the parliament of 1789 between the nobility and the commoner estates. He used the resentment of the latter as a means to curb his nobility and he succeeded, at the cost of a few concessions, which gave genuine advantages to the estate of the peasants, in having what was in reality an unlimited power conceded to him. Thus the unresolved problem of the former government of estates with regard to *the validity of the decisions of the three estates against the first* was finally decided by the intervention of the royal power but in a revolutionary and violent manner. The victory that the king had won by violating all his feelings and inclinations he hardly dared to admit to himself. It did also cost him his life.

It was a small revolution in a distant corner of the world compared to the great one that had simultaneously broken out in France and to which Gustaf III felt such hostility that he was for a time willing to take command of the campaign of the monarchs against it. His son regarded that enmity as his most sacred legacy. With a far better instinct for simple justice than his father, but lacking all martial abilities, he allowed himself to be diverted from a career suited only to times of peace by an ungovernable hatred, heightened even to fanaticism, against Napoleon and sacrificed his kingdom and his crown to that hatred.

Sweden, having come out of the conflict with the loss of a third of its territory and doomed to soon see the rest partitioned, rose with a newly awakened national consciousness, and one will in vain seek to deprive us of the fruits of that. The renunciation of old privileges that distinguished the parliament of 1809 and in which the Swedish nobility set a truly noble example, the extension of political rights that has since then gradually occurred by incorporating into the individual estates social classes hitherto excluded from representation, have already so fundamentally

411

changed the estates of the realm, the changes being so much in tune with the entire spirit of our time and demanding other more extensive ones, that anyone who, underrating them, would today adhere to the old principle of estates lacks any other basis than the uncertain one that can be conjured up through political passions.

But *those* passions are in every epoch subject to particular influences, according to the motives that prevail most widely at the time. In our own day all the political passions are subject to the influence of *demagogy*, even in the camps where apparently quite different banners wave. That is due to the newly-won political importance of the peoples, which no one can in reality deny. – There are now no politics that do not act in *the name of freedom*. Even the defenders of power and privilege are obliged to invoke it. Or can the phenomenon escape the notice of the observer that legitimists and ultras everywhere appear to extend a hand to the radicals, or at least try to speak their language, wherever it comes to checking the rising power of the middle class, and that in those representative systems where a class *below* the middle class already has a voice, the latter class is preferentially chosen as a field of operations, either in order to awaken in it a spirit of its own, hostile to the middle class, of being an estate, or else in order to arouse fear by the extremism of democratic demands? – In the French revolution one sees directly opposite tendencies operating to the same destructive end. It is a leverage of which foreign policy has often made use for its purposes. And that policy is not yet exhausted. Since the July revolution ever clearer symptoms of that kind have shown themselves in the internal party movements of Europe. – It is far from being the case that the dangers of anarchy primarily confront us in the concessions made to modern demands. They exist in a far more real form behind the development of society and conceal themselves in an ambuscade manned by its enemies. – It is better, then, to look the danger in the face and rationally consider how it can be not only combated but prevented.

One has to admit that a change in the system of representation has never hitherto occurred in Sweden except by means of and through a revolution, and of revolutions of our kind we have already had too many. A change in representation is in itself an act of *national independence*. Independence of the peoples can be both *internal* and *external*, but the connection between the two is *indissoluble* – and the evidence for that being so is unlikely to fail to appear among us either. – There are examples of *internal* political crises, happily overcome without also having been *external* crises. One sees such admirable examples in great nations, far advanced along the path of civic freedom, and they show what results may be achieved by a debate conducted with honesty and patience. The North American free states set such an example after gaining independence by a peacefully established central constitution. England has set another by the reform bill. – Reform without revolution must in general be the motto of the law-abiding friend of freedom, and a free discussion on the preconditions for freedom is not only assured to us through our constitution but that discussion is also at present a civic duty. – To me it is clearer what is *not* possible with regard to the forms and operation of our representative system than what *can* and *ought* to happen to change it. But an understanding of the former already throws light on the latter.

413

If the question whether our *present* constitution can function could be unconditionally answered with a *no*, then the matter would to that extent be decided. But that very question is far too indefinite and presupposes another: what *is* in fact the nature of our present constitution? – Whatever *is*, as an object of observation and experience, would seem to be easy to determine. Nonetheless, there is no subject on which one comes across more prejudices. If, for example, it is a matter of introducing an improved code of criminal and civil law, and if the original task was to combine into a whole and codify the changes that our general legal code of 1734 has undergone, one must find it obvious that the men to whom the work has been entrusted will not be able to realise how those changes that have occurred over the past hundred years can be amalgamated into a whole and be understood without taking into account the gradually modified principles in legislation that have in the meantime manifested themselves not only here but in Europe. They express those principles – and one accuses them of coming up with a tremendous novelty. The entire legal code of 1734, on the other hand, at once appears in an idealised light as the good old system, although it is the good in it that is not due to disappear but, on the contrary, the old that has already disappeared. – I already gave an example of that kind from an even higher level in the first of these lectures. Nothing is more certain than that the power of estates in Europe was curbed by the kings. Yet it is now throughout Europe the defenders of the privileges of the estates who wish to be regarded as the most reliable defenders and friends of monarchy.

What I call *impossible* in our present system of representation is *everything that aims at returning it to before 1809* – everything that now implies a denial of the basic principles that were articulated *then*, both with regard to the operation of the system of representation, as it was laid down in the government act of 1809, and to leaving the transformation of our system of representation to the future. The following will explain my meaning most clearly.

The significance of the estates as a state power depends on the definition of what is required for a *resolution of the estates of the realm*. That question has more than one aspect. First of all it requires a definition of what can become the *object* of a resolution of the estates. We have seen how indefinite the sphere of their activities formerly was – how, according to the parliament act of Gustaf Adolf, the king, in cases where the estates differed in their views, reserved the right to decide himself – how the nobility during the regencies made the same claim, and how the nobility finally demanded that it could not be outvoted. A more precise definition of the role of the estates in the legislative process coincided under Karl XI with the downfall of the aristocracy. It was then declared that all *regulatory* and *administrative* legislation was the sole prerogative of the king. The circumstances were such that that concession at the time covered everything. – After the fall of the autocracy the estates took control of *all* legislation. Gustaf III shared it with them, more in name than in reality, but could not prevent a differentiation from already being made in the resolutions of the 1778 parliament between the question of law which king and estates had the right to *jointly* decide and those that the king merely laid before the estates for their humble opinion. That was connected with a question that was already raised in the same parliament: *how the votes of the estates should be calculated on general questions of law* (one did not yet distinguish between them and constitutional questions). – According to the *letter*, as we have seen, that was already laid down in the parliament act of 1723; that was done again under Gustaf III in the parliament of 1786. In *reality* the situation was so undecided that the danger of a threatening majority of estates if the commoner estates acted together had provoked the revolution of 1772 and that the validity of the votes of those three estates *against* the first one could enter Swedish constitutional law only with a new revolution in the opposite direction, in 1789.

We have pointed out the rock onto which our ship of state has run *twice* within living memory. Those who wish our constitution to be preserved ought to be aware how to avoid such a shipwreck for the *third* time.

How to deal with issues on which no estate can be subordinated to the others or decide by itself and those that, even if two estates are opposed to two, can neither lapse nor be left to the discretion of the king, remained undetermined in our public law until the government act of 1809 sought to prevent the dangers that arise in such circumstances by establishing a special institution, later further developed, which I do not hesitate to regard as a basic precondition for the continuous functioning of our present constitution.

That is the establishment of the *expanded committees*, in which such issues are to be decided by members elected in equal numbers by all the estates – voting *per capita*, not *by estates*.

416

The government act of 1809 prescribed that expedient. It was first employed in cases relating to the administration of the state and the amount of the vote of supply appropriate to that. – For changes in the constitutional law the unanimous assent of the king and all the estates was required. But as one had also with the necessary prudence wished to leave room for improvements in the constitutional law (which could not be raised in the plenary sessions of the estates but were to be notified to the standing committee on the constitution), once the final report of the committee had been submitted, the decision ought only to be taken by the estates in the following parliament.[20] It soon emerged that the legislators of 1809 had relied too much on the decision-making powers of the standing committee on the constitution, in certain cases with the authority of the estates, as they appeared to presume that the estates would not be able to modify a proposal of the standing committee on the constitution in order to get it presented in the form in which they thought it should most appropriately be referred for a decision by the next parliament. The contradiction implied in that with the right otherwise generally allowed to the estates to scrutinise and modify the proposals of their committees before they were adopted or rejected led in the parliament of 1815, once the standing committees on the constitution both in 1810 and 1812 had delivered an opinion on that, to the addendum in § 56 of the government act that also created an *expanded standing committee on the constitution*. The clear intention of the addendum is that, just as each estate separately has the right to adopt or reject a proposed change in the constitutional law when it is submitted for a final decision, so also the opinion of

417

no estate, "if it does not comply with the others," can be suppressed with regard to the form of the proposal itself already in the parliament in which it is being prepared but should then become subject to a vote within the expanded standing committee on the constitution.[21]

There is thus a *possibility* that the meaning of a majority within an expanded standing committee on the constitution may be *different* from that of the estates and that, as a consequence of that, a *motion* on a change relating to constitutional law not approved by the majority of the estates may be left dormant in one parliament, to be decided in the next one. But that possibility can so little be assumed to be alien to our constitutional law that the essential distinguishing character of our form of government *is* precisely to have opened up that possibility, with the aim of thereby preventing those direct collisions between the individual estates by which our constitution of estates has more than once broken itself to pieces. – On questions of constitutional law nothing has yet been essentially decided by means of that possibility. It is only a *motion* that is prepared, which is open to public discussion until the next parliament and which, when it comes to be decided, the *veto* of a single estate can overthrow. If one or two estates then use their veto to defeat a motion that has otherwise won the support of many citizens, one may *wish* that the situation were different; but no one has the right to *complain* about the exercise of a *lawful* right.

What one could regret with every reason would be if one or two estates, because a motion such as the new proposal on representation tabled in 1840 was not in accord with the view of those estates, should seek to destroy the possibility provided by the constitutional law to get such questions prepared and instead wish to turn its *veto* against the *motio*n as such, or, if two estates stand against two, declare *the motion* to have *lapsed*. – That would not only be to push our form of government back beyond 1809; it would be to revive the principle of estates in a cruder form than it has had in Sweden since our unhappy era of party rule.

It cannot escape anyone that our constitutional law has sought by means of the rights of the *expanded committees* to reduce the acerbity of the old differences between the estates. It was in the *expanded committees* that it first removed the *voting by estate*, and it has since then permitted the same kind of voting for the committees of *all* of the estates.[22] – Generally speaking, a principle of estates modified by the influence of the civic principle reveals itself in our present constitution. That was the reason for the concessions by the estates in 1809; that was the reason for the incorporation, since then continued, of hitherto unrepresented social classes into our old estates.[23] It would be consistent of the reactionary sector that wishes to oppose the rights of the expanded standing committee on the constitution under constitutional law if it should also feel hostile to all those concessions. And if they had not already been made – would they, I wonder, be made *now*?

Our present constitution has left one major difficulty unresolved, namely the *relationship* of the civic principle in the system of representation to the principle of estates. One is a representative as a *Swedish nobleman, clergyman, burgher, peasant*; one is not so as a *Swedish citizen*, without any of those qualifications, however well suited one might otherwise be for that, and one cannot, according to the currently existing rules, become one. We have seen how one has attempted to *strengthen* the civic element in the

419

principle of estates. But is the principle of estates capacious enough to absorb into itself the concept of a citizen? Should the relationship not rather be *reversed*, so that citizenship becomes the *principle* and the qualification by estate an *element* subordinate to that? Should not the former determine the latter and not the other way round?

Our answer to that question cannot be ambiguous. In the first of these lectures I have shown in general that *such a reversal has already occurred* – that it is that from which the new state has evolved and is evolving, and that the new state therefore already *possesses* a *content* that seeks and must seek corresponding *forms* for itself. How that fact manifests itself *among us* has then been the object of our discourse. – We shall now begin to conclude it.

The abovementionèd situation did not escape the notice of the first standing committee on the constitution of 1809-10. Within two weeks it had, at a moment of extreme national peril, had to complete its assignment with the proposal for the government act that was subsequently adopted by the king and the estates, which introduced such important improvements to our old constitution. The committee, which had partly proposed, partly indicated the changes that were compatible with the retention of our constitution of estates, nonetheless concluded by admitting the inadequacy of its forms. It stated in its memorial on the *national representation*, to quote: that it *"has not been able to avoid admitting that the greater part of the reasons for the misunderstanding, the delaying and the disorder in the conduct of business, as well as for the disputes between the estates that have so often divided the nation, shaken the foundations of the social order and overthrown the constitution, lay in the division into estates,"* – That the *disputes between the estates* should recur at the very moment when that truth expressed within our representation by such an important authority thirty-five years ago are beginning to make themselves felt again, one might have expected – nor have they failed to appear.

I have quoted one of the most excellent official publications that have been penned in Swedish. Its main contents have for far too long been consigned to oblivion,[24] first when the great external political events occupied everyone's attention above all else and then, when peace had returned, a continued softening of the sharpness of the principle of estates by the extension of the representation (though always *within* the old categories of estates) appeared as the middle way that lay closest at hand. Only one attempt remained to be made, intended to move in the same direction but already falling *outside* the middle way: to retain our *four* estates but let the unrepresented form a *fifth* one alongside them, and that attempt is now under way.[25]

But already the *first* standing committee on the constitution declared that to be a *diversion*. After the section that we have just quoted in the memorial of the committee it says: "*the majority of the committee has on the grounds of those reasons viewed the division into estates as the chief fault in our representative system and has therefore to begin with, on the question of the claims of those who are unrepresented, held themselves obliged to entirely set aside the one for a fifth estate. As interests already diverge, the disadvantages of that are unlikely to be overcome by increasing them by a new corporation, and if it were thereby thought that one had prevented the occurrence of tied votes between the estates, one would perhaps soon enough find that the measure one had adopted to promote the conduct of business is more likely to prevent its being concluded. The competition to be the last to decide would, we fear, become a new cause of delays and discord between the estates. It is in any case never by means of the number of wheels in an already complicated piece of machinery that one improves its motion; it is by the regularity and power of its effect, by the removal of all unnecessary secondary matters that it can attain the strength that accords with its construction and with its purpose."* – My view is that even today nothing better could be said against the proposal to add a *fifth* estate to the four that already share our representation between themselves.

It is in reality the *middle class* that we are dealing with, and the more complete representation of which one wants to give to the form of a separate estate, alongside the old estates. But that is all the more unsuitable, even impossible, because the middle class has emerged by the progressive dissolution of the old estates, so that it can neither be absorbed by the latter nor be divided according to any new *differences of estate* or *class*, definable in advance. For the fact that all such differences within it have become *fluid* is precisely what constitutes the essence of the middle class. The cause of that, as we have seen, is that the middle class now represents the wealth that has remained mobile within society, due to the growing proportion of intelligence in work. That is why it claims that its very *wealth* is evidence of *education*. It now collectively embraces all the so-called *higher* classes in society, that is to say, all those citizens whose material affluence above all provides them with the leisure and opportunity to acquire the advantages of education. That is why it everywhere makes such a degree of wealth a precondition for the exercise of political rights and is all too inclined to establish that precondition as the *only* one. We see in all of this a new social standing, far removed from the old circumstances of the estates, the strong as well as weak sides of which I already attempted to describe in the first lecture.[26]

I have wished to establish what in our constitution is *not possible* – namely not possible without denying the preconditions on which it is based, and thereby *destroying* it. One will take up that statement of mine and ask *who* then are those who misjudge it to such an extent? The answer may first be given from a purely formal point of view. – It is undeniable that the constitution of 1809 itself opened up the possibility of its own *transformation*; it prescribed the legal forms for the preparation and adoption of that. That acknowledged possibility is one of the preconditions on which it is based. Those who utilise the constitutional means to achieve such changes are thus positioned *within*, not *outside* the constitution. The opposite circumstance applies to those who would deny or prevent the deployment of those constitutional means. Among them I count those who cannot even accept that the majority within an *expanded standing committee on the constitution* will be a *different* one from that of the estates, although the authority of the expanded committee does not extend further than to postponing a duly proposed change in the constitutional law until the next parliament, as its adoption requires the *combined* assent of the king and all four estates.

It will be objected that this answer, which disregards the content and nature of the changes demanded, is simply evasive. What is the destruction of the constitution if not changing the foundation on which it rests, namely *the principle of estates*? – The answer is that our representative system *no longer* rests on that principle in its former sense and that the principle of estates, by the means allowed by our constitutional law, will change places and be *subordinated to the civic principle* – at the same rate as the latter manifests itself within the estates themselves – that is the real *fundamental prerequisite* of our constitution; that is its *spirit* even as expressed in *writing*. It is bold, yet as noble as it is lawful, and it embodies the greatest tribute to the peaceful power of conviction that any people has yet paid.

I have attempted to show that the change has already occurred in the *matter* itself, so that the question now in effect relates to the most appropriate *forms* in which to express it. But precisely in that respect opinions are still so divided that the inherently slow progress of the constitutional debate must thereby be even further delayed.

It is by no means with the same confidence that I express my thoughts regarding the positive aspect of the question. What is *not possible* in our constitution without destroying it can be explained on general grounds. What is at present *possible* and *advisable* with regard to changing it is harder to determine, nor can it strictly speaking be decided simply according to what one regards as *right*. Every compromise between existing new and old interests is a political transaction, to a certain degree depending on mutual concessions. – To a certain degree, I say. For if a *new social principle* has established itself, all that remains is to accept it, and the modifications can only concern the more or less immediate implementation of its consequences. That *they*, however, should be explicitly *formulated* to their full extent as soon as they are *realised* is part of the honesty of the debate, and I therefore did not hesitate, as a member of parliament in 1840, to express convictions on the question of representation, the apparent paradox-

ality of which I could easily foresee would become a matter for ridicule. In these lectures I have tried to develop
them further, but would also wish not only to advocate
the modifications in the use of the political principle of
personality[27] that I have indicated from the beginning but
also to add others with the same purpose.

The main subject of the debate is whether the real content of the question of representation is compatible with
the form of *elections* by *estates* as *classes*, or not. – The former expression in reality includes two alternatives. *Elections by estates* would be *elections* within the old categories
of estates, as far as possible modified in accordance with
the demands of our time, or with the addition of a *fifth*
estate, in order to more fully satisfy the claims of the unrepresented. Our conservatives appear to be inclined to
deal with the matter on that basis. They seem not to realise that, by admitting the small word *elections* in *all* estates,
they have overthrown the entirety of our representation
by estates. The right of representation of the *nobility* is
not based on elections but on an *uncontested right*. If that
were to be *given up*, which the nobility once declared itself
willing to do on certain conditions, *the Swedish representative system would already be fundamentally transformed*. For
nothing seems more certain to me than that the Swedish nobility, which has for so long acted as a national representation in Sweden, can now only return its right of
representation into the hands of the nation, in order to
receive it back from them as a voluntarily given token of
appreciation for civic merit. That is the noblest, the most
worthy, the only possible procedure. If that is the case –
and I appeal in this regard to the innermost feelings of
the Swedish nobility – then the *nature* of the question of

representation is decided, for the other estates as well. The elections are placed in the hands of the nation and have thereby ceased to be *elections by estates.*

But what significance could one give to *elections by classes*, which would not be *elections by estates*? – There is in fact a new class in society that neither is nor can become an estate, like the old estates, and whose existence is nevertheless indisputable. We have already characterised it. The question of whether one wishes to recognise *the middle class* with its new social power comes too late. It is there, as a fact, which has to be accepted. The only doubt is whether one ought to recognise both everything that it *is* and everything that it *desires to be*. One can do one without the other, that is to say: one can accept *the middle c*lass in its newly-gained significance but reject its claim to exclusively represent *the people*.[28] – That would be to recognise a new social formation that is already completed – and at the same time leave room for a more extensive one, which is already on the way.

If one accepts the middle class, there is no way to avoid accepting its politically distinctive feature, which is wealth, as both the result of and a means towards education. One then has to consider an electoral register graded according to wealth. But from that concession it does not follow that such grading might not and ought not to be carried on from the *larger* property to the *lesser*, or even to the *lowest level of possible subsistence*. That again brings us on to the subject of the basic proposition, already formulated by our first standing committee on the constitution: "*that all Swedish citizens, without distinction of estate, professions or way of life, should be entitled to participate in the election of the nation's authorised representatives as custodians of its legisla-*

tion; and that the exercise of that electoral right should depend only on the qualities of being domiciled, independent and of age, which are considered requisite for society, as a surety for making use of such a right."[29] The only constitutional preferential right that I would allow the middle class, or everything that could roughly be included in it,[30] would be that of *direct* elections, whereas the elections at a lower level, on the other hand, ought to be, as they still largely are among us, *indirect*. I neither can nor wish to enter into the details of a proposal on representation but must add that, with regard to them, I largely agree with a proposal put forward by two respected citizens, which has been in the public domain for fifteen years. The following words in the introduction to it I would like to adopt as my own: "We have not been able to reconcile making the right to vote at once virtually *general* and the elections without exception *direct* with the knowledge that we have of the present condition and circumstances of the Swedish people. We have not for a moment hesitated to extend the right to vote as far as we have considered possible, and perhaps further than it has existed hitherto in any country in our part of the world, but we have neither found it advisable or possible to make the districts for direct elections too small nor believed that we can concentrate excessive numbers of electors in larger districts. We have therefore had to accept two kinds of elections of representatives: one, as hitherto, in rural areas, through *electors*, for the large number of those entitled to vote who cannot without inconvenience gather to a man, and the other *direct*, for those electors among whom one has the right to assume the interest in the matter, the leisure from daily cares of work and the general affluence that are required to spend toil, time and means on journeys to more distant meeting places. In the case of elections through electors we have restricted eligibility to the district alone, as we have wished that there will never be lacking in the representation a certain number of men from every particular province. In the case of the direct election we have left eligibility unrestricted, partly because we have considered the acquaintance of the electors with eligible men outside the district to be greater and more reliable here and partly because we have wished to give an opportunity to the individual who, for whatever reason or cause, may have been prevented from taking part in an election in his own district, to benefit in another from the trust to which his real merit may possibly entitle him.[31]

I would be speaking against my own conviction if I asserted that our age in particular is suited to carry out great changes. It should not do so. But the changes will impose themselves on it, and it will be strengthened and tempered by that necessity. Our age is a youthful age, but not a forceful age. In our time the young generation predominates, which, having come into existence after the great wars, is full of the claims of the new era, without having shared its dangers, and has now, during a long peace, found subjects for its restlessness rather than objectives for serious activity.[32] It will not turn grey without being tested. All tests emanate from real, not from imaginary circumstances, and the most testing reality of our age lies in the heightened, liberated influence of the spiritual forces. Being aware of that, which will leave no one unaffected, we can also be assured that *none of the great social questions that the most recent past has raised and our age has received – will lapse.*

And with that these lectures have reached their conclusion. The presentation has been incomplete but the subject elevated and well worthy of consideration by the sons of Sweden and to be carried in their hearts by its princes. I have summoned up ancient Swedish memories. May they inspire to new noble activity and bear fruit in deeds and pursuits worthy to be remembered by our posterity! May all the old Swedish virtues live that once gave us an honourable position among the peoples! And all the Swedish vices and faults die away, disappear, which more than once have brought us to the brink of destruction! – And may the saving, protective hand rest over us in which no one has yet trusted in vain! – Live ye well!

Notes

1 Dumont, *Souvenirs sur Mirabeau et sur les deux premières assemblées législatives*, Paris, 1832, p. 139.
2 Cf. *Det europeiska samhällets begynnelser, akademiskt program af E.G. Geijer*, Upsala, 1844. The entire legal system of antiquity, from which the slave was excluded, rests on the fact that the slave could not legally possess a family. *Servi gentem vel genus non habent* [Slaves have neither social status nor ancestry] say the Roman jurists. Thence the definition of *being well-born*: *gentem habent soli, quorum parentes nemini servierunt* (social status belongs only to those whose ancestors never served anyone); from which it follows that the freed slave and his descendants could never become well-born either. The prejudice still current in the North American republics, deriving from the slave states,

that the blood of a slave in however distant a degree is passed on and remains indelible with its stigma, is old or new paganism.

3 What is said here about the religions has, for the sake of context, been introduced from a subsequent lecture. For the same reason many additions have now been incorporated into this lecture, which originally was shorter and delivered ex tempore.

4 I Peter 2:9.

5 [That applies only to Germanic languages. The Swedish 'mässa' (like German 'Messe') is derived from the Latin *missa*.]

6 See above, p. 273. [Footnotes refer to the Collected Works of Erik Gustaf Geijer, Stockholm, 1874]

7 Cf. vol. 2, p. 95.

8 See above, p. 125.

9 Cf. *Feudalism and republicanism*, vol. 2, p. 269.

10 Cf. above, p. 52.

11 Cf. above, p. 148.

12 The rapid growth in population that has occurred during the calm of peace after the great wars, has in particular affected the class that depends for its needs on daily work. – The effect of vaccination in reducing mortality among the children probably manifests itself chiefly in its impact on the numbers. But the large-scale modern industry, with all the dominion it offers to capital over the worker, has also been a fairly active cause of the rapid rise in population. Mechanisation, for example, which would appear to reduce the need for workers, has so far increased production that it thereby *supports many more* than the old industry.

It is precisely in the manufacturing districts that
the population of England has increased to such an
astonishing extent.

13   See above, p. 242.

14   See above, p. 126.

15   An interesting analysis of the relationship between
bourgeoisie and *peuple* is to be found in Stein, *Der
Socialismus und Communismus des heutigen Frankreichs.
Ein Beytrag zur Zeitgeschichte.* Leipzig, 1842.

16   *Sentimens de Napoléon sur la divinité du Jésus-Christ. Pensées
recueillies à S:te Hélène par M:r le Comte de Montholon.*

17   *Tal i anledning af H. K. H. kronprinsens antagande af högsta
styrelsen öfver Upsala akademi 1818.* (See vol. 7 of this
edition.)

18   Cf. the abovementioned work (vol. 6, p. 101).

19   Cf. Winquist, 'Berättelse om riksdagen 1789' in the
journal *Frej*, 20, pt 21.

20   Exceptions were made for changes to the constitutional
law proposed by *the king*, which could be rejected in
the same parliament in which they were raised, that is
if the standing committee on the constitution at once
recommends their rejection.

21   It was finally the proposal for an addendum to § 56
of the government act from the standing committee
on the constitution in 1812 that was adopted in the
parliament of 1815. In the committee's memorial on
the matter it says: "As the unanimous vote of all the
estates is required for the enactment of constitutional
law, the committee has taken care to formulate the
rules in such a way that the ultimate decision must
be able to be reached on a motion answerable by *yes*
and *no*. That required that all adjustment of views,

if, in examining the original motion, they should remain divergent in the estates of the realm, should precede the definitive resolution, which could not contain anything but a complete approval or a straight rejection. The committee has therefore been of the opinion that such adjustment should occur in the same parliament in which the question is raised and tabled, so that it should be fully prepared for a decision by yes or no in the following one. The expansion of the standing committee on the constitution that has been proposed for the purpose of carrying out adjustments is thus of quite a different nature from the panels that are prescribed for the other committees in the government act. The same authority to decide that they possess could not be given to the former, as the ultimate authority to decide on these issues must belong to the estates themselves, among which the veto of a single estate is sufficient to prevent the adoption of a motion. On the other hand, if, after attempts made by the committee to unite the estates of the realm behind a unanimous report, that did not succeed, there ought to be a means of formulating, by a per capita vote, such a definitive motion that it could without any changes be adopted or rejected. In that way the committee has been of the opinion that it is able to provide every possible opportunity to examine the issues, compare the opinions, create a consensus and finally formulate the motion clearly, so that it should be possible to arrive at a definite decision."
– Cf. *Sveriges statsförfattningsrätt*, by C. Neumann, Stockholm, 1844, I: 386.

22 That, too, was recommended in the first proposal for
     a parliament act in 1809. The proposal was repeated
     until it was adopted in 1823.

23 A right to representation was granted by the
     parliament of 1823 to the universities and the
     academy of sciences in the estate of the clergy – by the
     parliament of 1828-1830 to the mining industry, even
     outside the Falun mining district, in the estate of the
     burghers – by the parliament of 1834-1835 to noble
     freeholders in the estate of the peasants. The additional
     inclusion in the estate of the peasants of commoners
     owning a manor who do not belong to another estate,
     recommended by the estates in 1840, has now received
     the royal assent.

24 The memorial is not included in the appendix to
     the protocols of the estates of the realm from the
     parliament of 1809-10 but is cited there "as separately
     printed." – It has now been reprinted in the new
     edition of *Sveriges grundlagar* etc. Stockholm, 1844,
     published by Norstedt & Söner. The memorial, dated
     24 March 1810, is signed by the members of the
     standing committee on the constitution, from the
     nobility by: Claes Fleming, A.J. Silfversparre, A.G.
     Silfverstolpe, A.G. Mörner, C. Pont. Gahn; from the
     estate of the clergy by: Carl G. Nordin, Sv. Wijkman
     C:son; from the *estate of burghers* by: Dan. Eberstein,
     J.G. Gahn, C.G. Broms; from the *estate of peasants* by:
     Anders Jansson Hyckert, Nils Håkansson, Jon Jonsson
     – countersigned by J.D. Valerius. Separate statements
     (not included in the new edition) by the gentlemen

von Stockenström, Silfversparre, Mörner, Wijkman, Silfverstolpe, Gahn af Colqhoun and von Rosenstein were attached.

25 Even in the parliament of 1840 the common view of the nobility and the estate of the clergy aimed chiefly at that, in contrast to the proposition of the then existing standing committee on the constitution for the transformation of the system of representation on the basis of joint elections.

26 It is not only the amount of the value of the property within an entire social class but also knowledge of how much of that value accrues to each of its members that determines the political tariff of the middle class. But a comparison of the total value of property within the individual social classes in Sweden can already be illuminating, especially with regard to the claims of the unrepresented. According to the latest statistical surveys the *nobility* in Sweden possesses property to a rateable value of 73,856,380 riksdaler. *The clergy*: 1,457,380 (though one should take into account here that the property that the members of the estate of the clergy, as such, have permanently at their disposal amounts to 7,847,300 riksdaler). *The burghers*: 38,821,400. *Members of the commoner estate* (unrepresented): 54,270,850; but as that includes neither the property of members of the commoner estate in the county of Stora Kopparberg, nor the portion owned by that class in company property together with the other estates throughout the kingdom, nor the property of minors within the same class, it is likely that the property of the unrepresented

can be assessed at about 60 million riksdaler. The rateable value of the property of the estate of peasants amounts to almost 160 million riksdaler.

27 They were *indirect* elections for the most numerous social class, *direct* elections for those of greater wealth and the interpretation of the latter under the category of a *reinforced personality*.

28 There is no doubt that the embarrassing situation in which both government and representatives appear to be increasingly involved is due to the exclusive claims of the middle class that have been pursued there, by which it has placed itself in an unnatural position.

29 Cf. the memorial of the committee in *Sveriges grundlagar* etc. Stockholm, 1844, by P.A. Norstedt & Söner, p. 119.

30 "The determination of the limit can in itself only be *approximate* and must nevertheless be set at a *certain* point. It is the same situation as, for instance, with the age of majority. There is no rational ground why that should begin specifically on reaching the age of 21 and not before or somewhat later. Such rules provide examples of what one might call that which is *lawfully arbitrary*. That is generally of greater importance than one would think. In the executive sphere and administration it turns out to be even more important than in legislation, where, although to a certain extent unavoidable, it is still restricted within narrower limits. If one exceeds the limits that the legislator and the judge have set for themselves, the scope of that arbitrariness, not definable by any rules, is necessarily enlarged. That is to say, the *trust* becomes increasingly *personal*, which is also its nature. That

applies most of all to the *ruler* and the government, including the council of the ruler, and next to them to the *representative*. From that we can draw an important conclusion. The representative, even if representing on the basis of authorisation, can and ought not, *within* the limits set by constitutional law for his activity, which are determined in advance, be bound in other respects by *instructions*. His personality, his way of thinking, the trust he inspires constitute the only surety that he ought to and in the nature of the case can give his electors." Cf. above, p. 269.

31 *Förslag till national-representation* by *C.H. Anckarsvärd* and *J.G. Richert*, Stockholm, 1830. As that proposal has gained far less attention than, to my mind, it deserves and that is likely to be partly due to the fact that it is set out in a legal form and without extended reasons being attached, I will here present the following summary of its main points:

1. The *estates of the realm* (perhaps they should in this proposal rightly be called the *national committee*) consist of two divisions:

a) The *grand committee*, which consists of at least 150 and at most 175 persons and

b) The *examining committee*, consisting of 75.

The total number will thus be at least 225 and at most 250.

2. To the grand committee members are elected

a) *by means of electors*, in smaller electoral districts:

  – for the countryside 88;

  – for the towns 32.

In the *electoral elections* all adult men participate who have reached 25 years and do not have a *direct* franchise according to letter b. – if they
– either *own* or possess real estate for an unlimited time or at least under a *ten-year right of occupation* in the country or in a town;
– or else for *property* or an annual income pay a rate of *at least five riksdaler*;
b) *by direct elections*, by counties, 55; in those elections all participate who pay a rate of at least 50 riksdaler and, where these do not amount to 50 for each election of a representative, as many of those most highly taxed among them as are required for such a number.

By establishing special electoral colleges one obtains the *only real* guarantee against the risk of the exclusion of the higher wealth and education; and when one leaves the lesser wealth by itself, one also removes the temptations of electoral intrigues, which would undoubtedly arise from the fact that both classes are invited to compete on one and the same track.

Among those who have a franchise for a 5 riksdaler rate one finds all *lesser* officials and the whole of the *younger* educated class, i.e. assistant vicars, schoolteachers, junior lawyers, junior officers, physicians etc. For these one could even omit any register.

Among those who have a franchise for a 50 riksdaler rate one finds not only the wealthy but also the whole of the *higher* and *older* educated class of officials and literary men. One would be able to reduce that class of voters to a 30 riksdaler rate, or perhaps to 25; there would be no risk attached to that, but one

437

would achieve the great purpose of lowering, as far as possible, the *direct* franchise, which, where it may *possibly* occur, must always be regarded as the most *certain* and thus also as the *best*.

The proposal can be compared to the French electoral law, if one substitutes between 25-30 and 50 riksdaler for 200 francs and provides that franchise with a *basis* of *indirect* elections, in which almost every *adult* and *free* man participates. It is precisely such a *basis* that is lacking in France, but which is so much opposed there, as one will not nowadays consider any other franchise than the *direct* one.

3. The examining committee is elected by the grand committee, *within* or *outside* the latter.

4. The grand committee is renewed every third year to its total number, the examining committee only to one third.

5. All elections occur per capita.

Count *Anckarsvärd* presented this proposal during the final debate on the question of representation with the modification that *one half of the examining committee*, the total number of which he proposed was to be 90, *should be chosen by the king*. – Baron *Hugo Hamilton* accepted that with the further amendment that the *other half* of the examining committee should be elected by *the currently existing estates of the realm*. But where is one to find them after half a century?

32 A friend who has had occasion to become well acquainted with the subject writes to me as follows, which I have every reason to believe applies not only to Sweden but to Europe: "As it is a matter of statistical information, I use this occasion to mention

a circumstance concerning the distribution of the
population by different ages, to which my attention
has been strongly drawn. That is, namely, that the
sections of the population that are in childhood, youth
and incipient manhood have increased enormously
in comparison with those of more mature age and
old age. That is to say, there have never been as many
young people in Sweden as during approximately
the past twenty years. The number stands in an
exceptional ratio to the number of those of mature
age and the elderly. Of that fact I am very sure. – It
should be mentioned, however, that that ratio appears
to be temporary. The last report of the statistical
commission shows an increase in the classes of more
mature age, which will without doubt continue, until
the exceptional ratio entirely disappears."

6. An Economic Dream

Published in Dagligt Allehanda,
26 February 1847

O NCE A RARE occurrence, I have for some time
now often dreamt. These dreams are not usually disjointed and fantastical. On the contrary,
they are distinguished by a logical context, which unfolds,
seemingly autonomously, behind the eyes of the dreamer.
It is as if the machinery of the mind had of its own volition
crafted the subject.

Recently, this was economic and left the, perhaps rare,
example of an economic dream; therefore I wish to tell of
it, briefly. It is a dream of national economy, which may be
added to the others.

The question concerned the influence of the natural
features of a country on its finances and the answering of
it undertaken with respect to the fatherland.

In that connection it emerged that the expanse of Sweden, with all its natural dissimilarities, could not avoid ex-
erting a profound influence on the economies of especial
places in the fatherland. The different lives of the plains-
man and the mountain-dweller were displayed. The min-
er, the farmer, the manufacturer, the merchant, the hunt-
er, the fisherman stepped forward, all under the various
conditions that the place and the distinct needs arising
therefrom prescribed for their activities. They gathered
into groups accordingly. The various groups were scattered, separated by great distances, in that way isolated

441

within themselves. It is no wonder that each regarded itself as *a whole unto itself!* Different needs and circumstances
had shaped each one. The force of habit had cemented it
and erected a wall, as it were, around each domain, beyond
whose horizon the gazes of the inhabitants need not extend. I said to myself: behold the origins of *corporative and
guild privileges!* – These are the children first of *need*, second
of *habit* and finally of *prejudice*. As *such*, they exist long in
the imagination, because their true validity has dissipat-
ed long before this. The various domains, by reason of an
omniprevalent enterprise, are now drawn together. Their
relationships to each other are utterly changed. He whose
gaze encompasses several such areas will see this at once.
He who lives by charity under the old conditions, however, does not see the change, or considers it a disorder and
thus cries out incessantly for order, the *old* order, that is;
even as the *new* is already, unnoticed by him, in full swing.

It is clear that he whose enterprise extends to *several*
objects of human industry will more easily arrive at this
insight, than he who is confined to one. For the insight is a
comparative insight and arises through the comparison. So,
it manifests itself soonest to the merchant, the manufacturer; latest, most reluctantly to the artisan, in whose life
change usually comes before he notices it, much less has
any inkling of its causes. Therein, he is like an animal star-
tled out of its hibernation, which charges its enemy to its
own destruction. Thereof the recently so common uprisings of workers against their masters. It is a blind impulse,
made yet blinder and angrier of the unaccustomed light.
And this usually turns out to the detriment of those who
surrender themselves in that direction and rush headlong
into new conditions, alien to them, which will soon take

442

them further than they could have imagined. What has been the result of all these assemblies? *Improved working methods*, in which *science* replaces the shortage of *reduced manual power* many times over; further, as a consequence thereof, *reduced wages*, and yet – oddly enough – *increased production and consumption* to the extent that the *freer distribution* puts food in the hands of many more than under the old, barbaric order. It is the leap into the midst of the new order of things, to which each and every one must resign himself. – Often, certainly, a hazardous endeavour. The transition reaps many victims. All who live in such a transition period must then be prepared – happily if he does not have eyes only for his losses, but also for the manifold and vital sources of new enterprise that run to meet him. Because that which is happening in the world now is: the *liberation of labour* – a true incarnation of the so-often odious *principle of personality*, which is increasingly encroaching upon reality. Judgements vary according to point of view! This *liberty* is tantamount with *disorder*, a thousand voices shout. On the contrary, she is a new, self-evolving order; so do others comfort themselves, the more industrious, the wiser. That liberty, even if she brings disorder for a passing while, follows her own rules and develops from within, implanted in her by the Creator, her own *law*: that is the full faith of *liberalism* and it leads to salvation. What is a *conservatism* that rejects this gift of God? An holding on to the corruptible in its corruption, no less fruitless than perfectly and immeasurably absurd. This way of thinking may very well console itself with its own, higher wisdom, incomprehensible to most. This wisdom shuns the rising light. To the degree this lowers itself from the heights to the vales, the faith of the many in the same

443

is lost, as the sunbeam vanishes in the fog; and thus is the supremely unnatural alliance between the so-called *conservative* and *popular* interests severed, whose loathsome delusion is still, on both sides, the so often invoked support for the most ignorant superstition.

What is the *new order of things*? With each day, its *law* evolves more clearly; its *substance* is already so apparent that one can thereof judge its nature and the spirit of progress. This substance is the *day-by-day, constantly evolving, all-encompassing fellowship and interaction of human powers and needs*. This new, but actually ancient law of labour is that of *intelligence*, which works in expanding circles. From there comes the dependency, from there the interaction in all occupations, equally familiar and acknowledged, and which, to the extent of this increasingly ardent acknowledgement, communicates ever more directly with its own essence and from this new, greater powers emerge, day-by-day and without surcease. Therefore, every seeming defeat is a true victory for it. It needs hardly touch the Earth to feel at home and rise again with renewed vigour.

One needs only to regard this immortal principle in detail in its effects to find oneself in the field of an infinite project that reaches in all directions and returns from all directions to its centre. – How could any occupation, any area of human enterprise, now be able to isolate itself? In so doing, it cuts itself off from its very breath of life, withers and inevitably dies. It thrives, flourishes, feels happy and promotes happiness utterly to the same extent that it both communicates and receives based on an enlivening influence.

6. AN ECONOMIC DREAM

And so, the separated groups of industries and trades finally flowed together before my eye. The artisan, not merely with his bodily strength, but with his intelligence, was the foundation of it all, for an enterprise that the factory owner used and distributed, that the merchant spread across the Earth. I saw a new day ascend above it. It was the rising sun; and the Dancing Hours moving around the sun, in measured heavenly-harmonious orbits, were the beautiful performance at which I wakened from my dream.

CL Press

A Fraser Institute Project

https://clpress.net/

Professor Daniel Klein (George Mason University, Economics and Mercatus Center) and Dr. Erik Matson (Mercatus Center), directors of the Adam Smith Program at George Mason University, are the editors and directors of CL Press. CL stands at once for classical liberal and conservative liberal.

CL Press is a project of the Fraser Institute (Vancouver, Canada).

CL Press includes a series called CL Reprints. CL Reprints was undertaken to make selected older works-no longer under copyright, chiefly-more available.

People:

Dan Klein and Erik Matson are the co-editors and executives of the imprint.

Jane Shaw Stroup is Editorial Advisor, doing especially copy-editing and text preparation.

Zachary Yost is Production Manager for CL Reprints.

An Advisory Board:

Why start CL Press?

CL Press publishes good, low-priced work in intellectual history, political theory, political economy, and moral philosophy. More specifically, CL Press explores and advance discourse in the following areas:

- The intellectual history and meaning of liberalism.
- The relationship between liberalism and conservatism.
- The role of religion in disseminating liberal understandings and institutions including: humankind's ethical universalism, the moral equality of souls, the rule of law, religious liberty, the meaning and virtues of economic life.
- The relationship between religion and economic philosophy.
- The political, social, and economic philosophy of the Scottish Enlightenment, especially Adam Smith.